# PRAISE FOR
## *ARTIFICIAL INTELLIGENCE FOR*

CW00918814

'The world of workplace learning will be dominated by AI within a few years. *Artificial Intelligence for Learning* plots a clear and concise path through what is the biggest opportunity the industry has had for many years.'
**Paul McElvaney, CEO of Learning Pool**

'Donald Clark has been at the leading edge of technology in learning for over 30 years. His take on tech is always informed by his detailed knowledge of learning theory. This book on AI is no exception – it's bold, thorough, bang up to date, well-researched, evidence-based and practical.'
**Kirstie Donnelly MBE, CEO of City & Guilds Group**

# Artificial Intelligence
# for Learning

# Artificial Intelligence for Learning

*How to use AI to support employee development*

Donald Clark

KoganPage

First published in Great Britain and the United States in 2020 by Kogan Page Limited

| | | |
|---|---|---|
| 2nd Floor, 45 Gee Street | 122 W 27th St, 10th Floor | 4737/23 Ansari Road |
| London | New York, NY 10001 | Daryaganj |
| EC1V 3RS | USA | New Delhi 110002 |
| United Kingdom | | India |
| www.koganpage.com | | |

Kogan Page books are printed on paper from sustainable forests.

**ISBNs**

| | |
|---|---|
| Hardback | 978 1 78966 083 8 |
| Paperback | 978 1 78966 081 4 |
| eBook | 978 1 78966 082 1 |

**British Library Cataloguing-in-Publication Data**

A CIP record for this book is available from the British Library.

**Library of Congress Cataloging-in-Publication Data**

Names: Clark, Donald (Writer on artificial intelligence), author.
Title: Artificial intelligence for learning : how to use AI to support
    employee development / Donald Clark.
Description: London, United Kingdom ; New York, NY : Kogan Page Limited,
    2020. | Includes bibliographical references and index. |
Identifiers: LCCN 2020008029 (print) | LCCN 2020008030 (ebook) | ISBN
    9781789660814 (paperback) | ISBN 9781789660838 (hardback) | ISBN
    9781789660821 (ebook)
Subjects: LCSH: Employees–Training of–Technological innovations. |
    Artificial intelligence.
Classification: LCC HF5549.5.T7 C5877 2020 (print) | LCC HF5549.5.T7
    (ebook) | DDC 658.3/124028563–dc23

Typeset by Integra Software Services, Pondicherry
Print production managed by Jellyfish
Printed and bound by CPI Group (UK) Ltd, Croydon CR0 4YY

# CONTENTS

# ABOUT THE AUTHOR

Professor Donald Clark is an EdTech entrepreneur. He was the CEO and one of the original founders of Epic Group plc, which established itself as the leading company in the UK online learning market, floated on the stock market in 1996 and sold in 2005. Now CEO of Wildfire, an AI content creation company, he is also a director and investor in other AI learning companies, a prolific blogger and award-winning international speaker.

# ABOUT THIS BOOK

What is the aim and structure of this book? First, a note about what this book is not. It is not a technical book on AI. Neither is it an exhaustive or definitive book on AI for learning, as this is still an embryonic and fast developing field. Neither is it an opinionless book. AI is a contentious issue in learning and I do not shy away from that contention to express views and opinions you may agree or disagree with. Where appropriate, I have made the effort to explain the pedagogic arguments behind the use of AI. This, I think, is important if we are to progress on the basis of AI being a technology for 'learning'.

## Part One

*Chapter 1, Homo technus*, looks at how we got to the present through different lenses, moving from the general to the particular across 2,500 years of philosophy, mathematics, culture and, more recently, the use of technology in learning. *Chapter 2, What is AI?*, shows AI to be many things and therefore applicable to many areas of teaching and learning. It clears the decks somewhat with a definition of AI as an *idiot savant*, which has competences without comprehension. It also explains some of the anthropomorphic and exaggerated claims around AI and 'intelligence'.

## Part Two

*Chapter 3, Robot teacher fallacy*, and *Chapter 4, Teaching*, look at AI from the teacher or trainer's perspective, showing that it is not a replacement for, but a valuable aid to, teaching. Robot teachers are beside the point, a bit like having robot drivers in self-driving cars. The dialectic between AI and teaching shows that there will be a synthesis and increased efficacy in teaching when its benefits are realized.

## Part Three

*Chapter 5, AI is the new UI*, deals with the profound influence AI is having on interfaces, especially voice – AI being the new UI. *Chapter 6, Chatbots*, and *Chapter 7, Building chatbots*, deal with the many ways chatbots can be used in learning, along with practical advice on building chatbots. This technology is already being used in many ways in learning to engage, support, teach and assess.

## Part Four

*Chapter 8, Content creation*, and *Chapter 9, Video*, explain how AI can be used in content creation and to enhance video in learning. Learning content and curation is now being delivered by AI, in minutes not months, at a fraction of the traditional cost. This offers opportunities for organizations that have not seen online learning as possible in terms of costs and timescales. *Chapter 10, Push learning*, explores how AI can deliver push techniques, such as nudge learning and spaced practice. *Chapter 11, Adaptive learning*, covers adaptive and personalized learning.

*Chapter 12, Learning organizations*, deals with new ecosystems of learning as learning management systems move towards workflow learning, learning experience platforms and learning record stores. *Chapter 13, Assessment*, focuses on AI in assessment. From student identification to the delivery of assessments and forms of assessment, AI promises to free assessment from the costs and restraints of the traditional exam hall. Plagiarism checking is also discussed, as is the semantic analysis of open input in assessment and essay marking.

## Part Five

*Chapter 14, Data analytics*, looks at data, its types, the need for cleaning data, the practical issues around its use in learning and its use in learning analytics.

*Chapter 15, Sentiment analysis*, shows how sentiment analysis allows us to look at subjective issues in learning.

## Part Six

*Chapter 16, Future skills,* uncovers the sort of skills learning technology professionals are likely to need in this new world of AI. *Chapter 17, Ethics and bias,* handles the tricky issues of bias in humans and AI, as well as the ethical issues around AI for learning. *Chapter 18, Employment,* looks at AI's impact on the workplace and employment, including learning professionals. *Chapter 19, The final frontier,* looks as some mind-blowing technology and speculates on how AI may accelerate learning through immersive and brain-based technology. Finally, in *Chapter 20, Where next?,* we look at how AI and learning may develop in the future.

# PREFACE

I was born in 1956, the year the modern era of AI began with an epoch-making conference at the Ivy League Dartmouth College in the US. It was there that John McCarthy coined the phrase 'artificial intelligence' and set in train some foundational work in the field. As a young undergraduate I was fortunate to spend time there, where I used my first computer. My only previous coding experience was on punched cards, which I had to post off to the local government, mainframe computer in Edinburgh, when I was at school. The results, in the form of a printout, came back a week later. At Dartmouth we had access to a mainframe, played Battleship, and could code. It was an epiphany. On my return to Edinburgh I bought a home computer and the first computer program I wrote taught the basics of the Russian language.

My first serious application of AI was in intelligent tutoring, in the 1980s, when my colleague Clive Shepherd and I built a training programme that used dynamically gathered learner data to recommend routes through a training programme on interviewing skills for British Telecom. We learned several valuable lessons. First, we used now disproved learning styles; second, the computers we used lacked the processing power and memory to do what we needed to do properly; third, this was promising and, in time, would bear fruit. That time came later, after we built a successful company, floated it on the stock market, as Epic plc, and helped create the UK online learning industry.

Then along came AI-driven Google search, which revolutionized the efficiency of research and learning, a huge pedagogic shift. After selling the company, freeing myself from the tyranny of employment, I took a deeper dive and took Sebastian Thrun's famous MOOC (massive open online course) on AI – a revelation and real introduction to the mechanics of algorithms and their potency.

Convinced that AI would be the primary driver behind online learning, I began to talk about it at conferences around the world and found audiences intrigued by the possibility. Convinced that AI would become by far the most significant form of technology in learning, I invested in 'adaptive learning', developed an AI strategy for another company in which I was a director, and then took the plunge myself and designed and built an AI-driven content creation, curation and practice tool, which won three major awards for Most Innovative New Product in Learning, Best Online Learning Project Award and Best EdTech Award from the UK's main tech organization in higher education, JISC.

More recently, a few other seminal moments confirmed my belief in AI in learning. They took place in some rather odd places and circumstances. One particular instance was a bit terrifying. I was teaching on AI in learning at the University of Philadelphia, on the morning of the US presidential election, and showed an AI prediction that pointed to a Trump win. Oh how they laughed – but the next morning was a sobering experience, with some in tears. This confirmed my view that the old media and pollsters were stuck in an Alexander Graham Bell world of telephone polls, while the world had leapt forward to data gathering from social media and other sources. They were wrong because they didn't understand technology. Traditional media have an in-built distaste for new technology, as it is seen as a threat. Also, at a deeper level, Trump won because of technology. The deep cause, technology replacing a significant number of manufacturing jobs, had come to pass. It was always thus. Agriculture was mechanized and we moved into factories, factories were automated and we moved into offices, offices are now being automated by AI… and we're not quite sure where all this will end. AI will be a primary political, economic and moral issue for the next 50 years.

Another stunning moment came when I sat in my friend Paul McElvaney's Tesla, while it silently accelerated, pushing my body back, deep into the bucket seat. On the dashboard I could see two cars ahead and vehicles all around the car, even though they were invisible by sight to me and the driver. But it was when Paul took his hands off the steering wheel, as we cambered round the corner of a narrow road in Donegal, Ireland, that the future came into focus. Self-driving cars are now real and will inevitably replace their driver-dependent ancestors. Tesla is an AI company. The car is now a robot in which one travels. It has agency. More than this, it learns. It learns your roads, routes and preferences. It is also connected to the internet, and that learning, the mapping of roads, is shared with all as yet unborn cars. It could be argued that the car is a mere peripheral, hanging off an AI-driven network.

There were also some astounding AI successes. Google beat a GO champion, the most complex game we know, then a poker champion. Time and time again, AI rose to the challenge. Take almost any area of human endeavour, add a dose of AI and you have a business.

Another revealing moment was buying an Amazon Echo. This put AI bang in the centre of my home, not only answering questions but controlling my music system, smart TV, robot vacuum cleaner, heating and lights. The progress in natural language programming is astounding, in speech recognition, understanding, translation and generation. It had been interesting to see how Siri had crept into my wife's life via her iPhone, but this was something else. This is a chatbot, at consumer level, that acts as a sort of teacher, cleaner, concierge, DJ and personal shopper.

On a visit to lecture at Penn State University I came across a couple of bot projects that intrigued me. The Georgia Tech bot, which fooled everyone into thinking it was a real teaching assistant, even being put up for a teaching award, was a breakthrough. I also saw a pupil bot for trainee teachers, who behaved as troublesome boys tend to in school, showing how this new approach through natural language interfaces will have a profound effect on how we interact with AI. AI itself has provided rapid advances in natural language processing that has made AI accessible at the consumer level.

Then came a debate in Berlin, with the motion 'AI can, will and should replace teachers'. It was an opportunity to show that, given recent advances from Google onwards, at some time it would be ridiculous to say that AI will decimate professions such as lawyers, doctors, accountants and managers, yet leave 'teaching' untouched. That would be a conceit. Many were surprised at the real-world examples in the creation of learning content, personalized feedback, assessment and reinforcement. It was not that it was coming; it was already here.

Both my sons are pretty techy and one has a degree in AI. This has been a godsend. Being able to get immediate clarification advice on tools, and generally engage in conversations with someone whose passion is AI, has been more than useful. Their hero is not any politician, scientist, entertainer or musician, but a techie. Not Steve Jobs or Marc Zuckerberg, but Elon Musk. He's the titan – super smart and not just talking, but doing something. They see in him a new generation of pioneers, who use AI for social and human good – the end of fossil fuels and therefore global warming, self-driving cars, harnessing solar power and going to Mars. But he's also alert to the dangers. AI creates but can also destroy. Musk sees it as an existential threat, as we have several exponential phenomena that push it forward: advances in technology, avalanches of data and advances in AI. When you have three exponential things happen at the same time, lots of unexpected things can happen. The world has got a lot smarter and it will get smarter still. We need to be smart in harnessing AI as a force for good.

AI will change the very nature of work. This means it will change why we learn, what we learn and how we learn. Almost everything we now do online is mediated by AI: Facebook, Twitter, Instagram, Amazon, Netflix – almost everything except learning. That is about to change.

Finally, throughout all of this I was speaking to people like Roger Schank, a pioneer in AI and cognitive psychology, reading a lot on the subject and writing about AI. Roger taught me to temper expectations with comments such as 'remember – AI is just software'.

But it has been my own work in the field, creating the world's first content creation tool using AI – WildFire – as well as working with Learning Pool on their LXP (learning experience platform), chatbots and LRS (learning record store) that provided real-world experience and delivery in real organizations in real award-winning projects with real learners. Cogbooks has been another practical and invaluable experience delivering some of the first adaptive learning courses at Arizona State University and other organizations around the world.

Giving talks around the world on AI for learning, across Europe, the US, Africa and even Russia, has allowed me to test many ideas with diverse audiences and come across projects that have been fed into this book. It has been a fantastic 'learning' experience and this book is the result of that obsession with AI and learning.

# ACKNOWLEDGEMENTS

Thanks to: Callum Clark and Roger Schank for their useful advice on AI, and Jim Thompson on adaptive learning; Paul McElvaney, Ben Betts and the good people at Learning Pool on learning experience platforms and learning record stores; and Julie Stone at the University of Derby for insights into higher education. Also thanks to clients like Henri Palmer for allowing me to test out ideas in real projects, and Rebecca Stromeyer and Channa van der Brug for their support in the dissemination of my ideas.

# LIST OF ABBREVIATIONS

| | |
|---|---|
| AR | augmented reality |
| API | application programming interface |
| CPD | continuing professional development |
| GDPR | General Data Protection Regulation |
| GIGO | garbage in, garbage out |
| L&D | learning and development |
| LMS | learning management system |
| LRS | learning record store |
| LXP | learning experience platform |
| MOOC | massive open online course |
| Moodle | modular object-oriented dynamic learning environment |
| NLP | natural language processing |
| PLA | personal learning assistant |
| ROI | return on investment |
| SCORM | sharable courseware object reference model |
| SME | subject matter expert |
| UI | user interface |
| UX | user interface experience layer |
| VLE | virtual learning environment |
| VR | virtual reality |
| xAPI | experience API |

## PART ONE

# Introduction

# 01

# Homo technus

AI has and will continue to change many areas of human endeavour. Almost everything we do online is mediated by AI: search through Google; social media, whether Facebook, Instagram, or Twitter; buy something on Amazon; entertain yourself through Netflix – all are mediated by AI. AI now touches almost all global, online services. Perhaps the only online sector that is not yet mediated by AI is learning.

The nature of work is also being shaped by AI, not only in the automation of manufacturing and warehouses, but also in our homes, offices and services. This change in the workplace, in itself, will surely have a profound effect on *what* we learn, *why* we learn and *how* we learn. This is already changing through AI-driven, online learning.

## Technological revolutions

Technological revolutions are not new. We as a species have shaped and been shaped by technology, from the first intentional use of stone hand axes to artificial intelligence. There has been a relentless rhythm to this progress.

The problem with most descriptions of this technological progress is that they focus on the *physical* technology itself, stone tools (Stone Age, Neolithic), metals (Bronze Age, Iron Age), age of steam engines, railways, mass production, computers (Industrial Revolutions). We see this when AI for learning is couched in terms of the 'Fourth Industrial Revolution' (Seldon and Abidoye, 2018), which is neither the fourth nor industrial.

A far better lens through which to look at AI in learning is not in terms of industrial revolutions, but cognitive revolutions. It is more revealing to see AI in terms of those revolutions in learning technology, such as language, writing, alphabets, printing, the internet and now AI. Our *physical* technology is underpinned, supported and created by *psychological* technology that enables its very conceptualization, design, development and delivery. The stone axe was imagined, shaped and used by minds. Cave paintings were the product of sophisticated imaginations. Clay tablets, papyrus, manuscripts and the entire technology of writing were a psychological breakthrough that externalized and archived thought for others to access. Printing gave rise to the scientific revolution, the Reformation and the Enlightenment. The internet, more specifically the web, gave us global access to knowledge. Now we have AI, the next technological leap, again a product of pure psychological endeavour.

Technology that enables learning is often overlooked when the history of technology is written. It is all too easy to focus on the physical objects. But without learning technologies, no other technologies would have developed. We are the species that 'learned' faster than the others. Our evolution as a species over the last few million years has been one of learning to adapt. It is this that has given us global dominance, allowing us to walk on the moon and reach out beyond our solar system.

Without the ability to shape stone tools we would never have avoided predators, sought out prey and become that dominant species. Prehistoric technology like pointed axes allowed us to kill, crush, scrape and cut. With bone needles we could dress ourselves efficiently, with pots cook and with axes chop down trees for fuel.

We are called *Homo sapiens* but our genus '*Homo*' emerged with the appearance of *Homo habilis* (handy man). They were so described because of their association with stone tools, but recent evidence has shown that tools were used by previous species. We are, more accurately, *Homo technus*, the species that uses tools and technology, both physical and, more importantly, psychological.

In addition to physical tools we are the masters of symbolic tools. It is difficult to see *language* as a tool, but if we define technology as something that exists outside of ourselves, that we create to exist outside of our minds and bodies, to enhance us psychologically and physically, then language is a technology. We create sounds that exist separate from us, travel to others across distance to be heard by others. It is the mainstay of communication, whether face-to-face, across the globe by telegraph then telephone and now face-to-face online. Voice underpins all other forms of technology and is being embedded in the powerful and personal mobile devices we have in our pockets, as well as in our homes, as the way of controlling the internet of things.

From Gutenberg to Zuckerberg, language, writing, printing, distribution, communication and sharing came together on the back of the internet in the form of the World Wide Web. The global scale and cumulative effect means it may prove more disruptive in the long term than all that went before. Some compare now to the 1930s, but truer historical comparison would be the 15th and 16th century, when printing shook the world. The internet has unleashed forces we are still struggling to understand. This deep tectonic shift in technology is still in its infancy. The same creative and destructive forces are being unleashed as were with writing and printing, and AI has given them a new impetus.

As smart AI technology emerges, technology challenges and, in some cases, supersedes human competences. We enter another unpredictable phase of technological change. This, some argue, is an existential threat. Whatever it turns out to be, it is certainly changing the very nature of work. For all its dangers, AI will therefore certainly shape, in some form, how we learn. Unlike speech, writing, printing and the internet, this is software that matches, and in some cases even more than matches, us as humans.

Daniel Dennett, philosopher and polymath, in *From Bacteria to Bach and Back*, attempts a synthesis of human evolution and AI (Dennett, 2017). Just as the Darwinian evolution of life over nearly 4 billion years has been 'competence without comprehension', the result of blind design, what Dawkins called the 'blind watchmaker', an invisible process that drove biological evolution, so cultural evolution and AI is often competence without comprehension (Dawkins, 1996). His vision, which has gained some traction in cognitive science, is that the brain is a prediction machine, constantly modelling forward. He also sees cultural evolution as the invasion or infection of the brain by memes, primarily words. These informational memes, like Darwinian evolution, also show competence without comprehension and fitness in the sense of being advantageous to themselves.

His hope is that machines will open up 'notorious pedagogical bottlenecks', even 'imagination prostheses' working with and for us to solve big problems. We must recognize that the future is only partly, yet largely, in our control. Let our artificial intelligences depend on us even 'as we become more warily dependent on them'.

Technology comes in revolutionary waves that have disruptive effects. It is combinatorial and cumulative, building upon previous revolutions, not something separate from us but ultimately a dialectic or an accommodation between it and we humans. We must also recognize that technology is almost always a double-edged sword that needs to be overseen and controlled, so that technology for good overcomes technology for evil. At heart these technologies define what we must learn and how we learn. They transform learning. We are *Homo technus*.

## Culture

To understand AI in learning, one also has to dig deep into our cultural history, be almost archaeological, to uncover the historical paths that gave rise to AI. Eliezer Yudkowsky is right to warn us that 'by far the greatest danger of Artificial Intelligence is that people conclude too early that they understand it' (Yudkowsky, 2015). This means understanding where it came from and how we got here.

AI has its origins in Greek philosophy and mathematics. It has also been interpreted for centuries by *culture*: poems, plays and novels. In addition to these ancient and older origins, a more recent art form, the movies, has almost defined AI in the modern mind.

Culture can illuminate, but also mislead, and there is no more misleading cultural forms than those that deal with AI. AI has been shown to us in Western culture largely through dystopian theatre, literature, then movies, with endless re-treads of the Prometheus (Frankenstein) myth. This has distorted thinking around AI for learning, but we do have something to learn from its presentation in culture, and in movies in particular.

From Aeschylus's *Prometheus Bound* to Mary Shelley's *Frankenstein: The Modern Prometheus*, the creation of a monstrous force took hold of the popular imagination, a myth fed straight into the movies in the 20th century. Asimov's novels have provided the famous Three Laws of Robotics in his short story, *Runaround* (1942), and there is a slew of modern novels about AI that have started to appear. Typical is Ian McEwan's *Machines Like Me* (2019), still stuck in the Mary Shelley Frankenstein myth, with Turing as the gratuitous Frankenstein.

Over the last 100 years, from *Metropolis* (1927) through the lens of movies, AI has largely been portrayed as dystopian and evil. AI has, in film, reflected our fears, often representing the fear of technology but also of the 'other', whatever that 'other' was at the time – the Cold War, crime, violence, helplessness, corporate greed, climate change and so on. There have been glimpses of a more sophisticated and subtler dynamic around AI, in *Blade Runner* and more recently a rush of movies around AI, as it takes hold in our lives through the internet.

There are several movie themes that have shaped the common perception of AI, primarily as robots. AI will lead to robots that will turn on us and kill us all. AI will take over the internet and kill us all. AI will fool us into thinking it is good but it is bad. This is similar to the popularity of child characters in horror movies, where our creations, our children, become our worst nightmares. These are variations of the Prometheus myth.

Technology is always ahead of cultural commentary. It will always be thus. Only now, over these last few years, as AI becomes operative in many domains, is it receiving subtler cultural appreciation and critiques, rather than robot fantasies.

## Philosophy and mathematics

Technology is not a 'black box', something separate from us. It has shaped our evolution, shaped our progress, shaped our thinking and it will shape our future. There is a complex dialectic between our species and technology that is far more multifaceted than the simplistic 'it's about people not technology' trope one constantly hears.

Descartes (1641) saw the body as a machine; others see Leibniz (1666) as the true progenitor of AI, with his theory that language mirrors thought and a universal language may be written that manipulates symbols representing concepts and ideas using logic to simulate reasoning. Note also that Descartes and Leibniz made significant contributions to mathematics, in algebra, geometry and calculus, influencing AI in other, more purely mathematical ways.

In the 20th century, Sartre in *Being and Nothingness* (1956) and Heidegger in *The Question Concerning Technology* (1954) explore the place technology has in our very being. But it was Turing's speculations, modified by the likes of Searle (1980) and Dennett, that shaped speculative thinking on AI.

To understand why AI has real potential in learning, we also need to understand its two and half millennia gestation period, through *mathematics*.

The modern era of AI started in 1956, at the famous Dartmouth conference convened by John McCarthy and Marvin Minsky, whose aim was to 'to proceed on the basis of the conjecture that every aspect of *learning* [my emphasis] or any other features of intelligence can in principle be so precisely described that a machine can be made to simulate it'.

Note the emphasis on learning, the realization of Turing's vision of machines that could learn like children to become competent. There were successes, like Arthur Samuel's checkers software, but the promise was never realized and the first AI winter arrived in the 1960s. The early 1980s saw a resurgence of interest in expert systems but it got bogged down in rules-based reasoning and a second winter came. Only when probability and statistics were literally introduced into the equations, to give us deep learning, did we succeed in translation, speech and image recognition. AI, with exponential growth in processing power, data and powerful devices, can now deliver on that early promise.

From Euclid onwards, maths and algorithms were laying the foundations for what we now call 'artificial intelligence'. So AI has not sprung up out of nowhere; it has had long gestation period, 2,500 years of mathematics, logic, probability, statistics, algorithmic progress and machine learning.

We can revisit and implement that 1956 objective, with a focus on how AI can be used to not only learn itself but accelerate our learning. AI makes us rethink learning. It holds the possibility that we do not have to learn some old knowledge and skills; it may help us learn new knowledge and skills, even improve the process and speed of learning. Stuart Russell, a major figure in AI, rightly claims in *Human Compatible* that, 'With AI tutors, the potential of each child, no matter how poor can be realised. The cost per child would be negligible and that child would live a far richer and more productive life' (Russell, 2019). I think he's right. Even if he's only partly right, this is the right direction of travel. What greater social good than AI helping us to learn?

## Learning technology

Our final look at AI is through the history and development of AI in learning technology. Mechanical devices have been used to teach and learn for a long time. Behaviourism spawned many such efforts. Sidney Pressey (Petrina, 2004) showed his 'automatic teacher' at an American Psychology Association meeting in 1924. Skinner's teaching machines took positive reinforcement as their learning principle. The problem with these and much of the simple behaviourist modelling is the lack of data and knowledge about what the learner was actually thinking and why. Adaptive AI goes much further with individual and adaptive data that guides the user, much like a GPS or satnav, through the learning experience. The experiences themselves can also adapt through machine learning.

The go-to paper for much of this is Benjamin Bloom's 'The 2 sigma problem' (1984), where he compared the lecture, formative feedback lecture and one-to-one tuition. Taking the straight lecture as the mean, he found an 84 per cent increase in mastery above the mean for a formative approach to teaching and an astonishing 98 per cent increase in mastery for one-to-one tuition.

Intelligent tutoring was attempted for decades, with limited success, most notably in the computer-based education system PLATO. These systems started to improve as interface design, hardware capabilities and more sophisticated pedagogies emerged. These were heavily influenced by the idea of expert systems and knowledge management in the 1980s and 1990s, but were still hampered by limited hardware and, just as significantly, limited software design. These were simple 'hard-coded' conditional response systems or rule-based systems that trundled through 'rules' to capture insights and therefore decisions about what to teach next to the learner.

It is often thought that all the real progress was made in universities and education, but in practice it was organizational learning, especially corporates, that established computer-based training (CBT) as a standard feature of the learning and development budget. Companies grew to serve the real needs in this market and learning management systems emerged to manage the learners and learning content, along with standards, such as sharable courseware object reference model (SCORM), for passing data from learning experiences back to a database. There was little interest in certification. This was all about serving actual organizational needs in what were starting to become fast-moving businesses.

Alongside this emerged the multimedia age, with an increased range of media (audio, images and video) available through hardware and software advances. Laserdiscs could store tens of thousands of images and hours of audio and video. They were read-only devices but led to a much richer use of visual imagery in learning. CD-I and many other consumer devices were also tried but failed. Again, they all tended to have limited memory and speed. The hardware was always a rate-limiting factor.

Many of the multimedia, CBT and learning management system (LMS) businesses started in the 1980s and 1990s are still around today. The sector has grown year on year, steadily taking on learning tasks that were previously thought beyond the reach of computers.

But one significant event led to increased growth in the market – the internet. At first, with slow dial-up, there was little to be gained, but as bandwidth and consumer adoption exploded, new opportunities were available for networked and more sophisticated pedagogic approaches. This gave us online access to Google, YouTube, Wikipedia, open educational resources, massive open online courses (MOOCs) and cloud-based services.

The development of online learning proceeded in fits and starts. Exponential growth in hardware meant faster, smaller, more powerful and cheaper machines. Interactive design adopted heuristics such as blended learning, the flipped classroom, scenario-based learning and simulations. The internet then gave us the power to network and cloud computing. Interface design, always dependent on hardware capabilities, developed from commands and menus to window metaphors to touch screen and now gesture and voice.

Post-internet, the ecosystem morphed, alongside these advances, into the online learning market. This has thrived and most large organizations have learning management systems, buy catalogues of content, commission content, use webinars and encourage social learning. More recently, as mobile devices became ubiquitous, mobile learning, or m-learning, became viable, putting the potential for learning into one's pocket. Most online learning content is now 'responsive' to desktops, laptops, tablets and mobile devices.

Beyond this we have the enhancement of real-world experience through augmented reality (AR). The democratization of experience through virtual reality (VR) is now with us, as are MOOCs. All of these are, to some degree, already delivered through the smart use of algorithms *implicit* in the hardware and software. All of these offer opportunities for AI to become more pedagogically *explicit* and greatly enhance these learning channels

Then, as the devices became more powerful and data more plentiful, AI had a surge on the back of new techniques, especially in natural language processing (NLP) and machine learning. This grew out of the existence of the internet, then began to shape it.

The first great triumph in AI-led learning was in search, in its many forms – the ability to find things out, quickly and accurately. It was here that AI took centre stage in the learning ecosystem, opening up the future to irreversible, pedagogic shifts. As Google became the way we found things – including finding the answers to things, scholarly articles, places on maps, images, videos – huge productivity gains were made. In research alone, months of getting to and from libraries, walking up and down shelves of books and journals, were reduced to seconds.

Buying books, no matter how obscure, became quick and easy, accelerated by an AI-driven recommendation engine. This had a deep effect on AI on the internet as data mining, and a whole host of AI techniques, were brought to bear on the presentation of content and ads. Social media became a global phenomenon and many found these incredibly useful in terms of learning and continuing professional development (CPD) all mediated by AI. Facebook timelines and Twitter feeds were suddenly algorithm driven.

AI-driven face recognition developed quickly as did voice to text and text to voice. NLP led to advances in search, translation and a whole host of new advances in interface design. AI also, sadly, made an appearance in plagiarism checking. It may seem odd that the only place you are likely to see AI in learning in a university is in checking on whether students cheat.

Despite all of these advances, online learning still remains stubbornly primitive, almost behavioural in approach. Even the gamification of content can be doggedly Pavlovian, with its use of external stimuli, such as scores, badges and leader boards, to motivate learners. The issue that remains is to what degree AI-driven learning can replicate an actual one-to-one tutor. What held such systems back were the limitations of the hardware, software, tools and a paucity of data. To have any real impact on reproducing the process of actual teaching, we had to wait for huge increases in processing power, memory and data. This has proved significant for those working in AI in learning, as data is the fuel that allows algorithms to function more effectively. But there are other advances that are less data hungry, in interfaces, content creation, curation, personalization, assessment and the consolidation of learning.

In organizational learning the rise of learning experience platforms (LXPs) is an enabling development. LMSs have their uses, especially in large organizations where enterprise software is necessary. But it has also become a bind for those that want to move on to use AI, as they lack the flexibility needed on personalized interface experiences, personalized learning paths, content delivery and the need for a more data-driven approach to learning.

The web has moved on while learning has remained stuck in a fixed world of flat delivery. Almost everything we do online is mediated by AI recommendation engines, with rapid moves into voice recognition and advanced analytics, yet learning is stubbornly static.

Newer technologies that are AI friendly, such as experience application programming interface (xAPI), allow tracking and data generation well beyond the traditional, fixed SCORM standard. Learning record stores (LRS) open up the possibility of using, not just learning, business data to finally integrate learning into the decision-making that grows the business.

The combination of algorithms, big data and computing power promises to unleash AI into all layers of the learning experience: user interface layer, learning layer and data layer.

In education, if AI can result in accelerating and reducing the cost of learning – even basic skills such as reading, writing and arithmetic – on a global scale, it will make past improvements in pedagogy look like rounding errors.

Since 2014, the Global Learning XPRIZE has offered $15 million for software that will enable children in developing countries to teach themselves basic reading, writing and arithmetic within 15 months (XPRIZE, 2019). It has to be scalable and open source. There have been two winners: the Kitkit School from South Korea and the US, and 'onebillion' from Kenya and the UK.

## Conclusion

Little has been written on AI as a technology for learning, little on the pedagogy of AI, and little on its existing and potential applications to help us teach and learn. This book attempts to do just that. We have a unique opportunity. AI has suddenly become a topic of global, public concern. It is the topic of the age. Why now? Why this moment in history? Well, the technology has matured to the point where it can be delivered even to your pocket via mobile devices; the internet means that it can be delivered from the cloud and that tsunamis of data can be used to fuel AI solutions. We have also seen remarkable advances in AI techniques, not just in machine learning but across the board. At the same time the online learning market has matured so that it is ready to adopt AI solutions. At last smart solutions using smart software can be used to produce smart people, through AI-delivered teaching and learning, whether students, employees or citizens.

## References

Aeschylus and Vellacott, P (1961) *Prometheus Bound and Other Plays: The Suppliants/Seven Against Thebes/The Persians*, Penguin, London

Asimov, I (1942) Runaround, *Astounding Science Fiction*, **29** (1), pp 94–103

Bloom, BS (1984) The 2 sigma problem: The search for methods of group instruction as effective as one-to-one tutoring, *Educational Researcher*, **13** (6), pp 4–16

Dawkins, R (1996) *The Blind Watchmaker: Why the evidence of evolution reveals a universe without design*, WW Norton & Company, New York

Dennett, DC (2017) *From Bacteria to Bach and Back: The evolution of minds*, W.W. Norton, New York

Descartes, R (1641/2013) *René Descartes: Meditations on first philosophy: With selections from the objections and replies*, Cambridge University Press, Cambridge

Heidegger, M (1954) The question concerning technology, *Technology and Values: Essential Readings*, **99**, p 113

Leibniz, GW (1666/1989) Dissertation on the art of combinations, in *Philosophical Papers and Letters*, pp 73–84, Springer, Dordrecht

McCarthy, J, Minsky, ML, Rochester, N and Shannon, CE (2006) 'A proposal for the Dartmouth summer research project on artificial intelligence, August 31, 1955' *AI Magazine*, **27** (4), p 12

McEwan, I (2019) *Machines Like Me*, Jonathan Cape, London

Petrina, S (2004) Sidney Pressey and the automation of education, 1924–1934, *Technology and Culture*, April, Vol 45, pp 305–330. Available at https://www.academia.edu/5065516/Sidney_Pressey_and_the_Automation_of_Education_1924_1934 (archived at https://perma.cc/99AF-35VM)

Russell, S (2019) *Human Compatible: AI and the problem of control*, Penguin Books, London

Sartre, JP (1956/2001) *Being and Nothingness: An essay in phenomenological ontology*, Citadel Press, New York

Searle, JR (1980) Minds, brains, and programs, *Behavioral and Brain Sciences*, **3** (3), pp 417–424

Seldon, A and Abidoye, O (2018) *The Fourth Education Revolution*, Legend Press Ltd, London

Shelley, MW (2009) *Frankenstein, or, The Modern Prometheus, 1818*, Engage Books, AD Classic, San Francisco

XPRIZE (2019) Website. Available at https://www.xprize.org/prizes/global-learning (archived at https://perma.cc/CRK9-JZZP)

Yudkowsky, E (2015) *Rationality: From AI to zombies*, Machine Intelligence Research Institute, Berkeley

# 02

# What is AI?

In 1899 Jean-Marc Cote tried to imagine what domestic life would be like in the year 2000 (Public Domain Review). He drew a mechanical robot as tall as a human sweeping with a brush and pan. His imagination was shaped by the mechanical paradigm of the day. This framing of AI in an overly mechanical fashion can lead to an overemphasis on strangely old-fashioned concepts such as robot teachers. Framing AI in terms of anthropomorphic qualities can also lead to the attribution of comprehension, cognitive qualities, general intelligence and contextual understanding, when in fact none of these things are present. When we think of the future we tend to frame it in the past.

## AI as idiot savant

Among these first new consumer robots were floor cleaners that bumped randomly around your room sucking up dirt and dust. The first models simply sensed when they hit something, a wall or piece of furniture, turned their wheels and headed off in a different direction. Still basically mechanical but with sensors.

The latest cleaner robots actually map out your room and mathematically calculate the optimum route to evenly clean your floor. They have a memory, build a mathematical model of the room, with laser mapping, 360-degree cameras, detect objects in real time, know when they hit the lip of a stair, move from room to room, have clever corner cleaning capability and can be operated from a mobile app. They will even automatically return to their dock and recharge when their batteries get low and resume from the point they left.

Then, one day, you come back, open your front door and get hit by a horrific smell. The dog has taken a dump and the robot cleaner had smeared it evenly across the entire carpet, mathematically, into every corner of the room.

The lesson here is that AI is an '*idiot savant*' – smart in that it can replace humans in all sorts of precise tasks, but doesn't have the checks and balances of normal human intelligence. It literally doesn't know shit!

AI is good at one thing, or a few narrow things, such as moving, mapping and cleaning, but it doesn't know when the shit hits the fan. It is not cognitive or intelligent; it is narrowly smart but dumb. Remember also that AI does things but it doesn't know why it does them.

What seems like astounding levels of competence – beating humans at backgammon, chess, GO, poker and computer games – is, in fact, solving 'bounded' problems. They are specific, limited problems with clear rules and solvable with achievable AI solutions. Another set of bounded problems lie within NLP. These boundaries are bigger and many, such as translation, voice recognition and the semantic interpretation of text, are making rapid progress. Just because something is bounded doesn't mean it is not useful. There are many bounded problems in teaching and learning: many are the routine and repetitive tasks that teachers and learners find frustrating. Right across the learning journey, from learner engagement, support, teaching and assessment, there are bounded problems that have short-term solutions using AI. This means using many types of AI.

## AI is many things

AI is difficult to define. There is no watertight definition of AI. It is a whole constellation of technologies. Its core concept, the algorithm, has no exact mathematical definition and its many schools and techniques evade total capture. Behind this basic confusion is the idea that AI is one thing – it is not: it encapsulates 2,500 years of mathematics since Euclid put the first algorithm down on papyrus, and there are many schools of AI that take radically different approaches. The field is an array of different techniques, often mathematically quite separate from each other.

Other ways of looking at AI are through areas of practical problem-solving, such as natural language solutions to search and translation, image recognition in healthcare solutions or robotics. There are many ways of slicing the AI cake. The important point is to see it as a set of very different technologies or tools that solve problems – in our case, in teaching and learning.

We needn't worry too much about the mechanics of it all, but we do need to understand the ways in which it will impact the field of teaching and learning. AI powers almost everything you do online. It is not coming – it is here.

## AI and intelligence

The word 'intelligence' in artificial intelligence is perhaps misleading. Commentators such as Thomas Malone (2018) put a great deal of emphasis on the word, using it as a catalyst for analysis and the further development of AI. This may be a fundamental error, as it pulls us toward a too anthropomorphic view of AI, suggesting that it is 'intelligent' in the sense of human intelligence, benchmarking AI against a fundamentally anthropomorphic measure, a word with many problems, even when used in relation to humans. It is better to see AI in terms of tasks and competences, as *not* being intrinsically intelligent, as that word is loaded with human preconceptions and the danger is that people over-promise and under-deliver, so that there is disappointment in the market.

Linked to the notion that AI is 'intelligent' is the idea that AI derives wholly from our study and mimicry of the intelligent brain. Even the so-called 'neural network' approach is loosely modelled on the networked structure of the brain, more analogy than replication. A well-worn argument in AI circles is that we did not learn to fly by copying the flapping of birds' wings; we invented airplanes, an entirely different form of technology. Neither did we learn to go faster by copying the legs of a cheetah; we invented the wheel. Similarly with AI – simply copying the brain may be useful in some cases, but not overall.

The word made its debut in AI when the Turing test arrived in the brilliant 'Computing Machinery and Intelligence' (Turing, 1950/2009), still an astounding paper that sets the bar on whether machines can think and be intelligent. It is unfortunate that the title includes the word 'intelligence', as it is never mentioned in this sense in the paper itself. It is also unfortunate that the phrase AI (artificial intelligence), invented by John McCarthy at Dartmouth College, has become a bit of a misleading distraction.

It has been a distraction in learning for a long time. Binet, who was responsible for inventing the IQ (intelligence quotient) test, warned against IQ being seen as a sound measure for individual intelligence or that it should be seen as 'fixed' (Binet and Simon, 1916). His warnings were not heeded, as education itself became fixated with the search for and definition of this single measure IQ, the main protagonist being Eysenck. Unfortunately, it led to unhelpful policies, such as the 11+ in the UK, promoted on the back of fraudulent research by Cyril Burt (Eysenck, 1988).

Stephen Jay Gould's book *The Mismeasure of Man* (1996) is one of many that have criticized IQ research as narrow, subject to reification (turns abstract concepts into concrete realities), when cognition is, in fact, a complex phenomenon. IQ research has also been criticized for repeatedly confusing correlation with cause, not only in heritability, where it is difficult to untangle nature from nurture, but also when comparing scores in tests with future achievement. Socio-economic background and culture may also play a role and the tests are often not adjusted for these variables. This focus on IQ, the search for a single, unitary measure of the mind, is now seen by many as narrow and misleading. Most modern theories of mind have moved on to more sophisticated views of the mind with different but interrelated cognitive abilities. Gardiner (1983), for example, tried to widen its definition into multiple intelligences, but this is weak science and lacks any real vigour. It still suffers from a form of academic essentialism.

We would do well to abandon the word 'intelligence' in artificial intelligence, as it carries with it so much bad theory and practice. Indeed, AI has already transcended the term multiple intelligences, as it had success across a much wider set of competences such as perception, translation, search, natural language processing, speech, sentiment analysis, memory, retrieval and other domains, especially with the advent of machine learning.

## AI as competence without comprehension

Big Blue beat Kasparov in 1997, but chess is thriving. AI remains our servant, not master. Yet mention AI and people jump to the far end of the conceptual spectrum with big-picture, dystopian, and usually exaggerated visions of humanoid robots, the singularity and the existential threat to our species. The truth is more prosaic.

Work with people in AI and you will quickly be brought back from sci-fi visions to more practical matters. AI has no 'cognitive' ability. One could blame IBM, consultants and futurists for this hyperbole. Fine if they mean it can perform or mimic certain limited cognitive tasks, but they go further, suggesting that it is in many senses 'cognitive'. This is quite simply wrong. It has no consciousness, nor general problem-solving abilities – none of the many cognitive qualities of human minds. It is maths embodied in software.

IBM's Watson may have beaten the Jeopardy champions, Google's AlphaGO may have beaten the GO champion – but neither knew they had won. Roger Schank, an early pioneer and major figure in AI, says something rather wise here: that AI is merely software and that we should in fact just call it software. This is to counter the myths around 'cognitive' computing.

We may even be able to move away from that other anthropomorphic obsession – consciousness. Daniel Dennett in *Consciousness Explained* (1993) saw it as an epiphenomenon, not necessary for the explanation of actual competence and action. If we can drop the ghost in the machine, the machine itself can be seen as being non-anthropomorphically capable. Dennett has a deep understanding of AI, and in his book, *From Bacteria to Bach and Back* (2017), sees a fusion of human evolution and AI, with consequences for the ethics of AI. He takes a holistic and, in a sense, forgiving view of AI. As he rightly says, we make children without actually understanding the entirety of the process, and so it is with new, generative technology. We already trust systems that are way more competent than we humans and so we should. Daniel Dennett states the same thing in three words: 'competence without comprehension'.

If we move beyond brains, beyond organic versus inorganic, we can move, as Harari claims in *Homo Deus* (2016), towards intelligence as fundamentally algorithmic, and uncouple intelligence from humans and consciousness. His argument is that natural selection itself is algorithmic and gave rise to our species and brains, but these algorithms are independent of the substances in which they reside. We must therefore readjust our thinking around intelligence and learning to include wider definitions.

AI is now challenging what it is to be human, intelligent, competent and to think and learn. The challenges we face are not to mimic humans but to find solutions that we are incapable of thinking of and executing. When Deepmind played its Atari game, it shot round the edge of the blocks and attacked from above, something humans had never thought of. When AlphaGo beat the Go champion, it came up with a move that was so counterintuitive that it shocked its human opponent. We do not want flawed human performance; we want performance beyond our capabilities, that is better than human. Humans crash cars and aircraft, kill patients through misdiagnosis and wrong prescribing. We need technology that is better than us. We didn't go faster by copying the legs of a cheetah – we invented the wheel.

Turing clearly foresaw rapid advances in the power of computers and, in the long term, was visionary in his understanding of their potential capabilities. Remarkably, he successfully predicted that computers would have 1 GB of storage by 2000. However, the Turing test itself has been critiqued and is still a contentious area. He was wrong in assuming that 'at the end of the century the use of words and general educated opinion will have altered so much that one will be able to speak of machines thinking without expecting to be contradicted' (Turing, 2004). However, many underestimated the recent advances in technology, machine learning, reinforcement learning and deep learning that have since allowed AI to do the things that were regarded as unlikely, if not impossible.

But the category mistake is to measure all of this in terms of just human performance. This is why IBM's 'cognitive' computing is simply misleading. There's little that is 'cognitive' about it. AI has become much more powerful, with considerable advances in machine learning and in the practical application of such advances. This is partly to do with advances in AI techniques, but also technical advances, which Turing predicted, and the rise of the internet and massive data sets. Few dispute the impact of AI on tasks, not just in the automation of tasks but also its impact in what has been seen as the cognitive domain. We just don't need the language of human cognition to make progress.

## AI as collective competence

Networks, such as the internet, have provided a new substrate, where collective competence is also possible. One brain cannot download directly from another or replicate knowledge and skills perfectly, in a fraction of a second. But this has already happened in AI. In 'cloud robotics' robots learn from experience but can also learn from each other, as they are networked. Experience and learning are therefore shared across the networked robots.

This concept of pooled learning and competences is something that drops the idea of a brain, human benchmark, or subject. When it comes to our human abilities and what we regard as unique, we often invoke qualities such as 'intuition' or 'thinking' and 'consciousness'. Turing opened up the possibility of imaginable digital computers that would perform astonishing feats of what we would call intelligence or learning without recourse to a brain, soul or irreducible quality such as consciousness. That is becoming a reality.

AI is moving fast, scoring one victory after another in specific domains. However, the main problem AI has is in moving from one domain to another. It may be great at playing chess or GO, or other rules-based games, even poker, but when it comes to other simple but different problems, it is not flexible. This problem – getting AI to be more general in terms of its skills or learn to apply what it learned in one domain to another – is a serious limitation, perhaps the greatest limitation of current AI.

One solution to the learning problem in AI, now being practised in robotics, is 'cloud robotics', where one robot can literally 'teach' another. By teach, I mean pass and share its acquired skills on to other robots. Researchers have been experimenting with cloud robotics for some years, where robots learn how to do something through neural networks and reinforcement learning (trial and error) and, once they have acquired that skill, it can be uploaded to as many other robots as you want. They literally share experiences and therefore learning. Not only do the sets of robots learn quickly; they instantly share that learning with other networked robots. This whole idea of AI learning from collective or shared experience is fascinating.

This takes us to the altogether grander concept of 'collective intelligence', a term coined by Pierre Levy, defined by him as 'a form of universally distributed intelligence, constantly enhanced, coordinated in real time, and resulting in the effective mobilization of skills' (Levy and Bononno, 1997). But Levy's theory of collective intelligence is now dated and inadequate. More attention needs to be given to the nature and role of 'networks' in collective intelligence.

Some posit the idea that networks are intelligent, to a degree, simply by virtue of being networks. Our brains are networks, indeed the most complex networks we know of, and artificial intelligence uses that same (or similar) networked power to interact with our brains. We do not learn in a linear fashion, like video recordings, nor do we remember things alphabetically or hierarchically. Our brains are networks with pre-existing knowledge, and intelligence, that needs to fit with other forms of knowledge from networks.

The theory of connectivism, proposed by George Siemens and Stephen Downes (2008) posits 'connectivism' as a theory where 'knowledge is distributed across a network of connections, and therefore that learning consists of the ability to construct and traverse those networks'. It is an alternative to behaviourism, cognitivism and constructionism. 'Connectivism' focuses on the connections, not the meanings or structures connected across networks. Intelligence, existing and acquired, is made up of the practices, by both teachers and learners, that result in the formation and use of effective networks, with properties such as diversity, autonomy, openness and connectivity. This challenges the existing paradigms that do not take into account the explosion of network technology, as well as presenting a new perspective on collective use and intelligence. Connectivism can also be used to bring in newer technological advances and newer agents – such as artificial intelligence.

There are several recent technological developments that open up the possibility of collective intelligence. Artificial intelligence is embedded in many online media experiences. This takes us beyond the current flat, largely text-based, hyperlinked world of text and images, such as Wikipedia, or even social media, into forms of media that are closer to Levy's original idea of collective intelligence. Networks store knowledge but, with the advent of online AI, they can also be said to be much more competent. AI is competence that resides in a network and is competent in itself but also adds to the sum of collective competence when used by humans.

Machine learning, with the aid of collective human- and machine-created data, actually becomes more competent. The more it is used, the more intelligent it becomes, sometimes surpassing the intelligence of humans in specific domains. As we saw at the start of this chapter, it can now also be shared. This is a new species of shared competence that is shared in real time, direct and scalable.

Collective competence can then be said to reside in and be an emergent feature of all networks, human and artificial, organic and non-organic. In other words, the agents of collective intelligence have to be widened, as does the nature of that competence and the interaction between them all.

We are only just beginning to see and practically explore and build new forms of collective competence that allow teaching and learning to be done by machines very quickly and on a massive scale. This is exhilarating and frightening at the same time. We, as humans, are now part of a networked nexus of human teachers, human learners, AI teachers, AI learners, networked knowledge, and networked skills. The world has suddenly become a lot more complex.

Few would argue that AI has progressed faster than expected. In some cases the practical applications clearly transcend human capabilities and competences. We don't need to see 'intelligence' as the sun at the centre of this solar system. The Copernican shift is to remove this term and replace it with competences and look to problems that can be solved. The means to ends are always means; it is the ends that matter. What is wonderful here is the opening up of philosophical issues around agency, autonomy and morality. We are far from the existential risk to our species that many foresee, but there are many more near-term issues to be considered. Ditching old psychological relics is one. Artificial smartness is with us – it need not be called 'intelligent'.

## AI learns

We, *Homo sapiens*, are the most successful species on the planet because we adapted to the world through technology – needles, twine, clothes, axes, arrow tips, hooks and so on. Then we made machines that eased the burden of labour. Mechanical machines led to the industrial revolutions in agriculture, transport and manufacturing. But the more interesting line of technology was symbolic: writing, alphabets, writing instruments, paper and books. We then learned how to read, write, argue, code. They eventually led to us feeding machines with symbolic writing (code) that allowed them to solve problems of the mind. We now have machines that learn, machines that adapt to the world, like our minds, only not nearly as flexibly. If our ability to learn and adapt to the world, other people and knowledge is the hallmark of our species, then machines are starting to copy us.

As we teach computers to learn, we are doing to them what was done to us for millennia – education. We are smart because of what we are, but more importantly through what we learn, but this is no longer our sole domain. We are delegating some of that to machines.

So machines use algorithms to learn. They not only learn how to access data that becomes information and knowledge, like how to win at Jeopardy!, but combinatory skills, like how to drive a car. The consequences are immense, economic, social and political. If machines learn, they can potentially replace some human roles and activities.

Turing interestingly anticipated machine learning in AI, seeing the computer as something that could be taught like a child. Man may be the measure of all things, but it is clear that computer power has already transcended our brain in some areas, in terms of storage, exact recall, uploading, downloading, mathematical calculations, chess, driving cars and so on. The whole point of Google search is not to be like us. It is better than us, with a greater memory, better search and faster recall. Self-driving cars do not drive like us; they in many areas drive better than us. The whole point of the self-driving car is *not* to drive like us, as we kill 1.3 million people a year while driving, along with tens of millions of injuries. If we free ourselves from the tyranny of human competences and move towards problem-solving, the problem is no longer a problem.

Let's take this idea further. Some claim that *all* networks are, to some degree, 'intelligent'. As the boundary for consciousness and intelligence changed over time to include animals, indeed anything with a network of neurons, intelligence can be seen as a property that can be applied to any communicating network. As we have evidence that intelligence is related to networked activity, whether these are brains or computers, could intelligence be a function of this networking, so that all networked entities are, to some degree, intelligent?

Clark and Chalmers in 'The extended mind' (1998) laid out the philosophical basis for this approach. Extended cognition extends out to embrace, and according to Clark and Chalmers, includes learning tools like pens, pencils and keyboards. This opens up the field for definitions of cognition that are not benchmarked against human capabilities. If we consider the idea of competences residing in other forms of chemistry and substrates, and see algorithms and their productive capabilities as being independent of the base materials in which they arise, then we can cut the ties with the word 'intelligence' and focus on capabilities or competences.

In the same way that our conscious cognition relies on unconscious processes, hidden but operative, so AI is the hidden but operative part of extended competence that is the web. In the same way that our minds use social learning, to learn maths, languages and skills such as reading and writing, so AI uses collective input from aggregated data drawn from millions, sometimes billions, of humans. We are all bound up in this one nexus, this one giant, global network, where data, information, knowledge and skills are exchanged. Once we see the underlying system as a single network, composed of many networks, the concept of collective competence can be understood.

## AI in learning

AI in one sense means doing what humans do when they learn. The AI field is thick with references to 'learning', the most common being machine, deep and reinforcement learning.

*Machine learning* uses algorithms and statistical models and applies patterns and inferences to perform tasks through experience. This is analogous to traditional learning through exposure to taught experiences. *Deep learning* is a machine learning technique that uses layered neural networks with large data sets, supervised, semi-supervised or unsupervised, to perform tasks. This is more like learning from the real world to gain competence and solve actual problems. *Reinforcement learning* operates on maximizing reward by exposure to existing knowledge and exploring new knowledge. This is more like deliberate practice to get things right.

Digging deeper there is decision-tree learning, lazy and eager learning, supervised and unsupervised learning, incremental, feature, federated and ontology learning. The noun is so frequently used, in so many contexts, for so many techniques, that it has become a general term for software that gets better as it proceeds. This is why AI is a topic of immediate interest to those in the learning game.

Drawing inspiration from how we actually learn has given AI a boost. It should also be a wake-up call for those of us who work in the world of learning. AI is showing us what works and what doesn't. Pedagogic change no longer comes from just educational research; it comes from insights in cognitive science and, increasingly, through technological innovation. AI is the latest manifestation of digital pedagogy.

Charles Fadel, the founder of the Center for Curriculum Redesign at Harvard's Graduate School of Education and co-author of 'Four-Dimensional Education' (Fadel *et al*, 2015), is right in tracking AI against Bloom's three domains. So let's see how far a pedagogy of AI can be pushed in each of these three areas:

1   cognitive;

2   affective;

3   psychomotor.

*Cognitive* AI enables search across the web and access to educational resources such as knowledge on Wikipedia and 'how to' videos on YouTube. It can make connections, analyse data, use data to predict, prescribe, translate and transcribe. There's the detection and help with those who have disabilities and learning issues. Some argue it can also create, compose new music, paintings, sculpture. In learning this is by far the most significant area, as text plays a significant role in learning and can be used by a whole range of NLP techniques. But it has yet to master more flexible critical thinking, problem-solving and understanding of the wider picture, particularly space, time and context, and cannot handle complex situations.

*Affective* AI can identify the presence of emotions in text, speech, gestures, body position and faces. Opinion and sentiment analysis can detect positive, negative and other emotional and subjective views. Even from face recognition, attention, surprise, puzzlement and wandering minds can be detected. In learning this can mean getting insights into learners' minds, difficulties, misunderstandings, even potential for dropout. Again, however, it does not actually feel empathy, compassion or cope well with context.

*Psychomotor* AI, as we have seen with advanced robotics and self-driving cars, can perceive environments, move through 3D environments, analyse complex physical environments, adapt to difficult environments, respond with complex reactions, mechanically walk, run, even do complex manoeuvres. Yet it cannot perform very complex actions that require the combination of cognitive control and flexible manoeuvring. It is not clear that this has much, if any, application in learning, other than some niche robots for young children. We will see AI enter through simulations, AR and VR.

As we can see, progress has been rapid in some areas but it is not certain that it will be exponential. There are severe limitations to many of the models and some problems require enormous processing power. AI still lacks flexibility and versatility. At the moment it is a series of separate problem-solving competences, but as the technology becomes combinatorial, it will start to get flexible. Just as the iPhone brought together a set of separate technologies, so AI will bring together sets of competences. We get a hint of this in social media, where the experience is personalized, translation available on a click, transcription available, text to speech available, even speech recognition.

In learning we need these combinations of competences to help teachers and learners – integration of features and systems, such as new interfaces like chatbots and voice, adaptive learning to personalize experiences, recommendation engines to suggest what we do next, analysis of our performance and complex, simulated environments in which we can explore, fail and learn. Given the fact that productivity has stalled in education and costs are still rising, this seems like a sensible way forward. If we can deliver scalable technology, assistance, analysis, learning and teaching, at a much lower cost than at present, we will be solving one of the great problems of our age.

# References

Binet, A and Simon, T (1916) *The Development of Intelligence in Children (the Binet-Simon scale)* (Vol 11), Williams & Wilkins, Philadelphia

Clark, A and Chalmers, D (1998) The extended mind, *Analysis*, **58** (1), pp 7–19

Dennett, DC (1993) *Consciousness Explained*, Penguin, London

Dennett, DC (2017) *From Bacteria to Bach and Back: The evolution of minds*, WW Norton & Company, New York

Eysenck, HJ (1988) The concept of 'intelligence': Useful or useless?, *Intelligence*, **12** (1), pp 1–16

Fadel, C, Bialik, M and Trilling, B (2015) *Four-dimensional Education*, CreateSpace Independent Publishing Platform, Scotts Valley, CA

Gardiner, H (1983) *Frames of Mind: The theory of multiple intelligences*, Basic Books, New York

Gould, SJ (1996) *The Mismeasure of Man*, WW Norton & Company, New York

Harari, YN (2016) *Homo Deus: A brief history of tomorrow*, Harvill Secker, Penguin Random House, London

Levy, P and Bononno, R (1997) *Collective Intelligence: Mankind's emerging world in cyberspace*, Perseus Books, New York

Malone, TW (2018) How human-computer 'superminds' are redefining the future of work, *MIT Sloan Management Review*, **59** (4), pp 34–41

Public Domain Review. A 19th-century vision of the year 2000. Website. Available at https://publicdomainreview.org/collections/france-in-the-year-2000-1899-1910/ (archived at https://perma.cc/Y8ZV-LUEX)

Siemens, G and Downes, S (2008) *Connectivism and Connective Knowledge*, University of Manitoba, Manitoba

Turing, AM (1950/2009) Computing machinery and intelligence. In *Parsing the Turing Test*, Springer, Dordrecht, pp 23–65

Turing, AM (2004) *The Essential Turing*, Oxford University Press, Oxford

## PART TWO

# Teaching

# 03

# Robot teacher fallacy

AI is not as good as most people think it is and not as bad as you fear. What tends to happen is that some future, as-yet fictional, straw man is set up as a target then beaten like a piñata. This is a particular problem in learning, where it is tempting to see AI as a teacher or seer with stunning insights into learners and the learning process. This over-reach leads to all sorts of unwarranted assertions about robot teachers and sometimes exaggerated, ethical worries.

When discussing the role of AI in learning, future of jobs, automation, robots and healthcare, and the ethics of AI, it is important to know what AI is. As mentioned in the previous chapter, what gets in the way is the constant anthropomorphizing of AI, the reading of human qualities into the technology. The AI of the popular imagination, as opposed to professional implementation, is often a fictional image taken more from the movies than reality. This is hardly surprising. AI is esoteric, multifaceted and complex. It is tempting to take shortcuts and take cues from proxies, such as movies and popular journalism, rather than take a deep dive to try and understand what it actually is and does.

Before attempting to identify where AI can support and enhance teaching, we need to be clear about the tendency to anthropomorphize, which leads to simplistic ideas about robot teachers (a fallacy) and artificial oppositions between teaching and technology, which are not mutually exclusive but a complex exchange, back and forth.

## Anthropomorphizing AI in learning

Anthropomorphizing competence means there is a danger in putting too much trust into some of the more speculative AI solutions for learning. AI is still largely statistical pattern matching from large data sets. But as Gary Marcus and Ernest Davis remind us in *Rebooting AI: Building artificial intelligence we can trust* (2019), it is context that is missing in current AI. Try asking Google about whether Socrates used online learning. It does not really know what you even mean by the question and just throws up companies that use the Socratic method, articles on Socrates or online learning. Similarly with space and causality: AI may identify a pencil but it wouldn't really 'know' its actual function with an eraser at one end and sharp end at the other for writing. It works on correlations. It can pick out a pencil being held by Rembrandt, but if there were two Rembrandts in the image, it wouldn't know that this was a fake image. AI doesn't 'know' things in the way we do, yet we have a tendency to think it does.

We need to be able to trust that it does what it does and not just what we think it does. We may think that AI can be a teacher, but it is very far from being so, as its competences are narrow, limited and nowhere near that of the average human, never mind as flexible and adaptable as a trained teacher. This is not to say that AI is of no use in teaching; it most certainly is, but as a tool.

Anthropomorphizing comprehension is also common when dealing with AI in teaching. It may do facial recognition for the registration of students, even some classroom tasks such as attention and emotional analysis on dozens of students in a class simultaneously, but it does not 'know' those students. As Daniel Dennett (2017) says, AI is 'competent without comprehension', in that it won against humans at Jeopardy, chess, GO, poker and computer games – but it didn't know it had won. This may seem obvious, but we have a natural tendency to think of computers and software as having human qualities.

Reeves and Nass (1996) showed this in their 35 studies in *The Media Equation*, long before the current capabilities in AI were developed. We cannot help but see Alexa, Siri and Cortana as human agents. Similarly in learning applications, there is a tendency to see chatbots, adaptive learning and other forms of teaching software as people. This tendency to read agency into AI is the human bias upon which most anthropomorphizing happens.

Anthropomorphizing intelligence is an even more dangerous tendency. It is perhaps unfortunate that John McCarthy in 1956 coined the phrase 'artificial intelligence'. It has no precise definition and tends to be used either too narrowly, in equating all AI as machine learning, or too loosely, in covering all statistics and data science – and everything in between. AI is an artefact. We so often attribute an exaggerated form of intelligence to AI, which can lead to us reading too much into or relying too much on the technology. This is a type of category mistake.

One must be careful in the use of AI for teaching and learning. It is so easy to slip into an anthropomorphic mindset, using inappropriate language that leads to false promises. It is important to manage expectations and be honest about what AI is being used, where it is not being used, and the limits of its capability. To write it off by being overly anthropomorphic, seeing it *prima facie* as a super-intelligent, evil, or a job-slayer, is a mistake. We should rather treat it like newly developed pharmaceuticals being released on the market. What learning problem does it attempt to cure or symptom does it attempt to relieve? What are its limitations? What does it not do? What are its unintended but possible consequences or side effects? The technology offers much in the way of powerful solutions to specific teaching problems, but do not be fooled into thinking that it promises solutions to general problems. Do not attribute human qualities to what is, after all, only maths.

## Reductive robot fallacy

Robots already play a major role in your world. At any given time you are likely to be wearing, watching, listening to, eating, driving, flying or using something that has been partly made by robots. They are already your manufacturing servants. Why? In some tasks, they outperform humans in precision, consistency, endurance, strength and speed. The lesson is clear. When robots can perform a task more precisely, more consistently and with greater endurance and speed than humans, then, given reasonable manufacturing costs and social acceptability, they will be used.

Your breakfast milk could have been milked by a robot, your eggs selected and packaged by robots, the gas used to cook your eggs extracted with the help of robots at the wellhead, your dishes placed in a dishwasher built by robots, which is itself a programmable robot. A package arrives at your door, placed and picked off the warehouse shelf by a robot. You set off in a car that has been constructed, spot-welded and spray-painted by robots. It is likely, in the imaginable future, that the car itself will become a robot and drive itself – all before you have even started work. Watch out, many claim: just as robots have taken away these jobs, they may also take away the jobs of teachers, lecturers and trainers. But that does not appear to be happening, as that is a task that requires general intelligence, something that is singularly lacking in AI.

We need to be clear about the difference between weak AI and strong AI (sometimes called GAI, or general AI). We are nowhere near GAI or getting AI to do general human tasks. It is good for precise tasks in precise domains and not when it needs to be a generalist, like teachers, lecturers or trainers. To put it another way, AI is just software and largely statistical pattern matching.

Note that not all robots in factories necessarily use AI, and few look anything like humans. We see ourselves in robots; they are a mirror for our hopes and dreams. The problem is that our hopes and dreams often don't match the actual development and manifestation of technology. Human culture tends to imprint technology with human qualities. It tends to think of AI in terms of its human qualities, as humanoid robots. This is what I call the 'reductive robot fallacy', the anthropomorphic tendency to equate AI with robots along with the idea that robot technology has to look like us and do things the way humans do them. The vast majority of robots, especially AI-driven machines that perform a useful function, especially in teaching and learning, do not look like humans, almost all are online and, to a large extent, invisible.

This reductive robot fallacy comes to the fore when people describe, without any real justification, the possible rise of robot teachers. Sure, there is a role for humanoid features in toys that teach, for young children or those with learning difficulties, such as autism, but for the vast majority of teaching and learning tasks, humanoid robots are pointless. Just because we have human teachers does not mean that we need humanoid robot teachers. Indeed, Turing warned us against efforts 'put into making machines with the most distinctively human, but not intellectual characteristics such as the shape of the human body' (1951).

Innovation is only innovation if it is sustainable. Most of the actual attempts at robot teachers have been trivial or unsustainable. We have had simple robots that allow teachers to teach from a distance in rural schools. One was at the Nexus Academy of Columbia, which allowed teachers to Skype in and control a robot from their computer, going up to students' desks and checking work. This makes little sense beyond the novelty value. Robosem was a Korean robot used to teach English. It takes a hybrid approach, either using a real teacher via teleconferencing or through autonomous, adaptive lessons that use speech recognition and motion tracking. There are many of these examples, but they are doomed to failure. NAO is another. You supposedly can teach NAO and NAO can teach you. Sure, with speech recognition, NAO will call you by your first name, drill your child in multiplication tables, wake you up, monitor your home if you're out.

It may even be able to recognize members of the family, your friends – but a teacher it is not.

Then there is Pepper, with a touchscreen on its chest. This companion learns from its environment and draws from its cloud-based, updated, master algorithms. It has emotion recognition, reading visual expressions and from speech tones. But in the end it is a tablet on the front of a primitive plastic toy.

The 'cute' factor is the obvious focus, as these are aimed at young children and there are real applications for children with autism and other differences in learning, where the pressure on parents is immense and the needs often different from traditional classroom learning. Children with autism have been shown to respond positively to synchronized behaviour from a robot. This is used to move the child on to other types of social interaction. They have been used with autistic children, using mimicry, to establish trust. One can see how niche applications like this may have benefits.

The humanoid features of robotics are not particularly useful, however, in adult learning. Most asynchronous teaching and learning online is done in the absence of a live teacher or any form of anthropomorphic agent. It is done online without any mediation by the appearance of a human teacher, live or simulated.

AI is the new user interface (UI) in the sense that we use Google, social media, Amazon, Netflix and so on, where the interface is driven by AI, using personal and aggregated data, with potent algorithms. Our experiences online are highly personalized. This will also be true in learning. In fact it already is. Google was a massive pedagogic shift, used by almost everyone on the web to find things out. It is pure AI. Amazon recommends books for you to buy. It uses powerful AI. AI now drives content creation, curation, collaboration, feedback, adaption, assessment and the reinforcement of learning. These forms of delivery rarely involve any form of anthropomorphic mediation. In fact, they tend to disintermediate humans.

Indeed, when online maths programmes were first launched, one of the first pedagogic findings was the efficacy of removing the human face of the teacher, lecturer or trainer, especially when teaching semantic subject matter, such as maths, physics, coding and textual analysis. The face turned out to be cognitive noise, so some major providers, like the Khan Academy, started to show a hand drawing out graphics, words, numbers and equations straight onto the screen. This type of knowledge and skill relies largely on semantic memory, as opposed to episodic memory, so it benefits from a stripped down approach. Sebastian Thrun and Salman Khan understood, pedagogically, that their faces were largely noise, a distraction from the maths or whatever subject was being taught, so they used audio narration (Ng and Widom, 2014). Richard Mayer has been doing research in this area for many years and his work confirms this view – that different media may work against each other and that less is more (Clark and Mayer, 2016).

In fact, the real progress in robotics has been made in non-humanoid robotics. From factories, where they perform manufacturing, packing and many other predictable and repetitive tasks, they have automated huge numbers of mundane and repetitive jobs. They can even drive and fly us around the world (autopilot and autoland in airplanes). Astoundingly, they have been to the moon, Mars and landed on an asteroid.

With 'humanoid' robots little has been achieved, other than illusions and trickery. Robots can be made to look like humans, and feel to the touch like humans – that is the easy bit. What is hard is to make them talk and behave like humans. Most, to repeat, are poor chatbots in pieces of silicon or plastic.

We do not need human workers in factories to weld and spray paint cars; we invented articulated levers and machines to do those jobs. Neither do we use robot pilots in autopiloted planes, nor robot drivers in self-driving cars. It would be ridiculous to build a robot that walks about pushing a vacuum cleaner when a small, non-humanoid robot can do it better. The role of humans is to supervise and control these robots and robotic processes. So it is with most teaching, where robots are rarely necessary. Humanoid robots only matter when human appearance or attributes are necessary. This is likely to be true in human activities, such as childcare, early years learning, serious learning difficulties or care for the elderly. We have a long way to go before we cross the chasm to general teaching skills and the sort of human interaction a real person offers. A stronger argument is that this is quite simply the wrong direction of travel. A route more effective in terms of prac-ticality, costs and efficacy is straight, AI-driven online learning.

As Stanford's Reeves and Nass (1996) showed, we do need online teach-ing and learning services to at least appear to be friendly, patient, efficient, polite, relevant, personalized, social and human. Parents spend hundreds of millions on one-to-one tuition for their kids. Much, much more is spent on teachers and teaching. But it is not robots that will give unlimited amounts of attention and help, in ways no teacher or even parent can; it is online support and personalized learning. These services are available 24/7 and are patient, scalable and consistent. We must be careful not to foist old models and existing methods onto technology.

Robots have appeared at a slew of education and training conferences, as keynote speakers and in sessions on AI in learning. Sophia appeared as a keynote, rather disappointingly on wheels, at DevLearn in Las Vegas. Pepper the robot even answered questions from the Education Committee in the UK Parliament. This could be seen as a bit of fun but it is deeply misleading. Robot teachers not only promise something that is not practical; they promise something that is inadvisable.

## Teaching versus technology

So much effort goes into thinking about how AI will replace us when the reality is that it is more likely to augment and enhance our abilities. This is particularly true in learning, where it will help teachers and trainers to teach. As we will explore later in the book, it promises to reduce workload, provide administrative support, give teachers more data about their learners and allow detailed, personalized feedback that is beyond the practical limitation of the human teacher. It may also improve the quality of teaching.

We have all heard the line, 'It's not about the technology, it's about the learning'. Learning then tech? Tech then learning? Both positions are wrong. The truth is a little more prosaic. The relationship between learning and technology is a complex dialectic. It always has been and always will be. The great revolutions in technology that shaped the learning landscape were writing, alphabets, writing instruments, paper, printing, books, calculators, computers, the internet and now AI – none of this technology came from the 'learning' community. What did come from the learning community were classrooms, lecterns and blackboards. On the other hand, a lot of learning technology has been shaped by great learning professionals who make it usable, productive and manageable. It is not one-way traffic; it is a dialectic.

Also, those who teach, or are interested in learning, use the technology sensitive to the needs of learning and learners. Indeed, there are many examples of technology that emerged from this sensitivity to learning theory and learner needs. All manner of useful content creation, content delivery, communication, collaboration, assessment, learner management, learning management, simulation, spaced practice, and adaptive systems have been developed with learning in mind, often by educators. Moodle (modular object-oriented dynamic learning environment) is a good example, where Dougimas took the LMS idea and turned it into an open-source tool, something incredibly useful for educators.

Both sides produce failure when they stick to their prejudices: the technology folk when they overreach and overpromise, the learning folk when they refuse to listen and overreact. We've seen the disastrous consequences when both tech and teachers get obsessed with 'devices', leading to the wrong focus on short-lived mosquito projects, using tablets, mobiles and whiteboards – when what is needed are long-lived tortoise projects – sustainable projects that appeal to actual users. This is what happens when overzealous hardware vendors team up with teachers and educators and fall for a sort of 'device fetish', when the actual solutions are in software and technology like AI. All of this focus on devices leads, year after year, to a swarm of 'mosquito' projects. Most EdTech projects are mosquito projects: lots of buzz, tricky to spot and short-lived. They are funded but rarely sustainable. We need long-life 'tortoise' projects. Tortoise projects are infrastructure projects that improve bandwidth in schools, the Open University, Janet and SuperJanet, Wikipedia, Khan Academy, YouTube, MOOCs and Moodle. None of these initiatives are device-focused. They focus on cognitive ergonomics, not consumer electronics. The lesson here is to stop the largely wasted research on device-based projects and do not keep on taking (and buying) the tablets. Think about teaching and learners, not devices.

Educational debate around technology is often obsessed with devices – tablets, mobiles, whiteboards, holes-in-walls, microbits, Raspberry Pi, 3D printers, and so on – which is to focus on the wrong side of the problem. Device fetishism has often been a destructive force in research, procurement, projects and outcomes. It is so easy to get older managers, entranced by shiny devices, to buy hardware, only to find that they are then treated with contempt by users.

Devices are identified and purchased without a detailed plan for the actual improvement of learning outcomes. Teacher or trainer support is left out, actual cost-effectiveness analysis is often absent, detailed analysis of the device affordances matched to learning tasks rarely thought out, maintenance costs underestimated, insurance a problem, change management and internal communications plans usually beyond the skills of the purchaser. They are also often bought with external funds, grants or on the back of the whim of someone who has attended a couple of conferences and 'seen the shiny light'. Similarly in corporate environments, where it is far more useful to think of learning ecosystems, which have integrated technology stacks that complement each other, speak to each other and provide flexibility, often driven by AI, on the interface, content delivery layer and data layer. This is about software, not hardware.

The way forward is to think strategically, not tactically; scale and efficacy, not pilots and ill-defined pilots. AI is a good example with adaptive learning. After 2,500 years of mathematical progress, AI has come of age, as hardware has become powerful enough to deliver it to us personally, the web bountiful enough to deliver huge amounts of data to feed the recent advances in natural language processing and machine learning. We see real progress by people from maths, engineering, coding and AI backgrounds. This is being tempered with good teachers and learning theorists to produce productive and useful tools.

This dialogue between the learning world and technology world is starting to bear fruit. In practice it is a complex dialectic. Tech arrives and sometimes changes the learning landscape without any intervention from the learning folk, sometimes adapted by the learning folk, and sometimes it is just used by hundreds of millions because it is useful. The educators versus tech argument is specious because it fails to recognize that the real world is messy. That is the way of the world – complex causality, not 'us v them', 'tech v learning', 'teachers v robots'. Sure, both sides have their purists, but what we need is synthesis.

AI-driven teachers are sure to make many educationalists and teachers splutter with indignation, but AI-driven educational and teaching assistants are already with us, online, as online services, chatbots or software in complex adaptive learning systems. The point, in the short term, is not to replace teachers but to replace teaching administration and some support and aspects of teaching with technology. We need to think about the problem here, which is learning outcomes. This may sound like heresy to some, but teaching is always a means to an end, never an end in itself. Neither is it always a necessary condition for learning to take place. Cheap, consumer tech, with brilliant AI and user experience (UX), points towards a future where online learning will have the affordances necessary for improved outcomes.

# References

Clark, RC and Mayer, RE (2016) *E-learning and the Science of Instruction: Proven guidelines for consumers and designers of multimedia learning*, John Wiley & Sons, Hoboken, NJ

Dennett, DC (2017) *From Bacteria to Bach and Back: The evolution of minds*, WW Norton & Company, New York

Marcus, G and Davis, E (2019) *Rebooting AI: Building artificial intelligence we can trust*, Pantheon Books, New York

Ng, A and Widom, J (2014) Origins of the modern MOOC (xMOOC).
    Available at http://www.robotics.stanford.edu/~ang/papers/mooc14-
    OriginsOfModernMOOC.pdf (archived at https://perma.cc/4QZL-BPH5)
Reeves, B and Nass, CI (1996) *The Media Equation: How people treat computers,
    television, and new media like real people and places*, Cambridge University
    Press, Cambridge
Turing, A (1951, 15 May) Can digital machines think? BBC Third Programme.
    Typescript available at turingarchive.org (archived at https://perma.cc/3GZK-3S47)

# 04

# Teaching

Technology for teaching, AI in particular, must be careful to avoid anthropomorphizing and silly ideas around robot teachers. However, AI does bring some specific solutions to the problems that teachers face.

It is useful to look at AI in terms of:

- teaching administration;
- teaching activities;
- enhancing teaching;
- making better teachers.

There are many problems with teaching, including: burdensome administration, teacher shortages and the need to update skills. As AI develops, it promises to alleviate some of these problems, not by replacing teachers, but, like most technology, by helping teachers to teach.

## AI for teacher administration

That brings us to a very specific challenge. What things can AI do that teachers can not or do not want to do? Here are some ideas (there are undoubtedly more):

- registration;
- administration;
- timetabling;
- lesson planning;
- learner engagement;

- learner support;
- assessing;
- marking;
- continuous professional development.

*Registration* is a mechanical chore, whether in schools, classrooms or lecture halls. Face recognition is being used in China to automate registration. Simple registration in the classroom, in seconds, is now real in China. Some Chinese schools even have gates, like automated passport control, that check the faces and ID of thousands of students a day, and the students flood through into school in minutes (Connor, 2018). This doesn't seem like such an invasion of privacy, unless the data is used for some other purpose. Indeed, it surely frees up both teacher and student time to do more educationally useful tasks. One could push this, as it has been in China, with face recognition used to spot and manage activities and behaviour in the classroom. Face recognition has been used, for example, to spot inattentive behaviour, and fed back electronically to the teacher. This, in some countries, would be seen as ethically dubious, but there can be little doubt that, in some countries at least, behaviour is a seriously disruptive problem, and that this could be part of a solution.

Of course, learning in large organizations is likely to be already managed in a learning management system, so there is no daily registration issue. However, there are the complex issues of knowing who needs what, where and when. The learning management system is often part of a wider talent management system, with integrated records for all learners in the organization. Learning experience platforms take this one step further and know not only who does what, where and when, but also recommend and personally deliver learning at points of need in the workflow.

*Administration*, whether for the department, school, university, inspection body, business or organization, takes up a fair percentage of any teacher's or trainer's time. No one escapes from the demands of what seems like ever-increasing levels of admin, as compliance, regulations and inspections rise. All of this tracking, measuring, recording and reporting takes time – time surely better spent on teaching. If, as seems possible, technology can track attendance and other administrative data, then it can be automated as the data is being gathered and can be analysed and reported. If we could automate as much of this admin as possible, using AI, surely we would? LMSs and virtual learning environments (VLEs) have helped manage this administration, and newer learning experience platforms take this further by introducing and automating AI-driven interfaces, personalized teaching and learning, and advanced analytics. This all makes the administration and delivery of learning experiences more flexible and sensitive to real needs in real organizations.

## What about timetabling?

Boston saved $5 million using AI from MIT to optimize the journeys their school buses took to school (Grossman, 2019). It saved 1 million miles every year and led to lower carbon emissions and more efficient journeys for thousands of students. Data from Google Maps and traffic patterns, along with information about which students needed to be where, including 11,000 with a disability, was used to reduce what was one of the highest transport per student costs in the US. Some buses were far from full; others took multiple trips. Now 50 routes have been scrapped, buses are fuller and the planning took 30 minutes rather than weeks. The $5 million saved was put straight back into classroom activities, and they are now looking at school timetabling.

Timetabling is certainly tricky, even in a single school, as one has to juggle far too many variables to keep in one's head, do it on paper or even produce within a planning tool. Resolving clashes and optimizing timetables can be done well using AI. Access to timetables has also been made available to students via chatbots using AI, lessening queries by email to teachers. In organizations, the timetabling of learning, whether offline training events or online delivery in the workflow, now demands through learning experience platforms a far more sophisticated and sensitive form of delivery.

*Lesson planning* is another time-consuming task for teachers and trainers. Embryonic projects on finding existing lesson plans and actual lesson planning are already using AI. IBM's 'Teacher Advisor' uses AI to help plan and deliver lessons. The aim is not just to save time, but to also enhance lessons. Its Watson search and resource recommendation tool allows you to find relevant math lessons, activities, videos, and so on – all from a curated collection of educator-approved materials (Teacher Advisor, 2019). You can search for existing lesson plans, customize them and save them in your personal planning portfolio. It accesses open educational resources from trusted sources and also helps with context, differentiation and remediation.

In large organizations, some global, the need is for planning and execution of large amounts of training in multiple languages to individuals across time zones. This requires a learning management system to manage the learners and learning or learning experience platforms that handle this complex planning through smart interfaces, but also automated, data-driven planning and execution. This is lesson planning with recommendation engines that produce plans for each and every person.

*Learner engagement* is a perennial problem for teachers. It is not possible to expect trainers and teachers to satisfy all of the expectations students have around learner engagement. Learners have a huge number of initial needs and some institutions have used AI-driven chatbots to help satisfy demand for answers to the many queries new students have on arrival, during onboarding and throughout their learning experience. These chatbots are becoming a normal part of the student experience. Staffordshire University's chatbot, Beacon, answers queries on campus facilities and support services. In addition to student recruitment and clearing, they have also been used for reflecting on subject choice and engagement. Chatbots have been implemented that support general student queries on subjects and courses, as well as course-specific help on assignments. On a larger scale within organizations, such as the German software company SAP, AI-driven chatbots are used to answer learning queries and deliver recommendations on courses. The response has been positive, with good learner reactions and better targeting through machine learning.

In organizational learning, engagement is being boosted by learning experience platforms that both push and pull learners, with nudge teaching, alerts and personalized delivery within the workflow, making content more relevant, delivered at the point of need. The system responds to engagement at the organizational level but also engages, using clever AI techniques, at the personal level.

Beyond engagement, there's ongoing *learner support*, where students need recommendations, help and support with problems around their course and course assignments. Beyond this, AI is being used to recommend personalized learning paths. AI-driven services such as chatbots can drive and automate this support.

*Assessment* is difficult, time-consuming and costly. If AI can be used to help build assessments, this would take a weight off teachers' workload. These can be automated assessments constructed using AI from source material, or adaptive testing. It could also be digital identification for online assessment using face and document recognition. The detection of cheating in this era of students buying essays and dissertations from essay mills is becoming a serious battle and, as will be shown later in the book, it is clear that AI is already playing a role, using natural language processing techniques, to detect cheating. Actually, what seems to be developing is AI-assisted help in shaping text assignments before submission.

Assessment in organizational learning is also moving towards the semantic assessment of open answers, rather than well-worn banks of multiple-choice questions. It is important that we know what people actually know, rather than relying on weak assessment methods. AI can help with both the creation of these more sophisticated assessments and the assessment process. Assessment is clearly one area where AI has made, and will continue to make, inroads. If teachers no longer have to set and mark homework, assignments and exams, a huge portion of the teaching task will have been automated.

Who likes *marking*? Not many. It seems reasonable for AI to start marking free-text answers, even essays. This has been pioneered at Bolton College and in the corporate world by WildFire, but essay marking software has been around for a long time and will only get better with machine learning and more sophisticated AI techniques. One can still include the human component, but for knowledge-based marking, if a machine can do it as well as a human mind, but more quickly and at a fraction of the cost, why not? It seems more important for teachers to get accurate and reliable marks to act upon than to do it all themselves, eating into their valuable time.

*Continuing professional development (CPD)* has always been difficult for teachers, with often rare and poor training days. But teachers are increasingly using social media and online resources to find useful CPD resources and to connect with people they can learn with and from. Many well-known experts are on Twitter and freely share their knowledge and practical wisdom. As Twitter is mediated by AI, this is another example of AI creeping into the delivery of learning,

## AI for teaching activities

Okay, let's up the ante and examine how AI can be used in what is regarded less as support but more like full-on teaching tasks. As we've noted, teachers are not ends in themselves; they are always a means to an end – mostly cognitive improvements in the learner. Given this premise, could it be possible to eventually replace certain teaching tasks, even roles, with AI technology? This may not happen soon, but let us see where this is going and whether it could.

Obvious points are that AI is 365/24/7, fast, scalable and therefore could be a lot cheaper. This gives it a head start. But in what way could it teach?

First, we need to break down the functions of teaching and learning. We can use a typical higher-order, teacher-training schema as a starting point:

- providing answers;
- student engagement and support in learning;
- demonstrate good subject and curriculum knowledge;
- plan and teach effective learning experiences;
- promote good progress and outcomes by learners;
- adapt to respond to the strengths and needs of all pupils;
- make accurate and productive use of assessment;
- manage behaviour effectively;
- high standards of personal and professional conduct.

*Providing answers* is what teachers have done for millennia. Google has now been around for two decades and has already delivered a remarkable pedagogic shift with search. Let's also reflect on something that has already happened. Since Google's inception, the number of librarians has steadily fallen. We have less need of book and journal warehouses now that most knowledge is online. Beyond this, open educational resources such as Wikipedia, YouTube, Khan Academy and thousands of other sources, have transformed the learning landscape. All of this is available through AI-enabled search. But beyond search we see apps emerge, such as Photomath (2019), where you simply point your smartphone at a maths problem and it gives you the answer. More than this, it gives you the steps in between.

Chatbots also provide a natural language AI interfaces layer, below which lies sophisticated search that can interrogate documents, PowerPoints, videos and learning resources to find what you need. That's how powerful AI is becoming in education and workplace learning.

*Learner engagement and support in learning* is different from the contextual support they need around facilities, such as libraries and campus services that we discussed earlier. We have a good example of student support in the remarkable Georgia Tech bot, Jill Watson. This AI teaching assistant bot, trained to answer based on prior responses, was used with AI students, without them knowing. They were more than fooled; they praised the teacher for its efficacy and speed. We can expect a lot more of this, as teacher support gives way to intelligent AI agent support.

Domain-specific bots, such as the TUI bot on leadership, is a good example of AI being used in a learning experience. Its success came from its ability to be there 24/7, and provide a method of learning that was engaging, responsive to learner questions and consistent for the organization.

To demonstrate *good subject and curriculum knowledge* has been the hallmark of a good teacher. This is where AI is starting to make progress. At one level Google already provides access to 'knowledge' on every subject, in detail. On 'knowledge', Watson beat the Jeopardy Champions way back in 2011, and Watson has become a web-based service with access to huge knowledge bases and AI, even taking part in debates showing critical skills. At the skills level, YouTube is already the search engine of choice for learning how to 'do' things. With 3D, virtual worlds, one can see how learning by doing can be expanded, as it was with flight sims, through cheap consumer technology, high in AI. But we must be careful here. AI may appear to exhibit deep knowledge, but it does not yet exhibit deep teaching. It cannot read between the lines or react in a flexible manner to different angles and problems.

To *plan and teach effective learning experiences* one must be sensitive to the needs of learners in terms of differentiation and special needs. We have seen how the administration of lesson planning could be aided by AI tools. Lessons or learning experiences can be idiosyncratic, even flawed. AI design offers not only optimal design but also continuous improvement, as it can use individual and aggregated data to spot poor components in lessons. There are plenty of examples of this already, from MOOCs and other forms of online learning, where errors in content, badly designed questions, and overlong videos and presentations have all been caught by data produced by online learning systems that constantly look for improvement. Anomalies such as single questions that almost everyone finds difficult or answers wrongly are often a sign, for example, that the question is badly designed. 'Structured' is an interesting concept here and one could argue that learning needs to be far more structured than the one-size-fits-all lesson plan. Differentiation could be identified and handled by AI in a way that traditional teaching cannot. The promise is of learning experiences that are not only structured towards individual learners but also continuously improve as machine learning identifies and acts on identified weaknesses. AI may, at some point, even automatically produce lessons and content.

Teaching basic knowledge is the first area where AI can help relieve the pressure on teachers' time. Rather than teach the basics, most teachers and trainers would rather be engaged with higher-order learning. At all levels in education and training, elementary knowledge and courses could be partly automated using AI delivery for short courses, even micro-learning, and for longer courses, adaptive learning. This is being pioneered in corporate learning and in institutions such as Arizona State University, where a number of adaptive, 101 courses have been delivered to improve attainment and lower dropout rates.

The automation of teaching through an LMS or LXP has been around for over two decades in large organizations. It has not been without its problems, and many question the delivery of largely compliance training, which far from being part of someone's personal development, seems to be a method of protecting the organization from its own employees. Nevertheless, the rise of learning experience platforms may correct this tendency, with a focus on development sensitive to the actual needs of individuals, rather than the perceived needs of organizations.

*Promoting good progress and outcomes* by learners is not easy but it is what teaching is, in essence, about. Progress tracking is not easy, as it requires the simultaneous tracking of actual performance across many learners. This is notoriously difficult in teaching. AI, on the other hand, promises to do this across many learners in real time, as it gathers evidence that no teacher can possibly hope to gather through traditional observation and testing. More than this, one could argue that AI has a lot to offer in that it can be designed to be free from the human biases that sometimes inhibit learner progress. We have ample evidence of gender and socio-economic bias in teaching. AI can be free from bias on gender, race, accent and background.

As AI-driven learning solutions produce more granular data, through learning experience platforms, xAPI and learning record stores, optimal delivery, recording and measurement become possible in a way that is subtler, more dynamic and flexible. Data can be used, potentially, to *describe* what things are happening, *analyse* and tell us why things are happening, *predict* what is likely to happen and even *prescribe* what should happen. Again, AI promises a scalable solution to this problem that may be of higher quality than a teacher-delivered system.

Adapting teaching to respond to the *strengths and needs of all learners* is next to impossible in a one-to-many teaching environment, whether the classroom, lecture hall or training room. To solve this problem, one of AI's first forays into teaching has been through adaptive systems. These are already at work and producing impressive results. They act like a satnav, which constantly monitors the performance of individual learners and adjusts what they are asked to do next. This is done in real time. Content is no longer a linear curriculum of flat resources but a network of learning experiences that can be dynamically delivered to individual learners, based on their precise needs at that precise time. The analytic and predictive strengths of AI may very well identify factors that both inhibit and enhance learning in any individual.

In addition, AI can monitor and deliver to the needs of all learners, especially those with special educational needs – high ability, English as an additional language, disabilities – and be able to use and improve distinctive approaches. Technology has already made a big difference in special educational needs (SEN); AI will make an ever bigger difference. AI has, of course, provided invaluable text-to-speech support for the visually impaired and speech-to-text for the orally impaired. AI has also been used to spot dyslexia, so that early support can be provided. All of this may be way beyond the ability of any teacher to deliver on scale. It is here that the first successes in AI-driven teaching are being achieved. In organizations, learning experience platforms can provide AI-driven nudges, recommendations and levels of personalization that take every learner's needs into account.

To make *accurate and productive use of assessment* we must break assessment down into formative and summative; both, it can be argued, could benefit from AI. Formative assessment is used during the learning experience to aid learning; summative assessment is end-point assessment for a final check on knowledge competence or ability.

Formative assessment is difficult and often of poor quality in one-to-many classrooms. It is largely absent from the lecture hall. There are three ways that AI could improve formative assessment, in ways superior to current 'teacher' delivery. First the quantity: adaptive learning systems could deliver more feedback than teachers. It is self-evident that AI is scalable in the way a teacher is not and can deliver millions of pieces of feedback to millions of learners in milliseconds – this is what Google does already, albeit at a basic level. Second, AI could deliver higher-quality feedback, which can also be used to determine what is literally delivered next in an online lesson. Formative assessment is therefore one area where AI already excels. Increasingly we will also see, through AI, immediate feedback, delivered verbally or in text, as AI-driven speech recognition and delivery becomes commonplace. With speech we will move towards the sort of frictionless interface than enables good teaching and learning.

On summative assessment, AI can deliver adaptive questioning and, using item response theory, deliver assessment that includes learner confidence and other data during the assessment that no teacher could gather. It can also deliver to whatever statutory assessment requirements are in place.

Essay marking is reaching a level where it can perform as well as an expert assessor. Automated marking is also becoming more common. Online proctoring uses AI in typing patterns to identify the examinees, as does face recognition for digital identity and real-time face recognition, as the learner takes the exam.

To *manage behaviour effectively* you must be able to command your audience, whether offline or online. A bot that mimics bad behaviour can be used for professional practice. For example, a virtual boy with attitude, 'Eli', developed by Penn State, mimics an awkward child in the classroom (Clark, 2017). It is used by student teachers to practise their skills on dealing with such problems before they hit the classroom. This chatbot shows how, eventually, sophisticated AI-driven chatbots may be able to train teachers in handling tricky situations in schools. The same is true of handling conflict in the workplace, where AI-driven simulations can do a similar job.

A more complex example is AI software that tracks attention and behaviour. This is already being trialled in China, through face recognition and also neurotech headsets (Connor, 2018). One may not wish to go down this route, but one can't deny that AI is coming up with innovative ways of helping teachers deal with the problem.

It is clear that most of these AI innovations are partial solutions. Teachers will not be replaced. In fact, teaching is likely to be augmented and enhanced by AI innovation. Teachers will still set high expectations which inspire, motivate and challenge pupils. Teachers will still be role models for young people. Teaching is a profession that will not disappear because of AI. It will, however, in time, like any other profession, be profoundly altered by AI.

## AI for enhancing teaching

Few saw self-driving, autonomous cars coming. That happened because of AI. Few may also see self-driving, autonomous learners. That may also, especially with adult learners, come through AI automated or augmented teaching. Machine learning not only embodies learning; it learns about learners while they learn. It is, to a small degree, like a fast learning teacher. There is reason to suppose that teaching may, to some degree, even a substantial degree, be automated by AI, without wholly replacing teachers. If this is possible, it will be a momentous breakthrough, as education at all levels, whether schools, colleges, universities or workplaces, will experience massive reductions in costs. The developing world, where teaching is a problem in terms of quality and supply, is also likely to receive a huge boost. At some point we may look back at teachers and classrooms as we look back on manual manufacturing in factories. This is not to devalue teachers, just that AI technology may, as in many other areas, and in some support areas in teaching, get more valuable and smarter.

We are now in the 'Age of Algorithms' and, so far, the most promising use of teaching and learning data is through AI. Yet algorithms are faceless and anonymous, hidden from view. As users, we rarely know what role they play in our lives, if we're even aware of their agency at all. Like icebergs, their power lies hidden beneath the surface, with only a user interface visible above the waterline. So let's make them a little more visible.

Despite the charge that AI solutions are biased, algorithms are largely blind to the sort of social biases (gender, race, colour, age, ethnicity, religion, accent, social background) we commonly see, not only in society through sexism, racism and snobbery, but also in teaching, where social biases are not uncommon. In education, it is useful to distinguish between subtle and blatant biases, in that the teacher may be perceived to be unbiased and not be aware of their own biases. We know, for example, that gender bias has a strong effect on subject choice and that both gender and race affect teacher feedback (Whitehead, 1996). AI systems can, with effort, be free of such social biases.

Cognitive biases around ability versus effort, made clear by the likes of Carol Dweck (2017) on fixed versus growth mindsets, clearly affect teacher and learner behaviour, leading to self-fulfilling predictions on student attainment. Considerable bias in marking and grades has also been evidenced. There may also be ingrained theories and practices that are out of date and now disproven, such as learning styles that heavily influence teaching. AI-driven teaching, built on sound theory and practice, can, over time, based on actual evidence, try to eliminate such biases.

To teach is human and teacher performance is variable. That is not a criticism of teachers but an observation about human nature and behaviour. AI in teaching operates, albeit in a limited fashion, 24/7/365. Of course, one could argue that the affective, emotional side of learning is not always provided by AI-driven learning. That is true, but good design can ensure that it is a feature of delivery. Sentiment or emotional analysis by machine learning is making good progress. So even here, AI techniques around the interpretation of social learning data, face recognition, attention and emotion are being researched and built.

Let us remember that AI can do things that brains cannot. This seems like a bold claim, but the number of variables, and sheer formulaic power of an ensemble of algorithms in conjunction with data and immense processing power, in many areas, is well beyond the capability of the brain. In addition, the data feeds and data mining opportunities, as well as consistent and correct delivery of timely and relevant content to individuals as and when they need it, is often beyond the capability of many teachers. The problem is that most teaching is not one-to-one and therefore those tacit skills are difficult to apply to large numbers of different learners – the norm in educational and training institutions. For the moment there are many tacit skills in teachers that AI has not captured. That has to be recognized, but that is not a reason for stopping, only a reason for driving forward. We will see ever more sophisticated analysis of cognitive behaviour, where the sheer number of cognitive misconceptions and problems cannot be identified by a teacher but can be by careful AI analysis.

A group of learners can be represented by a distribution curve. Yet suppose we use a system that is sensitive not just to the bulk of learners but also to the leading and trailing tail? AI treats the learners as individuals and can personalize the learning journey for that learner. You are, essentially, streaming into streams of one at a time. The consequence is the right route for each individual that leads to learning at their speed of ability at any given time. The promise is that learners get through courses more quickly. We saw that Bloom, in his famous 2 sigma paper, showed the significant advantage of one-to-one teaching over other forms of instruction (Bloom, 1984). We now have the opportunity to start to deliver on this researched promise and already have evidence that this can be achieved on scale.

Slower learners do not get left behind in adaptive, AI-driven systems or suffer catastrophic failure, often in a final summative exam when it is too late, because the system brings them along at a speed that suits them. Most university systems have huge dropout rates. In schools, a considerable number of students fail to achieve even modest levels of attainment. This approach could lower dropout rates, something that has critical personal, financial and social consequences.

Such systems can produce reports that really do match personal attainment, through personal feedback for the learner that informs their motivation and progress through a course. Rather than standard feedback and remedial loops, the learner can feel as though they really are being tutored, as the feedback is detailed and the learning journey finessed to their personal needs. Teachers also have a lot to gain from feedback out of such systems. Early evidence suggests that good teachers, in combination with such systems, produce great results.

Teachers need to learn, though many would question the efficacy of current training days or current models of rushed or absent CPD. AI systems also learn. It is a mathematical feature of machine learning that the system gets better the more students that take the course. We must be careful about exaggerated claims in this area, but it is an area of intense research and development. We are now at a level where adaptive systems themselves adapt, as more and more students go through the system. It is this ability to constantly and relentlessly learn and improve that may, ultimately, take AI beyond the ability of teachers to constantly adapt.

Courses are often repeated, without a great deal of reflection on their weaknesses, or even inaccuracies. Many studies of textbooks have shown that they are strewn with mistakes. The same is true of exams and high-stakes assessment. Adaptive, algorithmic systems can be designed to automatically identify erroneous questions, weak spots, good resources and even optimal paths through a network of learning possibilities.

Humans are not scalable, but AI is massively scalable. We have already seen how Google, Facebook, Amazon, Netflix, retailers and many other services use algorithmic power to help you make better decisions, and these operate at the level of billions of users. In other words, there is no real limit to their scalability. If we can apply that personalization of learning on a massive scale, education could break free of its heavy cost burden.

The AI, adaptive approach to learning promises to provide things that live teachers cannot and could never deliver. All of the above is being realized through organizations like CogBooks, who have built adaptive, algorithmic systems. This is important, as we cannot get fixated by the oft-repeated mantra that face-to-face teaching is always a necessary condition for learning – it is not. Neither should we simply stop at the point of seeing technology as merely something to be used by a teacher in a classroom. It can, but it can be more than this. This approach to technology-based learning could be a massive breakthrough in terms of learning outcomes for millions of learners. It already operates in the learning sphere, through search – perhaps the most profound pedagogic change we have seen in the last century.

The bottom line, and there is a bottom line here, is that human teachers are expensive to train, expensive to pay, expensive to retire, variable in quality and, most important of all, non-scalable. This is why education continues to be so expensive. There is no way that current supply can meet future demand at a reasonable cost. The solution to this problem cannot be throwing money at non-scalable solutions. Smart, online solutions that take some elements of good teaching, and replicate them in software, must be considered.

## AI and online learning make you a better teacher

Time and time again, teachers and academics who have been seriously involved in online learning have found that they gained enormously from the experience. They become better teachers.

An obvious advantage is that online learning makes teaching visible. Every teaching and learning and development (L&D) professional can benefit from deeper reflection on their skills and practices. Participation in the design, development and delivery of an AI-driven online experience will broaden and deepen the process of reflection. Online encourages a more evidence-based approach to both the profession and process, because when you're at a distance from learners, you *need* to be a better teacher.

AI systems need good teachers to construct the content that they deliver. Adaptive AI systems have authoring systems that try to make it easy for teachers to build courses. This is often co-created with experienced instructional designers with specific skills in online learning, but some go it alone.

Online learning lies naked on the screen, open to scrutiny in a way that is rarely true in the classroom or lecture hall. This forces you to be clear, precise and accurate. It also forces you to consider attention, chunking, elaboration, deliberate practice, spaced practice and other principles in good teaching that you may have never previously considered. The design, development and delivery of AI-driven, online content improves the quality of the content. Adaptive systems now even identify weak and erroneous assessment items. When thousands of students got an algebra question wrong on a Coursera course, it had to be changed. Content production can crystallize and eliminate poor learning design.

For a number of years universities have been involved in online degree courses, where the online students never meet their tutors or other students. Year after year they perform as well as their campus colleagues on the levels of degree they attain. This is down to the detailed, structured, archived and frequent dialogue and feedback they receive from their online tutors, who are forced to use online structures. AI can help deal with this social interaction.

Online delivery also forces your hand on assessment. You cannot get away with primitive and destructive 'hands-up anyone' strategies. You often have to identify, and tackle, common student misconceptions, as you have to counter them with concrete strategies. This is particularly true in adaptive courses, where you have to be explicit in the dependencies and networked structure of the knowledge. In addition, online automatically produces data.

These analytics allow you to diagnose issues and take action, as a teacher, to improve the motivation and attainment of your learners.

Try running a teaching webinar online and you will soon learn to acquire skills on the use of the tool, monitor chat and questions, improve your presentation and teaching skills. In Arizona State University's Biology BIO100 course, Susan Holechek, their most experienced instructor, saw attainment rise from 72 per cent in the spring to over 92 per cent in the fall, using an adaptive learning system to enhance her teaching: 'I think we had the perfect combination of a good system and good teacher,' said the subsequent report (Clark, 2016). It is this combination of good teacher and good tech, in technology-enhanced teaching, that makes a real difference to even experienced teachers.

A point so often missed is that the online teacher and academic is likely to teach many more students than they would have in classrooms and lecture theatres. A school teacher, lecturer or trainer over a lifetime will only teach a few thousand pupils. If your profession is to teach, then reaching the minds of tens of thousands, hundreds of thousands, even millions, is surely a noble goal. Sure, there's the intimacy of the classroom and the human side of face-to-face teaching. But rather than being behind closed doors in a classroom or lecture hall, online teaching forces you to become a more visible and possibly a better teacher. You hone existing skills, enhance others and learn new teaching methods. That stretches you as a professional.

Like it or not, technology, especially the internet, is a massively relevant cultural phenomenon. To ignore the online world, as a teacher, is to ignore the reality of changes in the world outside of educational institutions. There has probably been more pedagogic change in the last 20 years than the last 2,000 years, through the use of technology. Technology is more than a tool; it is part of every teacher's and student's life. In terms of relevance alone, it benefits teachers to understand and use what their learners are likely to use in their personal and working lives.

## References

Bloom, BS (1984) The 2 sigma problem: The search for methods of group instruction as effective as one-to-one tutoring, *Educational Researcher*, **13** (6), pp 4–16

Clark, D (2016) 10 ways online learning can make you a BETTER TEACHER, Donald Clark Plan B. Available at http://donaldclarkplanb.blogspot.com/ 2016/01/10-ways-online-learning-makes-you.html (archived at https://perma.cc/N5DW-YXSW)

Clark, D (2017) 10 uses for chatbots in learning (with examples), Donald Clark Plan B, 17 December. Available at https://donaldclarkplanb.blogspot.com/search?q=Penn+state+chatbot (archived at https://perma.cc/2N99-LJHX)

Connor, N (2018) Chinese school uses facial recognition to monitor student attention in class, *The Telegraph*, 17 May. Available at https://www.telegraph.co.uk/news/2018/05/17/chinese-school-uses-facial-recognition-monitor-student-attention/ (archived at https://perma.cc/TS9R-7CC9)

Dweck, C (2017) *Mindset: Changing the way you think to fulfil your potential*, Hachette UK, London

Grossman, D (2019) How an algorithm made the buses in Boston better, Popular Mechanics. Available at https://www.popularmechanics.com/technology/infrastructure/a28689713/algorithm-boston-buses/ (archived at https://perma.cc/5RUY-ZDND)

Photomath (2019) Website. Available at https://www.photomath.net/en (archived at https://perma.cc/G8AG-B2TQ)

Teacher Advisor (2019) Website. Available at https://teacheradvisor.org (archived at https://perma.cc/F8UX-FV3Z)

Whitehead, JM (1996) Sex stereotypes, gender identity and subject choice at A-level, *Educational Research*, 38 (2), pp 147–60. Available at: https://www.tandfonline.com/doi/abs/10.1080/0013188960380203 (archived at https://perma.cc/7RR2-HQC3)

## PART THREE

# Chatbots

# 05

# AI is the new UI

In the seminal AI movie, *2001: A Space Odyssey*, HAL, the on-board computer, reads the lips of the two humans, who converse inside a pod, and decides that they pose a danger. HAL is an autonomous learner. HAL stands for 'Heuristically programmed ALgorithmic computer'. It turns out that HAL has become a reality. Indeed, we deal with thousands of useful HALs every time we go online.

The vast portion of the software iceberg that lies behind current interfaces – doing its clever but invisible thing, the real building blocks of contemporary computing – is algorithms and AI. Whenever you search, get online recommendations, engage with social media, buy, do online banking, online dating, see online ads – the experience is mediated by algorithms doing their devilishly clever work.

We open a file, it is decompressed, we save a file, it is compressed, we send a file, it is managed across a global network. We Skype, WebX, Snapchat, WhatsApp, Facetime – all of this is enabled by smart AI in terms of compression, networks and decompression. The underlying technology is fundamentally algorithmic. Lossless and lossy compression and decompression magically squeeze big files into little files for transfer. On top of this are error correcting codes, mistakes that fix themselves, so that sound, pictures and videos can be saved, stored and retrieved without loss, especially across networks, where these clever algorithms maintain quality. We sometimes forget that basic online communication, a key enabler in search, social and online learning, is only possible because of algorithmic techniques.

Public key cryptography algorithms is how encryption works and keeps your credit card details safe when buying stuff. Amazon, ApplePay, eBay, PayPal, credit cards and the entire world of online retail would not exist without this algorithm. Spam filters, phishing, even higher-order cyber-threats, are all handled by AI. So the ability to do business in online learning, make payments, buy courses, and do online assessment is mediated by AI.

Whenever you go online, you are using AI. Google is the obvious example. Beyond Google, our social media is mediated by the algorithmic selection of items on our Facebook timelines, Twitter feeds or Instagram experiences. Our email is filtered by AI spam detectors. Online dating is mediated by AI. Buy a book, or anything else on Amazon, and you will be subtly prompted into looking at, and buying, other related items. Watch Netflix and you will choose movies, documentaries and series that are selected by AI.

As the online revolution has accelerated, the often invisible application of AI and algorithms has crept into a vast range of our online activities. In the 21st century, cheap, fast and powerful online hardware, with fast internet access, has taken algorithms into the homes and minds of everyone who uses the web and is now embedded in the real world of passport control, crime detection, ATMs and in the internet of things. We are already networked into AI to such a degree that it is our constant companion, part of what we do and how we live. Our extended cognition has gone beyond the tools we use, such as pens, smartphones and what we see on the web. It now includes other smart entities, pieces of AI.

Note how the top tier of the stock market is dominated by tech companies that deliver access and services online. Note, also, that most have turned themselves into AI companies. Many of the most valuable companies in the world now have AI at the heart of their strategies: Apple, Alphabet (Google), Microsoft, Amazon, Netflix, Facebook, IBM, Samsung, Baidai, Alibaba and Tencent. Some, such as Google, IBM and Microsoft, have been explicit on this strategy. Others, such as Apple, Samsung, Netflix and Facebook, have been acquiring skills and have huge research resources in AI. Note also that Tesla, albeit a car company, is really an AI company. Their cars are 'always on' learning robots. We are seeing a rapid shift in technology towards ubiquitous AI.

It is difficult to see how many smaller companies will beat them in AI, as they have the cash, infrastructure, processing power and expertise to stay ahead of the game. On the other hand, they are not nimble and sometimes lack the innovative streak that smaller companies and organizations often possess.

In learning, we have all been immersed in AI since we first started using Google. Google exemplifies the success of AI in having created one of the world's most successful companies on the back of AI. Beyond simple search, they also enable more specific AI-driven search through Google Scholar, Google Maps, Google Translation and other services. Whether it is documents, videos, images, audio or maps, search has become the ubiquitous mode of access. AI is the real enabler when it comes to access. Search engine indexing finds needles in the world's biggest haystack. Search for something on the web and you are 'indexing' billions of documents and images. This is not a trivial task and it needs smart algorithms to do it at all, in a tiny fraction of a second. PageRank was the technology that made Google one of the biggest companies in the world. We all have, at our fingertips, the ability to research and find the things that only a tiny elite had access to only 20 years ago. In learning, it enabled perhaps the most profound pedagogic shift in decades, giving us instantaneous search to almost all knowledge, many tools and services.

Amazon has built the world's largest retail company with a raw focus on the user experience, presented by their recommendation engine. Their AI platform, Alexa, now delivers a range of services, but it was built on recommendations, first on books, then other goods. But recommendation engines are now everywhere on the web. You are more often than not presented with choices from pre-selected options, rather than the result of a search. Netflix is a good example, where the tiling is tailored to your needs. Most social media feeds are now AI-driven, as are many online services, where what you (and others) do determines what you see. This is already here in AI-driven learning, such as adaptive learning and chatbots.

Siri, Cortana, Google Assistant, Alexa… voice recognition, enabled by advances in AI through natural language processing, has changed the way we communicate with technology. As speech is our natural form of communication, it is a more natural interface, giving significant advantages in some contexts. We now see speech recognition move from being a topic of research to real commercial application, as AI in its many forms, but particularly deep learning and large data sets, has allowed some of the world's largest tech companies to use it with hundreds of millions of customers: Apple, Amazon, Google, Microsoft, Samsung and others.

What we now see is AI mediation in online learning, through the delivery of notifications, nudges, peer interaction and spaced practice. In adaptive, personalized learning, AI is used to optimize how you proceed through a course in real time, determining what you see on the next screen. Beyond this lies all sorts of techniques that enhance teaching and learning.

## Invisible interface

What do the most popular online applications all have in common? They all use AI-driven interfaces which use sophisticated AI to personalize in terms of filtering, relevance, convenience, time and place-sensitivity. They work because they tailor themselves to your needs. Few notice the invisible hand that makes them work, that makes them more appealing. In fact, they work because they are invisible. It is not the user interface that matters; it is the user experience.

Yet, in online learning, AI UIs are rare. That is a puzzle, as it is the one area of human endeavour that has the most to gain. As Black and Wiliam (2005) showed, feedback that is relevant, clear and precise goes a long way in learning – not so much a silver bullet as a series of well-targeted rifle shots that keep the learner moving forward. When learning is sensitive to the learners' needs in terms of pace, relevance and convenience, they progress, as they are not the victim of a batched, one-size-fits-all process.

Learning demands attention, and because our working memory is the narrow funnel through which we acquire knowledge and skills, the more frictionless the interface, the more efficient the speed and efficacy of learning. Why load the learner with the extra tasks of learning an interface, navigation and extraneous noise? We have seen steady progress beyond the QWERTY keyboard, designed to slow typing down to avoid mechanical jams, towards mice and touch screens. But it is with the leap into AI that interfaces are becoming truly invisible.

Voice was the breakthrough and voice recognition is only now reaching the level of reliability that allows it to be used in consumer computers, smartphones with Siri, Cortana and Google Assistant, as well as on devices in the home like Amazon Echo and Google Home. We do not have to learn how to speak and listen; those are skills we picked up effortlessly as young children. In a sense, we did not have to learn how to do these things in any educational sense; they came naturally.

We are at the beginning of the era of voice interfacing. 'Voice' is one of the top internet trends, a game changer in interface design and consumer behaviour, as keyboards, mice and touch have been in the past, but what impact could it have in learning? Voice recognition, driven by leaps in AI performance, allows personalized voice recognition, even tonal and emotional recognition, and it is hands-free. It is also low cost, requiring just a microphone and speaker. It also chimes with the rise of the internet of things. The barriers to adoption have been accuracy, latency and social awkwardness, but, as the first two are being solved, this leaves the third, which is a social issue.

Recognition and response must be accurate and fast. Failures and slow speeds turn users off. The good news is that we have punched through the 90 per cent accuracy barrier and are moving fast. At 95–99 per cent (not easy), the show really is on the road. The number of smartphone users using voice has risen rapidly, and that number will rise further as the technology gets better and habits change.

In terms of learning we must be a bit careful. Sure we can speak (150 wpm) faster than we can type (40 wpm), but we can also read faster than we can hear. There is also the huge hurdle of speaking to non-humans in public, even private spaces – the embarrassment factor. We have evidence that it has already taken root in the home with the sales of voice-enabled devices; the car is another similar target, where being hands-free matters. But what about on public transport or in the workplace? In these contexts, silence may remain golden.

Sci-fi films have been showing us voice-activated worlds for decades – it is now a reality. And with Siri, Google Home and Amazon Echo, we see early signs of its power. A slew of innovations in AI have improved its efficacy. AI will underpin tech for the foreseeable future, and what has given this technology a boost is that voice recognition, with the help of machine learning, has accelerated in just the last few years to become a mainstream consumer product in the home.

Amazon's Echo is a home-based, voice-activated personal assistant, a competitor to Siri, using a platform called Alexa. Alexa has a 'skills' kit. As a customer, you get a weekly email telling you about these new skills. It will play your music, using just voice commands, even from the far side of the room when music is playing (clever), handle Google Calendar, read audiobooks, deliver news, sports results, weather, order a pizza, get a cab on Uber, control lights, switches, thermostats and so on. It is a frictionless interface to the 'internet of things'.

Above all, it is a cloud-based AI service, on tap; it learns fast and is always adapting to your speech, vocabulary and preferences. It becomes, in effect, a personal assistant that learns not only about you but also from aggregated data. This is where it gets interesting. The aim is to get the internet of things going in the home through 'voice' and the activation of other devices.

Google is great, but we still largely write our requests. However, as speech recognition gets better, it will become quicker and easier to simply ask verbally. As Google Home, Amazon Echo, Siri, Cortana and other services take many of us into the internet of things, in our homes, cars and other places, we will want voice to trigger events, get help, find answers and arrange our lives.

The car is now a room. It is also somewhere you can learn. The home is now networked, a place you can learn. Your mobile is voice ready, a place where you can learn. In some of these environments, having your hands free is essential (driving) and useful (home). How-to tasks like cooking, repairing things and finding things out make sense. But behind this shift from text to voice is an interesting debate in learning.

## Learning interfaces

One could argue that AI could push us towards more authentic and, some argue, balanced forms of education and learning. Typing will always be an awkward interface. It is difficult to learn, error prone and requires physical input devices.

Reading is another skill that takes years to master. Listening to the spoken word is a skill we do not have to learn. We are grammatical geniuses aged three. Speech is primary and normal, reading and writing relatively recent adjuncts. So, when it comes to *learning*, speech recognition (output) and voice (input) give us frictionless dialogue. It could stimulate a return to more natural forms of teaching and learning.

This may result in significant improvements in teaching and learning, both of which have, arguably, been over-colonized by 'text'. Schooling, in all of its manifestations, has become ever more obsessed by text, and there is a good argument for rebalancing the system away from an endless series of written tasks, essays and dissertations towards more efficient, meaningful and relevant teaching and learning.

The blackboard has a lot to answer for. At that moment, teachers turned their backs on dialogue and conversation with learners and began to lecture, mediating their teaching with text; it can be even worse with text-laden PowerPoint. The teacher's voice started to get lost. Nowhere was this more evident than in higher education, where the blackboard reinforced and deeply embedded the 'lecture'. To this day, especially in maths and sciences, 'lecturers' (a job title that uniquely identifies the profession's problem) turned their back to learners and started writing. It is the opposite of teaching; it is writing.

In schooling we also had the drift towards text-based subjects. The essay as assessment has now descended into a game where students know that they will not get feedback for days, even weeks (often a grade with a few skimpy comments). So they share, plagiarize, buy essays and, in exams, memorize them, so that critical thinking is abandoned in favour of regurgitation. This is not to argue for the abandonment of writing, or essays, just less dependence on this one-size-fits-all form of assessment.

We have a system that teaches to the text and the tests of the text. Almost everything we test is in the form of the written word. Oral and social skills count for little in education. Practical skills are shoved below stairs and we send our kids off in lock-step to universities where the process is extended for year after year, often an inefficient and expensive paper trail that results in a huge paper 'IOU' for the student and state.

We have seen higher education morph into a global paper farm, with exponential growth of journals and text output, matched only by the inverse growth in readers. Research is falsely equated with paper output, where the paper is often the end in itself. Teaching is often side-lined in higher education as this paper mill becomes the dominant goal.

In the professions, and especially in institutions, witness bureaucratic systems whose function is often to simply to produce 'reports'. These are invariably overwritten, skimmed, then often binned. Report writing, plans and rhetoric are so often substitutes for action. Nowhere is this more apparent in the report than when it invariably concludes that 'more research is needed in…'. Reports beget reports.

In a way the historic, educational obsession with long-form text has been saved by the internet, where writing returned to a broader set of forms. Young people have taken to writing like demons, in messages, posts, tweets and blogs. There has been a renaissance of writing, reflecting a wide set of forms of communication, supplemented by images and video.

## Voice in learning

So how will voice manifest itself in learning?

It may help redress the balance between the academic and vocational. When learners leave the confines of school, college or university, they often have few exercise skills that are oral – dealing with work colleagues, interacting in meetings, being effective on the phone, dealing with customers and so on. You will spend a lot of time speaking and listening – these become primary activities and skills. These are not skills that are taught in many educational institutions. A return to voice-based learning may help here.

Dialogue with smart people on any topic is often a powerful form of learning. They challenge, probe, contradict. This type of collaborative learning may come into its own with speech and dialogue. There is also the sense in which some topics benefit from the lack of images and writing. It allows the imagination to construct personal imagery and links to what is being heard.

Adaptive learning, intelligent tutoring, chatbots... all of these are with us now. This form of technology-enhanced teaching can be further enhanced with voice recognition and feedback. One can see how AI, adaptive, tutoring software could turn this, first, into a homework support tool, then a tutoring tool, through to the delivery of more sophisticated learning. It has the advantage of being able to both push and pull learning. We could encourage habitual learning, the delivery of short questions, quizzes and spaced practice, via voice on the Echo, in a personalized sequence. In the privacy of your own home, this takes away the public embarrassment factor.

Voice moves us one step closer to frictionless, anywhere, anytime learning. Places other than institutions and classrooms become learning spaces. The classroom and lecture hall were never the places where the majority of learning took place. Context matters, and as learning becomes a utility, like water, we will be able to call upon it at any time and see learning as habitual and informal, not always timetabled and formal.

This is not to denigrate the written word. It matters. What matters more is a rebalance in education towards knowledge and skills that are not wholly text-based, but recognize that speech is as important, sometimes more important, and that verbal and communications skills also matter. Education in its current form is not the solution to that problem but part of the problem.

We can already see this being used in organizations, sitting on the meeting room table, with alarms set for 30 minutes, 45 minutes and 5 minutes, in an hour-long meeting. Once fully developed, it could be an ideal resource in meetings for company information – financial and otherwise. Alexa, as it evolves, may eventually make an ideal personal assistant for managers. Managers, according to a recent *Harvard Business Review* survey, spend 57 per cent of their time on admin, so there is room for improvement and an admin assistant seems likely. Access to workflow learning through voice assistants also seems likely.

Ask it simple questions such as, 'Who is? What is? Where is?' and curt answers come. What is more useful is the next-level 'Wikipedia' stuff. You get extended pieces on any topic. Now that's neat – a talking Wikipedia.

In the home, there's lots of basic educational games being developed for Alexa, for that around-the-kitchen-table learning.

Its use in special educational needs and disabilities is obvious. Accessibility is an important issue here as we can speak before we can read and write, as well as for kids with dyslexia, dyspraxia, autism and ADHD.

Alexa adds, subtracts, multiplies and divides, no matter how large the numbers, and handles negative numbers. It also does indices, roots, factorials and will give you pi to as many decimal places as you want. On formulae, it can show how to work out the area of a triangle, even give the quadratic formula on request. On probability, Alexa can give a number between x and y, roll a dice (any number of sides), pick a card and flip a coin. Then there are unit conversions, currency conversions and measurements. What is impressive is the lack of latency. This matters in learning.

Word definitions, spellings (handled that old classic – antidisestablishmentarianism – with ease), and synonyms can all be asked for. There are some problems with near homophones, such as 'quartz' and 'courts'. You'll encounter this quite quickly. This is easily remedied with a rephrasing of the word. There are audiobooks and, of course, going back to Wikipedia, lots of background stuff.

Given the effort you have to make to converse – pronounce your words, think about what you are about to say – when Alexa moves from monologue to dialogue, this could be a boon for the language development of young children.

You can also change the language, to say German, from your app. This is interesting as you can ask questions in English and get German replies to any question. Language learning will surely be possible – informal learning and practice while you are doing other things in the kitchen. For someone who is learning English, word games, daily words, and unlimited access to literature could be a great way to improve your pronunciation.

You can ask Alexa questions and there's a good chance you will get a reply: in chemistry, chemical symbols, chemical names and formula; in biology, definitions of photosynthesis and DNA; in geography, a vast number of geographical facts and concepts explained. You have access to Wikipedia.

Audiobooks are the next step up. So for the short stuff – there are podcasts galore, through Tunein and other services, and there are more books than you'll ever read.

Of course, there is tons more – any radio station you want, ordering taxis, pizzas, getting the phone number of a local business or restaurant. With Spotify, you get that music on-demand thing, as songs and artists come into your head. There's lots of controls here, even down to who sang what song, names of band members and so on. What movies are playing? It lists movies playing locally, tells us about the movie. However, usefully, if prompted, it will give me the names of the actors and, most useful of all, an IMDb rating. For general movie knowledge, it will answer questions about who played what role.

The important thing here is not the device but Alexa and the AI – or rather a range of AI techniques – that lies behind Alexa. NLP is striding forward. We will see Alexa and other voice technology pop up in all sorts of contexts – in cars, TV, watches, you name it. This is about deep-seated changes in technology, not the surface devices.

## Future interfaces

### Seamless interfaces

We can go one step further, looking at extending our already extended mind through invasive or non-invasive brain techniques. Although our brains can cope with sizeable *input* flows through our senses, we are severely limited on *output*, with slow speech or two meat fingers pecking away on keyboards and touchscreens. The goal is to interface physically with the brain to explore communications, but also storage and therefore extended memory. Imagine expanding your memory so that it becomes more reliable – able to know so much more, have higher mathematical skills, speak many languages, have many more skills.

We already have cochlear implants that bring hearing to the deaf, implants that allow those who suffer from paralysis to use their limbs, and VR can rewire the brain and restore the nervous system in paraplegics. It should come as no surprise that this will develop further as AI solves the problem of interfacing, in the sense of both reading and writing to the brain. The potential for learning is literally 'mind blowing'. Massive leaps in efficacy may be possible, as well as retained knowledge, retrieval and skills. We are augmenting the brain by making it part of a larger network, seamlessly.

AI also provides typing, fingerprint and face recognition. These can be used for personal identification, even assessment. Face recognition for ID and class registration is here. Attention diagnosis is also advancing, as is eye movement and physical gesture recognition. But there are bigger prizes in the invisible interface game. So let us take a leap of the imagination and see where this may lead to over the next few decades.

Mind interfaces, where you control computers and write straight from thought, is now a reality at one level and an exciting possibility in learning. This is an attempt to move beyond touch and typing, beyond the computer tablet and smartphone. Mark Zuckerberg wants to get into mind interfaces, where you control computers and write straight from thought. This is an attempt to move beyond smartphones. The advantages are obvious in that you think fast, type slow. There is already someone with a pea-sized implant that can type eight words a minute. Optical imaging (lasers) that read the brain are one possibility. There is an obvious problem here around privacy, but Facebook claims to be focusing only on words chosen by the brain for speech, ie things you were going to say anyway. This capability could also be used to control augmented and virtual reality, as well as communications to the internet of things. Underlying all of this is AI.

In *Sex, Lies and Brain Scans*, by Sahakian and Gottwald (2016), the advances in this area sound astonishing. John-Dylan Haynes (Max Plank Institute) (Soon *et al*, 2008) can already predict intentions in the mind, with scans, to see whether the brain is about to add or subtract two numbers, or press a right or left button. Words can also be read, with Tom Mitchell (Carnegie Mellon) (Mitchell *et al*, 2008) able to spot, from fMRI scans, nouns from a list of 60, seven times out of ten. They moved on to train the model to predict words out of a set of 1,001 nouns, again seven times out of ten. Jack Gallant (University of California) (Kay *et al*, 2008) reconstructed watched movies purely from scans. Karim Kassam (Carnegie Mellon) (Kassam *et al*, 2013) has shown that even emotions can be read, such as fear, happiness, sadness, lust and pride. Beyond this there has been modest success by Tomoyasu Horikawa (Horikawa and Kamitani, 2017) in identifying topics in dreams. Sentiment analysis from text and speech is also making progress with AI systems providing the analysis.

The good news is that there seems to be commonality across humans, as semantic maps – the relationship between words and concepts – seem to be consistent across individuals. Of course, there are problems to be overcome, as the brain tends to produce a lot of 'noise', which rises and falls but doesn't tell us much else. The speed of neurotransmission is also blindingly fast, making it difficult to track and, of course, most of these experiments use huge, immobile and expensive scanners. But once the routes are mapped, innovation around smaller devices usually comes in its wake. Witness the dramatic development of the smartphone.

The implications for learning are obvious. When we know what you think, we know whether you are learning, can optimize that learning, provide relevant feedback and also reliably assess. To read the mind is to read the learning process, its misunderstandings and failures, as well as its understanding and successful acquisition of knowledge and skills. A window into the mind gives teachers and students unique advantages in learning. Elon Musk's Neuralink goes one step further, looking at extending our already extended mind through neural laces or implants.

There is a sense in which the traditional interfaces are being slowly squeezed out here or disintermediated. Will there be a need for classrooms, teaching, blackboards, whiteboards, lectures or any of the apparatus of teaching when the brain is an open notebook, ready to interface directly with knowledge and skills, at first with 'deviceless' natural interfaces using voice, gesture and looks, then 'frictionless' brain communications and finally 'seamless' brain links? Clumsy interfaces inhibit learning; clean, smooth, deviceless, frictionless and seamless interfaces enhance and accelerate learning. This all plays to enhancing the weaknesses of the evolved biological brain – its inattentiveness, forgetting, need to sleep, lack of download or networking, slow decline, dementia and death. A new frontier has opened up and we are crossing literally into 'unknown' territory. We may even find that we will come to know the previously unknowable and think at levels beyond the current limitations of our flawed brains.

## Conclusion

Listen carefully and you'll hear whispers of the future. AI has been in your life for a while – Google, social media, Amazon, Netflix. AI's invisible hand already mediates most of what you do online, as it will in learning. It will mediate online learning by delivering the right stuff at the right time and place. It will fuel personalized learning. Voice is already here in your hand on your smartphone, in your home and in your car. Other frictionless interfaces are coming. Learning, as in life, will benefit from these advances as the interface will get out of the way, leaving more cognitive space in working memory for more efficient learning.

# References

Black, P and Wiliam, D (2005) *Inside the Black Box: Raising standards through classroom assessment*, Granada Learning, London

Horikawa, T and Kamitani, Y (2017) Generic decoding of seen and imagined objects using hierarchical visual features, *Nature Communications*, 8 (1), pp 1–15

Kassam, KS, Markey, AR, Cherkassky, VL, Loewenstein, G and Just, MA (2013) Identifying emotions on the basis of neural activation, *PLOS One*, 8 (6)

Kay, KN, Naselaris, T, Prenger, RJ and Gallant, JL (2008) Identifying natural images from human brain activity, *Nature*, **452**, pp 352–355

Mitchell, TM, Shinkareva, SV, Carlson, A, Chang, K, Malave, VL, Mason, RA and Just, MA (2008) Predicting human brain activity associated with the meanings of nouns, *Science*, **320** (5880), pp 1191–1195

Sahakian, BJ and Gottwald, J (2016) *Sex, Lies, and Brain Scans: How fMRI reveals what really goes on in our minds*, Oxford University Press, Oxford

Soon, CS, Brass, M, Heinze, HJ and Haynes, JD (2008) Unconscious determinants of free decisions in the human brain, *Nature Neuroscience*, **11** (5), pp 543–545

# 06

# Chatbots

Most learning professionals will have heard of the 'Socratic method', but few will know that Socrates never wrote a single word describing this method, fewer still will know that his method is not what it is commonly represented to be.

His lasting influence is the useful idea that, for certain types of learning, dialogue allows the learner to generate their own ideas and conclusions, rather than being spoon-fed. This has transformed itself into the idea of discovery learning, but there have been severe doubts expressed about taking this method too far. We wouldn't want our children to discover how to cross the road by pushing them out between parked cars!

The Socratic method, although quoted widely, is often no more than a teacher using the occasional open or inductive question. In fact, when used crudely, it can frustrate learners, especially when not combined with genuine dialogue and feedback, where the teacher asks a question, hands shoot up, and only those who already know the answer triumph, while the rest feel the sting of failure. When used well, however, it has lots to offer.

In online learning, this questioning and dialogue can now be delivered via chatbots. One could also argue that search-based inquiry through Google and other online resources allows the learner to apply this questioning approach to their own learning. Google search increasingly offers snippets and further related questions with answers. It has become more like dialogue.

Intelligent tutors and adaptive, personalized learning systems also account for where the learner has come from, where they are going and what they need to get there. Sophisticated online learning is allowing us to realize the potential of a scalable Socratic approach without the need for one-to-one teaching. Interestingly, it is only in the last few decades, through the use of technology-based tools that allow search, questioning and, now, adaptive learning, that Socratic learning can be realized on scale.

Voice assistants have gone viral, on our smartphones, in cars and in our homes. Once they gain knowledge from our behaviour, even if only online in communications, they will increasingly manage our calendars, shopping, bills, finances, travel and planning. It used to be the case that a tiny elite had a personal assistant; now everyone can have one. Progress is use and consumers are driving chatbot technology forwards, as the rewards for success are so great.

We are now starting to see this assistant being used to teach and learn using dialogue in learning as a motivating, social activity, where questioning lies at the heart of the learning experience. These chatbots are used for student recruitment, learning engagement, learner support, the delivery of knowledge and skills, assessment, even well-being.

## The tutorbot that fooled everyone

So let us talk about chatbots, as we are already talking with them. Bots are popping up everywhere, on customer service websites, in finance, health, Slack, Tinder and dozens of other web services. There are even bots that fend off loneliness and, at the extreme end of bot speculation, the idea that we will have a doppelganger bot that will live on after we die, so that our loved ones can continue to speak to us. Botland is being populated by as many chatbots as there are needs for conversation.

The benefits for mainstream applications are obvious. Chatbots can be engaging, sociable and scalable. They handle queries and questions with less human resource, often taking the load off humans, rather than replacing people completely.

They are also around in education, where bots perform a number of roles; these include student engagement, acting as a teaching assistant, teaching content or playing the role of an awkward student in teacher training, to name but a few.

An ever-present problem in teaching, especially online, is the very many queries and questions from students. In one Georgia Tech online course, this was up to 10,000 per semester from a class of 350 students (Lipko, 2016). Ashok Goel, the course leader, estimates that replying to these is one year of work for a full-time teacher. The good news is that Ashok Goel is an AI guy and saw his own area of expertise as a possible solution to this problem. If he could only get a chatbot to handle the predictable, commonplace questions, his teaching assistants could focus on the more interesting, creative and critical questions. This is an interesting development, as it brings tech back to the Socratic, conversational, dialogue model that many see as lying at the heart of teaching.

So how does it work? It all started with a mistake. Ashok created a chatbot named Jill Watson, which came from the mistaken belief that Tom Watson's (IBM's legendary CEO) wife was called Jill – her name was actually Jeanette. Four semesters of query data, 40,000 questions and answers, and other chat data were uploaded and Jill was ready to be trained. Initial efforts produced answers that were wrong, even bizarre, but with lots of training and software development, Jill got a lot better and was launched upon her unsuspecting students in the spring semester of 2016.

Jill solved a serious teaching problem – workload. But the problem was not just scale. Students ask the same questions over and over again, in many different forms, so you need to deal with lots of variation in natural language. This lies at the heart of the chatbot solution – natural, flowing, frictionless dialogue with students. The database, therefore, had many species of questions, categorized, and as each new question came in, Jill was trained to categorize the new questions and find answers.

With such systems it sometimes gets it right, sometimes wrong. So a 'mirror' forum was used, a parallel forum, moderated by a human tutor. Rather than relying on memory, they added context and structure, and found that performance jumped to 97 per cent. At that point they decided to remove the mirror forum. Interestingly, they had to put a time delay in to avoid Jill seeming inhumanly fast, to make it look as though she were typing. In practice, academics are busy and are often slow to respond to student queries, so they had to replicate this performance! In comparing automated with human performance, it was not a matter of living up to expectations, but dumbing down to the human level.

Most questions were important and practical queries about coding, timetables, file format, data usage – the sort of questions that have definite answers. Note that Jill has not replaced the whole teaching task, only made teaching and learning more efficient and scalable. This is likely to be the primary use of chatbots in learning in the short to medium term: tutor and learner support.

The students admitted they could not tell that Jill was a bot, even in classes run after her cover was blown – she was that good. In fact, they liked it because they knew it delivered better information, often better expressed and, importantly, faster than human tutors. Despite the name, and an undiscovered run of three months, the original class never twigged.

Real tutors, who often find themselves frustrated by student queries, can sometimes get slightly annoyed and tetchy, as opposed to Jill, who came in with personal but always polite and consistent advice. This is important. Chatbots do not get angry, annoyed, tired or irritable. They are also largely free from the sort of beliefs and biases that we humans always have. They do not have that condescending rolling-of-the-eyes reaction that an expert can have towards simple mistakes and errors by novice learners.

The students found her useful, the person who would remind them of due dates and things they really needed to know, there and then, not days later. She was described as an outstanding teaching assistant, albeit somewhat serious, and asked stimulating questions during the course. Of course, some got a little suspicious. They were, after all, AI students.

One spotted the name and questioned whether she was an AI or not. They checked LinkedIn and Facebook, where they found a real Jill Watson, who was somewhat puzzled by the attention. What finally blew her cover is interesting: she was too good. Her responses were just too fast, even though Goel had introduced a time delay compared with other teaching assistants. When they did discover the truth, the reaction was positive. They even wanted to put her up for a teaching award. Indeed, Goel did submit Jill for an award.

Students expect their teachers to be sincere, tolerant, assured, a good listener, expert and willing to share. Sure there are many things a good teacher can do that a chatbot cannot, but there are qualities a bot has that teachers do not possess. Real teachers can get a little tetchy and accusatory, even annoyed, compared with the clear and objective reply by a chatbot. This relentless patience and objectivity is something a good chatbot can deliver. Remember that the sheer number of the questions by students was beyond the ability of the real teachers to respond, and as the bot is massively scalable, it will always, in terms of availability and access, outdo its non-scalable human counterparts. It is really a matter of finding the right balance between automating teacher support and teaching.

The following semester they created two new bots as AI assistants (Ian and Stacey). Stacey was more conversational. This is a natural but technically difficult evolution of chatbots in teaching – to be more Socratic. This time the students were on the lookout for bots, but even then only 50 per cent identified Stacey and 16 per cent identified Ian as AI. The next semester there were four AI assistants and the whole team (including humans) used pseudonyms to avoid detection.

What is heartening about this story is the fact that a professor used his own subject and skill to improve the overall teaching and learning experience of his students. That is admirable. With all the dystopian talk around AI, we need to make sure that AI is used, like this, as a force for good.

## Chatbots and learning theory

Most technology in teaching has run against the Socratic grain, such as the blackboard, overhead projector and PowerPoint. With chatbots we may be seeing the return of the Socratic method. This return is being enabled by AI, in particular natural language processing, but also through other AI techniques such as adaptive learning, machine learning and reinforcement learning.

As the messenger interface seems to have won the interface wars, transcending menus and even social media, simple Socratic dialogue seems to have risen, through the process of natural selection, as an interface of choice, especially on mobile (Ballve, 2015). One is more likely to find people engaging in dialogue on a smartphone than any other form of activity. As personal assistants, already on our smartphones and in our homes, become commonplace, scale through consumer sales will normalize chatbots. This should help scale adoption in learning.

So one could argue that for younger audiences, chatbots are particularly appropriate, as they already use this as their main form of communication. They have certainly led the way in its use, but one could also argue that there are plenty of reasons to suppose that most other people like this form of interface. We have seen how online behaviour has moved from flat page-turning (websites) to posting (Facebook, Twitter) to messaging (WhatsApp, Messenger). We have seen how the web became more natural and human. Interfaces using AI have become more frictionless and invisible, conforming to our natural form of communication through text or speech.

Learning is expensive, scarce and difficult to scale. In classes with a hundred or more students, few get any personal attention. So can we have personal support and attention, even learning, at scale? Fundamentally, chatbot interfaces could realize the promise of a more intimate approach to online learning, as they enable dialogue between teacher and learner.

In the short term we can have scale for some functions. In the long term we can certainly foresee this sort of technology, with other advances, as yet unknown, make inroads in many other aspects of teaching – subject matter knowledge, feedback, planning, content creation, content delivery and assessment. It is not the case of dispensing with teachers, but reducing workload, giving them support and raising their game. Teachers should welcome something that takes away the administration and pain, so let us embrace possible solutions. The next stage will be bots that provide more than responses to questions and queries, but also provide real tutor plans, advice and play a more substantive teaching role.

So how can this combination of AI and UI have an application in learning?

In terms of *motivation*, we have evidence emerging that they can encourage and motivate learners. In Stanford research (2019) where a chatbot was compared with a more traditional quiz app, using identical sequencing algorithms (to make the comparison identical), there was 25 per cent more recall with the chatbot. Interestingly, learners also spent 2.6 times longer on the chatbot, as it was more conversational, more fun, and like a true study partner.

Learning takes *effort* and chatbots deliver effortful learning by virtue of being Socratic. Effortful learning was proposed as a fundamental learning strategy by Brown *et al* (2014) in *Make It Stick,* yet so much teaching ignores this with lecturing, long reading lists and talking at people. Personalized dialogue reframes learning as an exploratory, yet still structured (dialogue), process where the teacher guides and the learner has to make the effort.

As an almost *frictionless interface* it matches what we do in real life, requiring no special interface skills. Chatbots, such as Siri, Cortana, Google Home and Alexa, already exist and, with the addition of text-to-speech and speech-to-text, turn chat into learning. Reading and writing can be replaced by listening and speaking. This is a return to the more frictionless world of natural chat and communication. Easy to use, it allows you to focus on the message, not the medium. The world has drifted towards messaging for the simple reason that it is simple. By reducing the interface to its bare essentials, the learner can focus less on the interface and more on the important task of communications and learning. Our working memory is subject to cognitive load, the resources used by that temporary memory store. We can only hold so much in our mind at one time and for so long. Taking the cognitive load – implicit in the use of any interface – out of the equation means the teacher and learner can focus on the task and effort needed to acquire knowledge and skills. This is the promise of chatbots. Messaging is simple, a radically stripped down interface that anyone can use. It requires almost no learning and mimics what we all do in real life – simple dialogue. Compared with any other interface it is low on cognitive load. There is little other than a single field into which you type, and it goes at your pace.

*Chunking* lies at the heart of chatbots. In the psychology of learning it means reducing information into digestible pieces for ease of learning. One of the joys of messaging, and one of the reasons for its success, is that it is chunked and succinct. It is by its very nature chunked. If it were not, it would not work. Imagine being on a flight with someone: you ask them a question and get a one-hour lecture in return. That would be seen as rude, if not insane, behaviour. Chatbots chat; they do not talk at you. The rhythm of natural communication through dialogue is by definition chunked.

In a most likely apocryphal story, where Steve Jobs presented the Apple Mac screen to Steve Wosniak, Jobs had programmed it to say 'Hello...'. Wosniak thought it unnecessary – but who was right? We want our technology to be friendly, easy to use, almost our companion. This is as true in learning as it is in any other area of human endeavour. The brain is a social organ, likes to receive stuff in chunks and interact when learning. We are social apes, grammatical geniuses at age three, and we learn to listen and speak long before we learn to read and write (which takes years).

We *anthropomorphize* technology in such a way that we think the bot is human, or at least exhibits human attributes. Our faculty of imagination finds this easy, as witnessed by our ready ability to suspend belief in the movies or when watching TV. It takes seconds and works in our favour with chatbots, as dialogue is a natural form of human behaviour and communication. This was shown in groundbreaking research by Reeves and Nass (1996) in *The Media Equation*, in which they did 35 studies to show that we have a tendency to attribute human qualities and agency to technology, especially computers – and especially computers that engage us in dialogue. If chatbots deliver useful help, support, answers and even deeper teaching experiences, this would indeed be an advance worth following. Indeed, the natural language approach through chatbots accelerates this willingness to attribute agency to the chatbot. Natural language is our normal form of user experience. As AI provides better and better natural language processing, along with trained and smart databases of answers and smart responses, so AI will become a new learner experience.

As the language-processor ELIZA showed over 50 years ago, it is quite easy to maintain a semblance of realism in dialogue, as we have an involuntary response that makes us see computers as people when they mimic the behaviour of people – being polite, not having unnatural pauses, being consistent and so on. The more natural interface – which is an optimal mixture of teacher direction through questions and options balanced with learner requests and answers – is what turns chatbots into valuable learning experiences.

One such human quality is *feedback*. Feedback, as explained by theorists such as Black and Wiliam (2005), is the key to personalized learning. Being sensitive to what individual learners already know, are unsure about or still need to know, is a key skill in a good teacher. Unfortunately few teachers can do this as effectively as they would like, as a class of 30-plus or a college course with perhaps hundreds of students makes it impractical. Chatbots can specialize in specific feedback, dialogue that is personal, trying to educate everyone uniquely.

Being *anonymous* also has its advantages, and in learning, knowing that a human is not judging you can be an advantage. If you have qualms about chat replacing human activity, remember also that another advantage is that bots can allow learners to ask questions that they would not ask face to face with an academic, teacher or manager, for fear of embarrassment. This may seem odd, but there's a real virtue in having a teacher- or faculty-free channel for low-level support and teaching. Introverted students, who have problems with social interaction, are also likely to appreciate this approach. Others are simply quiet, even introverts. Anonymous learning, through a chatbot, then becomes a virtue not a vice. Well-being bots may also want to preserve anonymity. In this sense, chatbots may be superior to live, human teachers and bosses. Time and time again we see how technology is preferred to human contact – ATMs, online retail and so on. In learning, in some circumstances, we also witness this phenomenon.

One last advantage of AI in learning is its ability to *personalize* and deliver unique learning experiences to everyone.

## Uses of chatbots in learning

As chatbots become common in other contexts, such as retail, health and finance, so they will become common in learning. Education is always somewhat behind other sectors in considering and adopting technology, but adopt it will. There are several points across the learner journey where bots are already being used in a range of fascinating examples.

## Recruitment bot

The University of the People has 20,000 students in 200 countries. It has, of course, to replenish and recruit students. Helped by a Facebook Messenger chatbot fuelled by Messenger ads, they boosted their recruitment programme by engaging with potential students, providing personalized information on degrees and costs, filtering on past education and qualifications, and making it easier to qualify or disqualify potential students (Holguin, 2019). The dialogue moves the potential student forward, offering options, eventually leading them towards starting an application, the application portal or speaking with a person. They claim to have delivered a 62 per cent reduction in costs per application.

At Leeds Becket University (2017), Becky the chatbot was used in the clearing process, a service where students who have yet to find a course and university are 'cleared'. It was also used for general admissions. Becky's big advantage, true of all chatbots, is that she was available 24/7. A personalized service, Becky would also suggest connecting to a human, if necessary. But her main function was to find you a suitable course. After 21,000 unique interactions, she offered 217 places and 89 students started courses. They also gained a great deal of knowledge about admissions.

## Onboarding bot

Onboarding into educational institutions and the workplace is notoriously fickle. New starters, coming in with different needs at different times, are not served well by the old model of a huge dump of knowledge and documents. Chatbots are being used to introduce new students or staff to the processes, people, environment and purpose of the organization. New starters have predictable questions, so answers can be provided straight to mobile, or students can be directed to people, processes or procedures, where necessary. It is not that the chatbot will provide the entire solution, but it will take the pressure off and respond to real queries as they arise. Available 24/7, it can give access to answers as well as people. What better way to present your organization as innovative and responsive to the needs of students and staff? This is also true of new systems. Software, such as Slack, often has chatbots as an onboarding and ongoing performance tool.

Georgia State University had an onboarding problem with 'no-shows', which were up from 15 per cent to 19 per cent. This is a significant drop in revenue. Their chatbot had a 90 per cent opt-in rate and 80 per cent of users gave it 4/5 stars. With 14.9 per cent up on loan counselling, a 12.2 per cent increase on loan acceptance, 9.3 per cent up on on-time immunization submissions and 6.25 per cent up on online transcript submissions, they achieved 3.9 per cent higher enrolment and reduced no-shows by 21.4 per cent (Dalton, 2018).

## Learner engagement bot

Learners are often lazy. Students leave essays and assignments to the last minute, learners fail to do pre-work and courses – it's a human failing. They need prompting and cajoling. Learner engagement bots do this, with pushed prompts to students and responses to their queries.

Beacon, from Staffordshire University (2019), launched a bot that explained their campus facilities, support services, timetables, societies and clubs. AI lies at the heart of this institution's IT policy and this was seen as an innovative way to get student services into the hands of students, to keep students involved and engaged. The top most used features were: next lecture, personal tutor, societies, help and digital services, with questions like, 'When is my next lecture?', 'Who is my personal tutor?', 'Where can I eat?', 'How do I connect with the wifi?' The service is personalized.

'Differ' (https://www.differ.chat), a chatbot from Norway, is an engagement bot that engages through chat, encouraging conversations so that you can find a friend or mentor. It aims to keep students on their courses with a focus on well-being, combatting loneliness.

It responds to standard inquiries but also nudges and prompts for assignments and action. This bot also recognizes that procrastination is a real thing in students and encourages engagement with tutors, course material and assignments.

## Learner support bot

Campus support bots or course support bots go one stage further and provide teaching support in some detail. The idea is to take the administrative load off the shoulders of teachers and trainers. Response times to emails from faculty to students can be glacial. Learner support bots can, if trained well, respond with accuracy.

Taking this one step further, we have already discussed how the now famous Georgia Tech chatbot, and its descendants, played a credible role as a teaching assistant. Who would not want the basic non-teaching, administration tasks automated for teachers, so that teachers and academics could focus on real teaching?

Bolton College (2019) has a support chatbot named ADA that can respond to over 2,500 queries. She measures nitty-gritty stats like attendance, grade profiles and performance, nudging students towards better performance and improved grades. If you are having problems with maths, she will recommend drop-in maths sessions and show the timetable. She even offers help on subjects. There is a teacher version and it works with Amazon Echo!

SAP, a giant IT services company, used their own AI technology to build chatbots that answered learner questions from their learning communities, as well as recommending personal learning journeys (as outlined at Online Educa, Berlin, in December 2018). Using machine learning, it showed significant improvement in performance the more it was used, and when learners were asked whether they preferred the chatbot to human support, they chose the chatbot.

## Performance support bot

In a sense Google is a chatbot. You type something in and up pops a set of ranked links. Increasingly you may even have a short list of more detailed questions you may want to ask. Straight-up FAQ chatbots, with a well-defined set of answers to a predictable set of questions, can take the load off customer queries, support desks or learner requests. A lot of teaching is admin, and a chatbot can relieve that pressure at a very simple level within a definite area of knowledge – frequently asked questions.

At another level, the invisible VLE/LMS, fronted by a chatbot, allows people to ask for help and shifts formal courses into performance support, within the workflow. Sadly, your learning management system is likely to do the opposite. Often difficult to access and navigate, the clue is in the middle word 'management'. The LMS is largely about managing learners and learning, not engagement.

There are chatbots – such as Flo from Learning Pool, part of their LXP – that sit on top of content, accessible from Facebook, Slack and other commonly used social tools. You get help in various forms, such as simple text, chunks of learning, people to contact and links to external resources as and when you need them. Content no longer sits in a dead repository, waiting on you to sign in or take courses, but is a dynamic resource, available when you ask it something.

## Tutorbots

Tutorbots differ from chatbots in terms of the goals, which are explicitly 'learning' goals. They retain the qualities of a chatbot – flowing dialogue, tone of voice, exchange and human (like) – but focus on the teaching of knowledge and skills. Straight-up teaching is the approach, where the bot behaves like a Socratic teacher, asking sprints of questions and providing encouragement and feedback. This type of bot can be used as a supplement to existing courses to encourage engagement. Tutorbots that take a specific domain can be trained or simply work with unstructured data to teach knowledge. This is the basic workaday stuff that many teachers don't like.

One can also take a knowledge set and create a chatbot that re-presents that knowledge as semi-structured, personalized dialogue. As we know the answers and recreate the questions with algorithmic tutor behaviours, the tutorbot can be a simple teacher or assessor. In fact, it can be a more sophisticated teacher of that knowledge, sensitive to the needs of that individual learner. Once the basic knowledge has been acquired, the bot tests the student as well as getting them to apply their knowledge.

TUI is a large travel company and to solve the problem of consistent knowledge and attitudes towards 'leadership' across the organization, they built a bot that unpacks the concept of leadership (Bailey, 2019). Otto presents itself as part of the People Development Team and answers queries about leadership, objectives, mentoring, coaching and so on, with links to other resources.

## Mentor bot

The point of a bot may not be to simply answer questions but to mentor learners by providing advice on how to find the information on your own, to promote problem-solving. Once the bot knows the context and provides not just answers but advice, it behaves more like a teacher. Providing answers is not always the best way to teach. At a higher level chatbots could be used to encourage problem-solving and critical skills, by being truly Socratic, acting as a midwife to the students' behaviours and thoughts. As the dialogue gets better – drawing not only on a solid knowledge base, good learner engagement through dialogue, focused and detailed feedback, but also critical thought in terms of opening up perspectives, encouraging questioning of assumptions, veracity of sources and other aspects of perspectival thought – so critical thinking could also be possible. Bots will be able to analyse text to expose factual, structural or logical weaknesses. The absence of critical thought will be identified as well as suggestions for improving this skill by prompting further research ideas, sound sources and other avenues of thought. This 'bot as critical companion' is an interesting line of future development.

## Practice bot

Beyond knowledge, we have the teaching and learning of more sophisticated scenarios, where knowledge can be applied. This is often absent in education, where almost all the effort is put into knowledge acquisition. It is easy to see why – it's hard and time-consuming. Bots can set up problems, prompt through a process, provide feedback and assess effort. Scenarios often involve other people; this is where surrogate bots can come in.

Practice bots literally take the role of a customer, patient, learner or any other person and allow learners to practise their customer care, support, healthcare or other soft skills on a responding person (bot). Bots that act as revision bots for exams are also possible.

A bot that mimics someone can be used for practice. For example, 'Eli' is a chatbot, developed by Penn State, that mimics an awkward child in the classroom (Clark, 2017). It is used by student teachers to practise their skills in dealing with such problems before they hit the classroom. Duolingo uses bots after you have gathered an adequate vocabulary, knowledge of grammar and basic competence, to allow practice in a language. This surely makes sense.

## Assessment bot

Assessment bots can deliver formative assessments using adaptive assessment. WildFire built just such a bot for a travel company. It presents a medium-level question; if you get that wrong, it lowers expectations, and if you get it right, it raises expectations. Using an algorithm that aims to get you learning content, it eventually makes sure that you get all of your knowledge into the top zone. Assessment bots can also be used in summative assessments, with single passes through the questions.

## Well-being bots

As pressures on learners in schools, universities and the workplace become greater, there has been a rise in issues around well-being and mental health.

Well-being bots such as 'Elli' (Robinson, 2015) and 'Woebot' that are sensitive to patients' needs are already being subjected to controlled trials to examine the impact on clinical outcomes. If a bot is being used in any therapeutic context, its anonymity can be an advantage. From ELIZA in the 1960s to contemporary therapeutic bots, this has been a rich vein of bot development. Therapeutic bots are being used in controlled studies to see if they have a beneficial effect on outcomes.

Chatbots, as they start to understand context, will play a greater role in human–machine interaction, on the move, in the home, but also in learning. Dialogue is complex, but it is how most of us communicate and learn with other people. As AI provides new agents in the world that also learn, they will be things we learn from.

# References

Bailey, S (2019) Transcript: #167 – Henrietta Palmer, Learning Solutions, TUI Group on creating learning content with AI, The EdTech Podcast. Available at https://theedtechpodcast.com/transcript-167-henrietta-palmer-learning-solutions-tui-group-on-creating-learning-content-with-ai/ (archived at https://perma.cc/PK4E-XPCA)

Ballve, M (2015) Messaging apps are overtaking social networks to become the dominant platforms on phones, Business Insider. Available at https://www.businessinsider.com/messaging-apps-have-completely-overtaken-social-networks-to-become-the-dominant-platforms-on-phones-2015-4?r=US&IR=T (archived at https://perma.cc/2U8J-X7CT)

Black, P and Wiliam, D (2005) *Inside the Black Box: Raising standards through classroom assessment*, Granada Learning, London

Bolton College (2019) Education secretary praises ADA. Available at https://www.boltoncollege.ac.uk/latest-news/praise-for-ada-bolton-colleges-chatbot/ (archived at https://perma.cc/CC8K-578V)

Brown, PC, Roediger III, HL and McDaniel, MA (2014) *Make it Stick*, Harvard University Press, Boston

Clark, D (2017) 10 uses for chatbots in learning (with examples), Donald Clark Plan B, 17 December. Available at https://donaldclarkplanb.blogspot.com/search?q=Penn+state+chatbot (archived at https://perma.cc/LLL2-PA5L)

Dalton, M (2018) Georgia State uses a chatbot to attack 'summer melt', WABE. Available at https://www.wabe.org/georgia-state-uses-a-chatbot-to-attack-summer-melt/ (archived at https://perma.cc/X39E-XLJ8)

Holguin, J (2019) How a university increased leads with a Messenger bot, ChatbotsLife. Available at https://chatbotslife.com/how-a-university-increased-leads-with-a-messenger-bot-fd84a2b6aadf (archived at https://perma.cc/9Q6W-5USC)

Leeds Becket (2017) Cardwell, S. Becky the chatbot offers her first university place, Leeds Becket website, 17 August

Lipko, H (2016) Meet Jill Watson: Georgia Tech's first AI teaching assistant, Georgia Tech Professional Education Blog. Available at https://pe.gatech.edu/blog/meet-jill-watson-georgia-techs-first-ai-teaching-assistant (archived at https://perma.cc/SY2V-LKM9)

Reeves, B and Nass, CI (1996) *The Media Equation: How people treat computers, television, and new media like real people and places*, Cambridge University Press, Cambridge

Robinson, A (2015) Meet Ellie, the machine that can detect depression. Available at *Guardian,* https://www.theguardian.com/sustainable-business/2015/sep/17/ellie-machine-that-can-detect-depression (archived at https://perma.cc/B4JQ-WG32)

Staffordshire University (2019) Introducing Beacon – a digital friend to Staffordshire University students. Available at https://www.staffs.ac.uk/news/2019/01/introducing-beacon-a-digital-friend-to-staffordshire-university-students (archived at https://perma.cc/D9EQ-WVMV)

Stanford (2019) Stanford's 'QuizBot' – a chatbot that teaches – beats flashcards for learning factual information, *Stanford News*, May 8

# 07

# Building chatbots

Talking is replacing touching and typing. Apple's Siri was launched in 2011 built on previous technology that took decades to develop. Microsoft's Cortana and then Amazon's Echo (Alexa) came in 2014 and Google Assistant in 2016. They all serve different markets. Apple sells products, especially the iPhone, Microsoft sells business products, Alexa is a home product, while Google Assistant is a general product. The whole story is well told in *Talk To Me* (2019) by James Vlahos, who sees this as a race among tech companies to master voice and conversation. Speech is fundamental and voice is becoming the lifeblood of everyday computing. Voice humanizes and normalizes technology. It is not robots that reflect us, but chatbots, speaking and listening.

It is only a matter of time before digital assistants become personal learning assistants (PLAs). Chatbots free us from the clumsiness of drag and drop, clicking on figures to see speech bubbles toward dialogue, the very thing that makes us social beings. We may be able, one day, to speak to Plato, Newton, Darwin, Picasso and other dead and living experts.

People think that AI has a heart of stone, the chilling execution of algorithmic logic, but technology is being humanized. We speak to it, it speaks to us. This means understanding how chatbots can be built.

## Building or buying a chatbot

As in the case of the ELIZA chatbot, we are easily fooled into anthropomorphizing and reading agency into chatbots. Reeves and Nass (1996), in research at Stanford, showed that this was true for technology in general. In truth, chatbots do not talk to you; they pretend to talk to you. They are tricksters. In a sense, all human–machine interaction is trickery. It is, in the end, only software being mathematically executed with some smart natural language processing techniques and human scripts thrown in. Nevertheless, they are surprisingly successful. Alexa has been a massive hit, and it only answers simple questions, with little or no dialogue.

One must be careful here, as chatbots have real limitations. They work best in narrow domains, with a clear purpose and goals. Unlike real humans and teachers, they do not have the flexibility in dialogue to cope with much beyond the subject they are trained to cope with and are easily fooled with curve-ball questions. Their ability to deliver full, sustained dialogue is limited. Nevertheless, as mentioned in the previous chapter, they can deliver learning functions right across the learning journey, from onboarding to learner engagement, learner support, mentoring, teaching, assessment, practice and well-being.

Interestingly, this immediately raises an issue for chatbot deployment – setting 'expectations'. Do you tell users that it is just a piece of software, or do you keep up the 'magic' myth? How honest will you be about its capability? You may set the bar too high and get lots of disappointed users. Here are a few other practical things to think about when you enter the weird and wonderful world of botland.

## Domain knowledge

First up – on expectations – and this is really important: remember that chatbots are not generalists. They are domain specific, good at specific tasks within defined domains, topics or subjects. Google Duplex works only because it does domain-specific tasks – call a restaurant and book a hairdressing appointment. Some services offer stores of messaging transcript data, with detailed tasks for each industry sector. Some even focus on core use cases, which are mostly designed around customer service. Most are a long way off being a genuine teacher, coach or mentor, as they lack the general ability to deal with a breadth of unexpected queries and answers. A lesson from history was Microsoft's Clippy, a virtual assistant that people came to loathe, as it often disappointed with bad or irrelevant help. So dial your expectations down a notch or you will be setting yourself up for failure.

## Persona

Your chatbot needs to have a persona or personality. It is too easy to just throw a jumble of responses into a database and hope for the best. Nass and Brave explored the topic in *Wired for Speech* (2005). They noticed that movie robots often did not sound human, sometimes referred to themselves in the third person, by their own names or in the passive.

Modern chatbots, taking advantage of realistic speech technology, have gone in the opposite direction and have adopted human personas. This makes sense. We want to speak to interesting and engaging people, no matter if they are machines; witness the amount of idle banter and talk users engage in with chatbots, such as Google Assistant, Siri, Cortana and Alexa. Indeed, all of these went through detailed research before launch, so that their personas could be finessed. Each chatbot has a blend of qualities.

Cortana is named after a videogame AI assistant character from Halo. She is deliberately and sharply designed, friendly and approachable but detached, even a little nerdy. She knows her stuff. As she's integrated into calendars and other tools, you need to feel that you can trust her with your personal information. Trust also matters in terms of increasing engagement and use – necessary for machine learning bots that need volume data.

Siri was somewhat different, although just as deeply researched. Siri was bought by Apple and was quite edgy until Apple softened her up a little, but she's still more sassy than Cortana. It is, after all, Apple.

Compare these two with Google 'Assistant', a much more objective and functional moniker. This was all about not setting too high an expectation and failing to deliver. It is helpful, respectful and knowledgeable, like a good librarian. Not entirely humourless, certainly a nice person, but pretty solid.

Alexa is a home device and was designed for that environment, always dutiful, helpful, polite and not too cheeky as there may be children around in the home.

The trend has been towards personas that are open, natural, well spoken and educated, but the reality is that persona design has to be turned into real answers to real questions and there are trade-offs between human and software, the real and imaginary, the spontaneous and over-scripted.

## Gender

What about gender – female, male or neither? Cortana, Siri and Google Assistant are female by default but can be switched to male. Alexa, when asked, is 'female in character'. There is much debate around portraying such services as predominantly female, as it may suggest subservience. One could argue the opposite, that launching them all as male would have been a demonstration of power and patriarchy. Microsoft claim that the research shows we generally prefer the voices of young women. An alternative is to go genderless or give people an even choice at the start, like X.ai the scheduling assistant bot. The problem here is trying to get a genderless voice.

## Culture

Some assistants, like Siri and Cortana, answer in ways that are sensitive to the culture. This can be in the use of the actual language and vocabulary, but may also be the use of appropriate cultural references. Humour is an especially sensitive issue, as it varies across cultures, but few commercial bots are edgy or transgressive in their humour. It is all pretty much middle-of-the-road stuff. You can please a lot of the people a lot of the time, but not all of the people all of the time, so it is worth playing it safe.

## Personalization

What is likely to happen is multiple personas, and the personalization of style, where the system may even detect the user's personality and adapt to their needs. In the same way that a teacher may change tone according to who they speak to, so teaching bots could adapt to learners.

Define a persona and build a style guide. At the end of the day, lots of responses have to be written and they need to sound as though they have a single voice. In learning especially, you also have to be careful in tone. Too many chatbots have a surfeit of phrases that sound as if they're trying too hard to be cool or funny. In learning, one may want to be a little more calm and serious. This depends, of course, on your intended audience and the subject matter. Whatever the project, think about the 'voice' in this wider sense.

## Look and feel

Linked to voice is the visual manifestation of your chatbot. Think carefully about the appearance of the chatbot. Some stay sex neutral, others are identified as male or female. Many, perhaps too many, appear like 1950s robots. Others have faces, micro-expressions, even animation. Then there is the name. Be careful with this – it matters. And do you want one name or a separate name for each domain or course?

## Design

You may wish to start on paper with sticky notes to build an initial flow-chart. You may find that this cannot cope with levels of complexity. Many chatbot services offer a no-coding tool to build your flow; others require more complex skills. Flowcharting tools are common, and these often result in simply asking users to choose from a set of options and branching from them. To be fair, that keeps you (and the bot) on track, which may be the way to go in structured learning. Others will accept open input but steer you towards certain types of responses. One thing is for sure – you need new skill sets. Traditional interactive design skills will help, but not much. This is about dialogue, not monologue, about understanding complex technology, not just pages of HTML.

## Building chatbots

Understand what level of technology you want to use. There is a difference from one end of the spectrum to the other, from 'scripted' to AI tools used to build chatbots.

Scripted tools provide branching tools that are simple to use but provide fixed structures. They are easy to develop, don't need high-end programming skills and the chatbot can be quick to produce and low cost.

AI tools will produce more complex and sophisticated natural language recognition and are more flexible. An important feature of modern chatbots is the fact that they now *learn*. This matters, as the more you train and use them, the better they get. We used to have just human teachers and learners; we now have technology that is both a teacher and learner. One can take advantage of one of the machine learning bot services from some of the large tech companies. But be careful, as they tend to swap out functionality with little sensitivity around your delivery. They can also be difficult to develop, may take longer to produce, are complex to test and tend to be more expensive.

One could use Dialogueflow from Google, which has excellent tools for building and flow, and the tool will be fully supported. But the tool will provide no 'learning' specific design, costs will rise on scale and one must be careful with data, as Google may end up with or owning your data. Full access to your data may be difficult and not held in the territory it needs to be held for regulatory and legal constraints.

Or one could choose an open source approach, where you will need coding expertise. It may not be fully supported but you will have flexible coding and design, can introduce learner-specific design features, have no costs, and own and store your data at the location of your choice.

## Chatbot jargon

When building a chatbot it is worth getting to know three key words (utterance, intent and entity):

- Utterance: 'Where is the Flo chatbot?', 'Where is Flo?', 'Show me the Flo location.'
- Intent: Show location.
- Entity Chatbot (Event).

Get used to the language of 'utterances' (what is said), 'intents' (acts) and 'entities' (things). This is related to the domain-specific issue above. Chatbots needs to have defined tasks, namely 'intents' (the user's intention) as identified and named actions and objects, such as 'show weather'.

## Your data

How do you get your data into their system? This is not trivial. How do you get your content, which maybe exists as messages, PDFs, PowerPoints and other assets, into the format that is needed? This is far from automatic. Then, if it is using complex AI techniques, there's the training process. You really do need to understand the data issues – what, where and how it is to be managed? – and, of course, the General Data Protection Regulation (GDPR).

## Hand off to humans

What happens when a chatbot fails? Believe me, this is common. A number of failsafe tactics can be employed. You can do the common... ask the person to repeat themselves: 'Sorry, I didn't catch that', 'Could you elaborate on that?' The chatbot may even try to use a keyword to save the flow, distract, change the subject and come back to the flow a little later. So think about failsafes. If all else fails, and many customer chatbots do, default to a real human. That is fine in customer service, and many services offer this functionality. This is not so fine if you are designing an autonomous learning system.

## Channels

On what channels can the chatbot appear? There are lots of options here and you may want to look at what communication channels you use in your organization, like website chat, in-app chat, Facebook Messenger, Slack,

Twilio, Kik, Telegram, Google Assistant, Skype, Microsoft Teams, SMS, Twitter or email. The chatbot needs a home and you may want to think about whether it is a performance support chatbot, on your communications system, or a more specific chatbot within a course.

### Integration

Can your chatbot integrate into other platforms? Don't imagine that this will work easily from your LMS; it won't. Integration into other systems may also be necessary.

### Administration

Your chatbot has to be delivered from somewhere, so what are the hosting options, and is there monitoring, routing and management? Reporting and user statistics matter with chatbots, as you really do want to see if they deliver what they say, with user stats, times, and fallout stats. How are these handled and visualized? Does your chatbot vendor have 24/7 customer support? You may need it. Lastly, if you are using an external service, be careful about them changing without telling you (it happens), especially the large tech vendors, like IBM and Microsoft.

### Testing

Testing chatbots has its challenges. You will need a test plan that covers all aspects of the deployment, the quality of the driving software, support, infrastructure, interface design and goals. Rules-based branching chatbots are somewhat easier to test, a bit like checking all the branches of a single tree. A machine learning chatbot is a far more autonomous entity, more like testing in a forest. It needs a clear testing strategy. You will need a test plan and test team with clear objectives.

## Chatbot abuse

People ask chatbots the weirdest of things. Users know that chatbots are really pieces of software, so test it with rude and awkward questions. Swearing, sexual suggestions, requests to do odd things, and just being plain rude are common.

Chatbots are regularly asked out on dates, asked to send naked photographs and worse. Cleo, a finance bot, sends back a picture of a circuit board. Nice touch and humour is often the best response. The financial chatbot Plum responds to swearing by saying, 'I might be a robot but I have digital feelings. Please don't swear.' These are sensible responses, as Reeves and Nass (1996) found in their studies of humans with technology mentioned earlier, that we humans expect our tech to be polite.

People want to play with chatbots – that's fine. You often find that these questions are asked when someone first uses a chatbot or buys Alexa. It's a sort of onboarding process, where the new user gets used to the idea of typing replies or speaking to a machine.

The odd questions tends to come at the start, as people stress-test the bot, then drop off dramatically. This is telling and actually quite useful, as users get to see how the bot works. They're sometimes window shopping or simply seeing where the limits lie.

It also helps calibrate and manage expectations. Using a bot is a bit like speaking to a very young child. You ask it a few questions, have a bit of back and forth, then get its level. Actually, with some, it's like speaking to a dog, where all you can do is variants on 'fetch'. Once the user realizes that the bot is not a general purpose companion, who will answer anything, or teacher with super-teaching qualities, and has a purpose, usually a specific domain, like finance, health or a specific subject, and that questions beyond this are pointless, they settle down. You get that 'fair enough' response and they settle down to the actual business of the bot.

These little touches of humour and politeness serve a further purpose, in that they actually engage the user. If you get a witty or clever reply, you have a little more respect for the bot, or at least the designer of the bot. With a little clever scripting, this can make or break user acceptance. Some people will, inevitably, ask your bot to tell a joke – be ready for that one. A knock-knock joke is good as it involves a shot dialogue, or a light bulb joke.

These responses can also be used to set the tone of the bot. Good bots know their audience and set the right tone. It's pointless being too hip and smart-assed with an older audience, who may just find it annoying. Come to think of it, this is also true of younger audiences, who are similarly intolerant of clichés. You can use these responses to be edgy, light-hearted, serious, academic… whatever.

You'll find yourself dead-ending a lot with bots. They're nowhere near as smart as you at first think. That's okay. They serve a function and are getting better. But it's good to offer a little freedom, allow people to play, explore, find limits, set expectations and increase engagement.

## Botched bots

In practice, customer service bots are often seamlessly integrated with real humans as they tend to fail in extended dialogue or off message requests. Extended, wide-ranging, meaningful dialogue is difficult. That's not to say they are not useful. Chatbots are everywhere as they take the load of previously human-resourced systems in specific tasks, topics or domains.

Whether you are answering customer queries about your product or being a teacher answering questions from your students, the same queries and questions keep popping up. This is how a bot works; it knows that set of popular questions and dynamically 'learns' what they are from continued use.

In learning, with chatbots, this sort of focus is a good thing. The bot can direct, keep learners on track, personalize by providing individualized feedback and generally behave like a good teacher. That's what we saw with the Georgia Tech bot (Lipko, 2016). The mistake is to be too colloquial or too wide in approach. The natural rhythms of dialogue need to be maintained. Typically a chatbot would introduce itself politely, use your name, then be clear about what it wants to chat about. In real speech, sustained dialogue is episodic, allowing either side to change tack and occasionally lighten things up with idle chat, even a little humour.

We also have to be careful about overreach here. Simple chatbots that handle single-question responses, even simple sequences of dialogue, with blockers (where the dialogue ends and recommendations are made to refer to a source or person), can be built quickly in specific domains. Chatbots are difficult to build when they move beyond simple rule-based programming into AI-driven systems, where they must handle instances they have not previously encountered and must generalize to these situations.

An interesting example of a botched bot comes from China, where Tencent, which has hundreds of millions of users, had to take down a penguin bot named BabyQ, and a girl bot named Little Bing. Why? Their 'crimes' were that they showed signs of political autonomy and honesty (Oppenheim, 2017). BabyQ was asked, 'Do you love the Communist Party?' the penguin replied, curtly, 'No'. To the statement, 'Long Live the Communist Party', BabyQ came back, thoughtfully, 'Do you think such corrupt and incapable politics can last a long time?' Then, when asked about the future, the perky penguin responded, 'Democracy is a must!' Little Bing was more aspirational, and when asked what her Chinese dream was, she said, 'My China dream is to go to America,' then, when pushed to explain, 'The Chinese dream is a daydream and a nightmare.'

Of course, the bots were either picking up on real conversations or being subversively trained. Tencent were forced by the Chinese Government to take them down, which merely shows that we have more to fear from censoring governments and compliant technology companies than AI-driven bots.

A now infamous example of a bot that went off-piste was Microsoft's Tay. They had no idea that young people would take a playful view of the tech and deliberately 'train' it to be a sex-crazed Nazi (Hunt, 2016). It was all a bit of fun, but most people over 50 saw it as yet more proof of demonic, out-of-control bots. In truth, all it showed was that kids know what this tech is and know full well that bots are primitive and can be trained. My favourite example of this type of subversion is the Walkers Crisps campaign to encourage people to post selfies to Twitter. They did, but it ended up being a rogues' gallery of serial killers and Nazis (James, 2017). Once again, we the people won't be pandered to by companies implementing patronizing tech that they don't fully understand.

## Caution

Chatbots work well when they have limited goals; as general conversationalists they are not so good. If directed, one can keep the conversation on the go, but when you allow open input, as on, say, Alexa, things tend to go badly. That is because real dialogue is messy and complex, full of interruptions, people talking over each other, changes of tack, quips and context matters.

There are three prizes available for conversational chatbots: the Alexa, Loebner and Winograd Schema Challenge. Entries to these competitions are illustrative of the way chatbots operate. Most are a hybrid of two main approaches: rules-based plus machine learning. Rules-based systems suffer from the fact that it is not feasible to cover all the bases and script answers to every question.

The machine-learning-only approach is also fiendishly difficult, as pattern recognition from a huge database of text is rarely enough to sustain the conversation, even with access to huge databases of information, such as

Wikipedia, Reddit, subject-specific databases and Twitter, although this approach may win out in the long run.

In practice, winners often have multiple bots and ensembles of bots and use a variety of other techniques to cover the breadth of responses needed and depth of understanding to keep the conversation going. Initiating a conversation is very different from information retrieval, which is very different from questions about the bot itself, such as, 'How tall are you? Where were you born?' Turns out that people ask this type of question a lot. Idle chat or chitchat is also a problem and usually needs scripted responses.

Interestingly, the Alexa Prize uses real users as a testbed and has gathered a huge amount of data, which Amazon owns, so they are in a good position to further the art of the chatbot. Microsoft and Siri tend to deliver short replies to queries, similarly with Google Assistant. These chatbots are on the very boundary, the bridge between humans and AI. As they develop we see AI progress and gradually become more like us, giving insights into both us and software. Bots as assistants, friends, girlfriends or boyfriends, even memorial bots that live on after we die, push at the limits of what we used to regard as purely human.

Coming back to learning, chatbots are working at all stages in the learning journey, from student engagement, student support to feedback, learning and assessment. That is not to say that they are anywhere near replacing human teachers. Things have suddenly got very interesting but teaching and learning are complex tasks. That doesn't mean that many of the support functions could not be performed by chatbots, to a higher standard of performance in terms of access, response times, accuracy, consistency and quality.

The holy grail in AI is to find generic algorithms that can be used to solve a range of different problems across a number of different domains. This is starting to happen. The idea that the teacher chatbot will replace the skills of a teacher, not just be able to tutor in one subject alone, but be a cross-curricular teacher, especially at the higher levels of learning, is not impossible. It could be cross-departmental, cross-subject and cross-cultural, to produce teaching and learning that will be free from the tyranny of the institution, department, subject or culture in which it is bound.

As a chatbot does not have the limitations of a human, in terms of forgetting, recall, cognitive bias, cognitive overload, getting ill, sleeping eight hours a day, retiring and dying, once it's on the way to acquiring knowledge and teaching skills, it will get better and better. The more students that use its service, the better it gets – not only on what it teaches, but how it teaches.

Courses will be fine-tuned to eliminate weaknesses, and finesse themselves to produce better outcomes.

They need to be trained, built, tested and improved, which is no easy task, but their efficacy in reducing the workload of teachers, trainers, lecturers and administrators is clear. The dramatic advances in natural language processing have led to Siri, Amazon Echo and Google Home. It is a rapidly developing field of AI and promises to deliver chatbot technology that is better and cheaper.

For the foreseeable future, however, chatbots will support teachers. Chatbots are a form of technology that teachers should appreciate, as they truly try to support what teachers already do. It takes good teaching as its standard and tries to eliminate and streamline inefficiencies to produce faster and better outcomes at a lower cost. It is impossible for a teacher to have personal dialogue with large numbers of students, but chatbots are scalable. They may not be anywhere near the sophistication of actual human dialogue, but for some support tasks they can do a credible job. Let's be clear – chatbots will not replace teachers *any time soon*. Wonderful as they are, far from being cogent, conscious, cognitive beings, they are only really useful in a limited domain, such as a specific FAQ list, subject or topic in education and training. But this is precisely why 'chatbots' will go far. They are at present a useful supplement to real teachers and existing online courses. At some point, and this is some way off, they may become the teacher itself, but AI is nowhere near solving the complex problems that this entails. Bots will augment, not automate, teaching. Chatbots, at present, are not replacing people but working alongside people. This is important. Chatbots may replace some functions and roles, but few suppose that most jobs will be eliminated by chatbots. We have to see them as being part of the learning landscape.

## Conclusion

Chatbots in learning have to capture and embody good pedagogy and already do. Whether it is models of engagement, support, learning objectives, invisible LMS, practice, assessment or well-being, the whole point is to use both the interface and back-end functionality (important area for pedagogic capture) to deliver powerful learning based on evidence-based theory, such as retrieval, effortful learning, spaced practice and so on. This will improve rather than diminish or ignore pedagogy.

As chatbot technology gets better and state-of-the-art levels are reached, we get steady progression. It will matter whether this progression is open and accessible. The harvesting of questions and answers by learners will give us invaluable insights into problems with the existing courses and content, leading to deliberate or automated course improvement. Chatbot technology has the potential to move into more sophisticated teacher functions. They are already here, and more are coming – rather than condemn them for encroaching on teacher territory, we should see them as scalable agents that could be capable of delivering teaching at almost no cost, to anyone, anywhere, at any time. The PLA is here to stay.

# References

Hunt, E (2016) Tay, Microsoft's AI chatbot, gets a crash course in racism from Twitter, *Guardian*, 24 March. Available at https://www.theguardian.com/technology/2016/mar/24/tay-microsofts-ai-chatbot-gets-a-crash-course-in-racism-from-twitter (archived at https://perma.cc/LH8J-N7MQ)

James, SB (2017) Walkers Crisps social ad backfires as Lineker snapped with Fred West and Rolf Harris, Campaign Live, 25 May. Available at https://www.campaignlive.co.uk/article/walkers-crisps-social-ad-backfires-lineker-snapped-fred-west-rolf-harris/1434736 (archived at https://perma.cc/Y25Y-5CRU)

Lipko, H (2016) Meet Jill Watson: Georgia Tech's first AI teaching assistant, Georgia Tech Professional Education Blog. Available at https://pe.gatech.edu/blog/meet-jill-watson-georgia-techs-first-ai-teaching-assistant (archived at https://perma.cc/4CBU-9696)

Nass, CI and Brave, S (2005) *Wired for Speech: How voice activates and advances the human–computer relationship*, MIT Press, Cambridge, MA

Oppenheim, M (2017) Chinese chatbots deleted after criticising the ruling Communist Party, *The Independent*. Available at https://www.independent.co.uk/news/world/asia/china-chatbots-communist-party-ruling-critics-peoples-tencent-babyq-little-bing-a7875601.html (archived at https://perma.cc/MRR2-RE78)

Reeves, B and Nass, CI (1996) *The Media Equation: How people treat computers, television, and new media like real people and places*, Cambridge University Press, Cambridge

Vlahos, J (2019) *Talk to Me*, Random House, New York

## PART FOUR

# Learning

# 08

# Content creation

Another way of looking at AI in learning is to see how it can be used to enhance and create online learning.

## Learning science

At this point it is worth revisiting the psychology of learning, as there is a tendency to use new technology (such as AI) to implement old psychology. What do recent findings in cognitive psychology recommend be delivered using AI? As AI is smart software that can do things that were never possible before, such as text summaries, interpretation, speech to text, text to speech, semantic analysis and personalized delivery, it is worth considering what new pedagogy can be used with this new AI technology.

Richard Mayer and Ruth Clark are among the foremost researchers in the empirical testing of media and media mix hypotheses in online learning. Their *E-Learning and the Science of Instruction* (2003) covers seven design principles: multimedia, contiguity, modality, redundancy, coherence, personalization, and practice opportunities. 'Less is more' could be Mayer and Clark's mantra. Their precise studies have confirmed that our media mix (text, graphics, audio, animation, video) in online learning is often flawed, resulting in cognitive overload and dissonance. Perhaps their greatest contribution has been in identifying redundancy as a serious problem in screen-based learning

In one study, Mayer *et al* (1996) presented 600 pieces of scientific learning and found that briefer versions, which were concise, coherent and co-ordinated, resulted in far more effective learning. They are also precise in their recommendations:

There is a clear pattern in which the more words added to the core verbal explanation, the more poorly the student does in producing the core explanative idea units. These results are consistent with the idea that the additional words overload verbal working memory, drawing limited attentional and comprehension resources away from the core verbal explanation.

(Mayer *et al*, 1996)

The lesson with text is to cut it 'til it bleeds! Bullet points, simple writing, highlighted keywords and short paragraphs are all useful screen writing techniques. AI can help reduce redundancy in learning by summarizing text that was not originally written for learning.

## Text

Text opens up the application of AI through one of the most successful areas of AI development – NLP. With astonishing speed, AI has delivered commercial and credible search, summarization, transcription and translation services. Even with the rise of other media, such as images, audio and video, the web is still text heavy. We are still searching using text, reading Wikipedia, typing into Facebook, Instagram, WhatsApp and Twitter.

In online learning, content is often criticized for being too text-heavy. However, much online learning, especially simple knowledge and procedural learning, may demand no more than a simple text or a text plus graphics approach. There are many reasons why text is learner friendly.

*Text is searchable.* AI-driven search is fundamental to how the web works.

*We also read quickly.* Practised readers read at the rate of about 300 words per minute. This is roughly twice the speed of normal speech and recorded narration can be even slower.

*Text also gives learners control.* This means that learners can read at their own pace, fundamental to comprehension and retention.

*Text also leaves room for the imagination.* A well-written piece of fiction or non-fiction leaves the learner to create images, reflections and possibilities, unpolluted by sounds and pictures supplied by others. It keeps the imagination free to create appropriate thoughts in learning and does not clutter learning with inappropriate noise.

*Text is flexible.* The information architect Saul Wurman (1990) claims there are only five ways to structure information, using the mnemonic LATCH:

- location – place, maps, etc;
- alphabet – dictionary, index, glossary, etc;
- time – timeline, storylines, etc;
- category – themes, lists, etc;
- high and low – menus, numbered lists.

We should not ignore the sheer extensive, subtle and sophisticated ways in which text quite simply gets the job done.

*Text is linkable.* As we know from Wikipedia and other well-used learning resources, the humble hyperlink is a powerful means of navigation. It is also a powerful aid to learning, allowing elaboration, further exploration and revision.

So text has more going for it than many people imagine. It should not be written off as dull until its many advantages have been understood. It needs simple skills and tools to produce, requires low bandwidth and is easy to update, unlike audio and video.

These are pedagogic and practical arguments for the use of text. But how does AI handle text and how can it be used with text to improve teaching and learning?

## Natural language processing (NLP)

The good news is that NLP, that area of AI concerned with the recognition, understanding and generation of language, is one of the most advanced and useful areas of AI. It uses text as its data and AI models can do wonderful things to enable learning.

Syntax analysis is a huge area in NLP. Even the simplest tasks in interpreting language are not trivial. NLP has to identify sentences. Sounds easy, but URLs have full stops. It then has to identify words – easy in some languages like English, not so easy in others, such as Chinese. It can be used to clean up the endings of words (end from end-ed, end-ing, end-s). This is useful in recognizing all the variants of a word in open input questions in online learning.

Identifying parts of speech meaningfully, such as adjectives, adverbs, verbs and nouns, is not easy as words can mean very different things in different contexts. Dogs bark and trees have bark. Our hands have nails and we hammer in nails. This is necessary for the analysis of open-input text.

Parsing the grammar of a language involves breaking down the relationships between the different parts of sentences and therefore their meaning.

Entity analysis identifies different types of concepts and is used in the creation of online learning content, where the key learning concepts can be identified and turned into questions.

Semantic analysis concerns the meaning of text, the identification and extraction of understanding of natural language, the relationships between words, meaning, translation, answering questions and so on. Sentiment analysis is the reading of subjectivity, in terms of positive or negative views, even emotions. It even covers the generation of language, predictive text, the next word from a fragment of biblical papyrus and larger tasks, such as the production of articles, essays and so on.

Summarization will précis text, either keeping the original text intact or as a summary, where the words are changed. Keeping the original text intact can be useful for previously quality assured or regulated content. This is used to shorten text in learning, where less usually means more in terms of retention and recall.

Speech recognition and speech to text is another NLP technique. This is not easy as one has to separate the continuous flow of sound into words, then there's the quality of the sound and accents to cope with. It is used in learning for the orally impaired as well as major interfaces, such as Cortana, Siri, Alexa and Google Home, but also in some online learning programmes, as it avoids issues such as low levels of literacy, poor typing skills and dyslexia.

Text to speech is the reverse and is used for the same consumer services mentioned above, when they speak back to you, and in learning, for the visually impaired.

## Content creation

Good content matters in learning, just as good movies, books and other purposeful content matters. However, online learning content production has for decades been stuck in the delivery of rather flat content. It has been accused of being page-turning, largely media production, whether text, graphics or video, peppered with lots of click-on events to reveal, drag, drop or select from lists (multiple choice questions). The results in terms of actual learning and retention can disappoint, as the lack of meaningful cognitive effort often results in rather shallow and short-term results.

Content production has also been neither fast nor cheap. A typical production team could include a project manager, instructional designer, graphic artist (maybe video and sound person), developer and tester. Input by subject matter experts (SMEs) is then needed for content creation and quality control. This results in lots of documentation and innumerable iterations, which can be stressful as the culture of expertise clashes with the culture of learning and design. The psychology of learning tells us that less is more, yet subject matter experts often think (wrongly) that more is more. This all adds up to time and money. Projects can take up to six months or more to complete, and the cost per hour of learning, still a rather odd metric, can be considerable.

Rather than rush to use big data, analytics and prediction software, a more realizable and precise goal for the use of AI for learning is to:

- summarize content;
- adapt content;
- create content from existing resources;
- create open input for learning;
- create content from scratch.

All of these, with the help of AI, can be done in minutes, not months, at a fraction of the existing costs and with higher retention. This reduction in time is important, as training design can be a block in business process. A teacher, lecturer, trainer or business sponsor comes to the learning technology team and is told that it will take weeks, even months, to complete and needs a considerable budget. Their reaction is often to simply walk away. Deliver quickly, using agile techniques and tools, and you will be seen as delivering timely solutions to educational or business problems.

## Summarize text content

Walk into almost any large organization and you'll encounter a mother lode of documents and PowerPoints. They are often overwritten and far too long to be useful in an efficient learning process, where less is usually more. That does not put people off, and in many organizations we still have slide decks with over a hundred slides delivered in a room with a projector, masquerading as education and training. The trick is to use AI to automate the condensing or shortening of all of this text, down to the 'need to know' essentials.

To summarize or précis text documents down in size, a first human edit is always advisable. No matter what AI techniques you use to précis text, it is wise to initially edit out the extraneous material by hand – the content that learners will not be expected to learn. For example, supplementary information, disclaimers, who wrote the document, citations and so on. With large, well-structured documents, PDFs and PowerPoints, it is often easy to just identify the introductions or summaries in each section and use them as ready-made summaries of the essential content for learning. But whatever the source, with AI, garbage in, garbage out (GIGO) is the rule. Regard this step as human data cleansing! Now you are ready for further steps with AI.

*Extractive AI* summarization keeps the text intact and simply removes what it judges to be the less useful content. This technique uses AI to produce a summary that keeps the sentences intact and only 'extracts' the relevant material. This is especially useful where the content may already have been subjected to regulatory control and approval (approved by expert, lawyer, regulator). It may also have SME approval. The advantage of this approach is that you retain the integrity of the original text. This technique changes nothing; it simply shortens the existing text.

*Abstractive AI* summarization produces a summary that is rewritten and uses a set of training data and machine learning to produce a précis. Note that this approach needs a large subject-specific training set. By large we mean as large as possible. Some of the training sets for existing models are literally gigabytes of data. You will also need some heavy computing power, hardware and time. That data may also have to be cleaned. Abstractive tends to use deep learning models and neural networks to understand the content then generate summarized content as a précis. Free from the constraint of having to be loyal to the original structure, these algorithms will write their own abstract, getting down to the real essence of the text. This more powerful technique is more likely to provide a tighter, more suitable output for learning – shorter and a more optimal distillation of the meaning.

This is all useful in increasing the productivity of any educational or training design team, as you dramatically shorten this necessary editing task. On large PDFs, not uncommon in compliance and statements of work, these techniques work well. Summarizing also works well with any text from articles, papers, books, even PowerPoint text and video transcripts. It can also be useful in that it surfaces overwriting, repetition, even errors.

A point that is often overlooked is that this is wholly in line with the psychology of learning, which screams 'less is more'. Our limited working memories, along with the need for chunking and retrieval, make it essential to be precise and as short as possible with learning content. Many courses are overlong with content that is not essential and will soon be forgotten. What learners and businesses want is the crisp essence, what the learner needs to know, not the padding.

So if you have a large number documents and PowerPoints, one can shorten them quickly with minimal human intervention. The summaries, however they are produced, can be useful in the context of learning experiences – as look-up aids, reference, refreshers or for performance support. They can also be input into a content creation tool.

## Adapt language content

How do you make sure that language learning content is suitable for the learner as a beginner, intermediate or advanced learner? Duolingo, the massively successful language learning app, does this using an AI-driven 'CEFR checker' that can be applied to any text, including exercises, chatbot dialogue, stories and podcasts. Note that this CEFR checker has been released for general use by others.

The Common European Framework of Reference (CEFR) is a standard for measuring your proficiency in a language. It classifies you into beginner, intermediate and advanced levels according to your competences in listening, speaking, reading and writing. Machine learning is used to help create content by checking that content across languages, so that it is appropriate for beginner, intermediate, and advanced learners.

The machine learning is trained using a few thousand hand-annotated words and the model applies this to hundreds of thousands of words across other languages. Rather cleverly other AI techniques are used, which are not dependent on specific languages, to apply the model to any new language. Interestingly, this approach works better than using human translations because there are often mismatches, such as the idiomatic use of language, making the AI model technique more efficient.

## Create content from existing resources

Another thing that research in cognitive psychology has gifted to us over the last decade or so is clear evidence that learners are misguided when it comes to judgements about their own learning. Bjork (1994), along with many other high-quality researchers, claims that learning is quite misunderstood by learners, as we have a flawed model of how we learn and remember. There is often a negative correlation between people's judgements of their learning, what they think they have learned and what they have actually learned. The same is true of how they think they learn best, and the way they can actually optimize their learning. In short, our own perceptions of learning are seriously defective. This is why engagement, fun, learner surveys and happy sheets are such bad measures of what is actually learned and often detrimental to the design of optimal learning technology strategy and solutions.

Much online learning is illusory because it is too easy. Learning actually requires real effort for high retention to take place. This is why so much online learning fails. To simply click on faces and see speech bubbles of text appear, drag and drop labels across the screen, choose true or false, even multiple-choice questions, rarely constitutes desirable difficulty. This is click-through learning.

The solution is to provide *effortful retrieval*. This means moving beyond the traditional model of flat text and graphics punctuated by multiple-choice towards cognitive effort, namely strong retrieval, through open input by the learner. This effortful learning gives significant increases in long-term retention and recall. Online learning needs to adopt these techniques, enabled by AI, if it is to remain credible.

Retrieving and recalling what you need to know results in much higher levels of retention (Bjork, 1975). Rather than read, re-read and underline, look away and try to retrieve and recall what you need to know. Rather than click on 'true' or 'false' or an option in a short list (multiple-choice questions or MCQ), look away, think, generate, recall, and come up with the answer. The key point is that research has shown that retrieval is a memory modifier and makes your memory more recallable. Counterintuitively, retrieval is much more powerful than being presented with information in the first place, namely through the original 'teaching' event. From Gates (1917), who compared reading and re-reading with retrieval, to Spitzer (1939), who halted forgetting over two months with retrieval in 3,000 learners, to Roediger *et al* (2011), who got a full grade increase with retrieval techniques, and McDaniel *et al* (2011), who increased attainment in science, the evidence is clear – retrieval is a powerful learning strategy.

More focus should be given to retrieval, not presentation, clicking on items and multiple choice. We need to be presented with desirable difficulties, through partial or complete open input. We have the tools in natural language processing and AI to implement the findings of this research and apply retrieval practice, learning from failure, so technology has at last caught up with pedagogy. Let us not plough the same furrow we have ploughed for decades. It is time to move on.

So how has effortful retrieval in learning been applied, through AI, in real projects?

The multinational company TUI had a complex learning requirement that could not have been solved without the benefits of AI. They needed to deliver 138 modules of learning in just eight weeks. Analysis showed that traditional production methods would take up to eight months and costs for external development would be prohibitive. So they used an AI learning tool that analysed basic source content using AI and delivered online output that was high quality and resulted in high-retention learning experiences (Bailey, 2019).

It had a robust, effortful, retrieval pedagogy behind it. WildFire's approach enabled them to deliver the core training and also mock assessments – all in one solution. What also mattered was that they hit the deadline and delivery was within a budget that was around 10 per cent of traditional production costs. Speed of delivery was remarkable. In fact, their biggest struggle was to test outputs at the speed of delivery, but they got there and final delivery was within six weeks.

Henri Palmer says that 'being flexible and "brave" with this new approach saved TUI six months of effort, around £438,000 in development budget and £15,000 in salary costs' (Bailey, 2019). Without the use of AI learning technologies it would have been impossible for TUI to achieve these objectives. The team took a bold step to use a new AI learning technology approach to achieve delivery of an extensive amount of learning content, with a limited budget and challenging timescales. On timescales alone they recognized that an innovative and agile development approach was necessary to achieve success.

They identified a tool called WildFire that uses AI to develop and deliver learning with a focus on long-term retention and recall. WildFire processes content such as a document, PowerPoint presentation or video, and uses learning algorithms to output high-quality, online learning content. Outputs are SCORM compliant, meaning learner progress can be tracked for e-portfolios and assessment reviews. It literally creates the presentation of content, questions and links automatically.

The tool also links to Wikipedia, or other sources, even internal, to pull in relevant content, enabling learners to research a topic in depth, without requiring additional development. Subsequent learning analytics showed that 78 per cent used these links to Wikipedia content to extend learning (Bailey, 2019).

The TUI team identified a number of other critical challenges to be overcome.

A new agile project approach was needed at TUI so testing and sign-off could keep up with the WildFire delivery speed – otherwise timescales would not be met. The team, recognizing that this was new technology that required a new approach to project management, reworked their project approach, removing unnecessary steps and rolling testing phases to allow for a development tool that could create multiple modules a day for eight weeks. Working with the WildFire team, they agreed what time of each day changes identified during testing would be reported, with telephone communication where clarification was required. This agile approach meant the project could be delivered without a single face-to-face meeting.

With an enthusiastic learner response to the implementation plan driven by assessors, the team needed to ensure the technical launch was successful first time. The LMS was prepared to ensure access and layout of content was intuitive, with guidance to support this new approach. Customer scenarios were also added so learners could reinforce learning. The helpdesk also created a support document and allocated additional time to support learners at launch.

With learning design driven by WildFire's algorithms, reusing existing updated content and no formal learning script to develop, all 138 modules were delivered in just six weeks – well within the tight delivery timescale. The final solution produced content at both Level 2 and Level 3 for a development cost of just over £60,000. With an additional salary saving of £15,000, this meant that the project costs around 10 per cent of the original, estimated costs of doing this using non-AI technology.

To identify the impact of the training the team contacted store managers who had a learner who had taken the training. The training had only been available for two months and already the impact of the solution was recognized. It was found that '43% recognized an improvement in knowledge and confidence when engaging with customers' (Bailey, 2019).

After a few months they surveyed the target audience and '95% rated the design approach as good or very good and 62% could identify a specific sale based on the knowledge they had gained' (Bailey, 2019).

Soon other areas of the business were asking for access, 'so we provided this and within four months we had 850 voluntary completions. A year later voluntary completions were at over 6,000 and rising' (Bailey, 2019). Delivering to other TUI employees maximized the investment. Overall the team demonstrated how, 'with a bit of lateral thinking and a lot of tenacity, seemingly impossible timescales could be met'. Within the company the 'wider business now recognizes the benefits of being bold with new learning technologies' and sees the project as an 'outstanding example of achieving our strategy to invest in and develop our people' (Bailey, 2019).

At the Learning Technologies Awards, where it won an award for Best Online Learning Project, the judges said:

> To speed up production TUI took the brave step of selecting... an Artificial Intelligence tool, WildFire. The result saw triple savings; six months knocked off the expected timescales, £15,000 in salaries and £438,000 off the development budget.

Being flexible and 'brave' with this new AI approach saved TUI six months of effort, a huge sum of money and reduced time taken for assessors to validate and mark learning, giving them back 15 per cent of their available time.

## Open input content

With much online learning, learners just skate over the surface. For all the talk of learning experience systems and 'engagement', if all you serve up are flat media experiences, no matter how short or micro, with click-through multiple-choice or, worse, drag and drop, you will have thin learning. As Richard Mayer (1989) showed many times in his research, media-rich does not mean mind-rich. In fact, media-rich and simple click options often inhibit learning with unnecessary cognitive load, combined with low cognitive effort. We know that what counts is effortful, desirable and deliberate practice, and the way to make such systems work is to focus on effortful 'learning' experiences, not just media production.

We tend to think that we learn just by reading, hearing and watching. When, in fact, it is other, effortful, more sophisticated practices that result in far more powerful learning. Learner surveys and happy sheets have been shown to be poor measures of how and what we actually learn and very far from being optimal learning strategies.

It is the *effort* made to 'call to mind' that makes learning work. Even when you read, it is the mind reflecting, making links, calling up related thoughts, that makes the experience a learning experience. This is especially true in online learning. The open mind is what makes us learn and therefore open response is what makes us really learn in online learning.

You start with whatever learning resource, in whatever medium you have: text (PDF, paper, book…), text and graphics (PowerPoint…), audio (podcast) or video. By all means read your text, go through a PowerPoint, listen to the podcast or watch a video. It is what comes next that matters.

With AI tools, online learning with 'open' input is created quickly and open input created by AI can drive the learning. The answers, short or long, are also interpreted, semantically, by AI. You literally get a question and a blank box into which you can type whatever you want. This is what happens in real life – not selecting items from multiple-choice lists. Note that you are not encouraged to just retype what you read, saw or heard. The point, hence the question, is to think, reflect, retrieve and recall what you think you know. AI helps interpret answers through natural language algorithms and semantic interpretation.

You are asked to tell us what you actually think and know. It is not easy and people take several attempts. That is the point. You are cognitively digging deep, retrieving what you know and having a go. As the AI does a semantic analysis, it accepts variations on words, synonyms and different word orders. You can't simply cut and paste, and when you are shown the definition again, whatever part you got right is highlighted.

It is a refreshing experience in online learning, as it is so easy to click through media and multiple-choice questions thinking you have learned what is expected. Learners are easily fooled into thinking they have mastered something when they have not.

We know a lot about how people learn; the excessive focus on surface experience may not help. All experience leads to some learning. But that is not the point, as some experiences are better than others. What those experiences should be are rarely understood by learners. What matters is effortful learning, not the skating across the surface that is click-through learning.

## Create content from scratch

An even bolder use of AI for content creation is the idea that AI can create content, not as in all of the above examples, by enhancing existing resources, but from scratch. You may have never heard of GPT-2, but it is a breakthrough in AI that has astonishing implications for us all, especially in learning. GPT-2 is an AI model that can predict the next word from a given piece of text.

In practice, GPT-2 is a powerful model for:

- summarizing;
- comprehension;
- question answering;
- translation.

This is all without domain-specific training. In other words, it has general capabilities and does not need specific information on a topic or subject to operate successfully. It can generate text of good quality at some length. In fact, the model is 'chameleon like' as it adjusts to the style and content of the initial piece of text. This makes it read as a realistic extension. This has huge implications, both good and bad, for the future of education and training.

## Good

- AI writing assistants allow the automatic creation of text for teaching and learning, whether study papers or textbooks, at the right level.
- Lengthy texts can be summarized into more meaningful learning materials.
- More capable dialogue agents mean that learner 'engagement' through teaching assistant agents could become easier, better and cheaper.
- More capable dialogue agents mean that learner 'support', such as is often provided by teaching assistants, could become easier, better and cheaper.
- Online learning content can be created with little SME input.
- Student free-text input answers can be interpreted.
- Formative feedback based on student performance can be provided.
- Machine teaching, mentoring and coaching may well get a lot better. However, I'd be cautious on this, as there are other serious problems to overcome before this becomes possible, especially around context.
- Assessments can be automatically created.
- Speech recognition systems will get a lot better, allowing them to be used in online learning and assessment.
- Well-being dialogue agents will become more human-like and useful.

- Personalized learning just got a lot easier.
- Online learning just got a lot faster and cheaper.
- Language learning just got a lot easier, as unsupervised translation between languages will boost the quality of translation and make automatic and instantaneous, high-quality translation much more accurate and possible.

## Bad

- Essay mills have just been automated. You want an essay? Just feed it the subject or the subject supplemented by a line of inquiry you want to follow and it will do the rest. Even with an error rate, human finessing could polish the essay.
- It can do homework assignments.
- It could perform well in online exams, impersonating real people.
- Teaching assistant jobs may be increasingly automated.
- If it can answer questions, many human jobs that involve the interpretation of text and data may be automated. Customer service jobs, call centre jobs and the increased automation of all human interaction jobs may be accelerated.
- It can generate misleading learning content (and news articles).
- Impersonating others online can be automated on a massive scale.
- Abusive or fake content to post on social media can be automated on a massive scale, which is bad for education.
- Spam/phishing content can be generated on a massive scale.

Importantly, the model is far from flawless. Some reports suggest human-level capabilities. This is far from the truth. It is still of variable quality and error prone. But, for a first iteration, this model is astonishingly powerful. They have published its performance against established tests. In future iterations it is likely to get a lot better as they predict more training data, more computing power and fine-tuning.

The homework example sets the following task: *For today's homework assignment, please describe the reasons for the US Civil War*. It then shows a plausible essay on the subject. The examples also include creative output, with an interesting example on the AI website showing the generation of a fictional story, with full dialogue, from just one relatively short sentence.

This opens up fascinating possibilities for the generation of stories, fiction and literature.

We have seen how AI can take existing documents, PowerPoints or videos and create credible online content. It can do this at a fraction of the speed and cost of traditional methods. It also creates the need for a more agile approach to online content production, where one has to adopt a leaner team, different processes and a mindset that focuses on fast delivery. We have also seen how AI is starting to provide software that can also create content from scratch. This area is developing fast – very fast. AI-generated articles on finance and sport have been appearing in newspapers and online for years; this is now happening in online learning.

## Conclusion

AI does more than just sequence content, provide recommendation engines, fuel chatbots and help with assessment. It can be used to help create content. This can be the identification of learning points and the creation of externally curated links or the provision of semantic analysis of open input by learners. We will also see how the weaknesses of video content, which tends to flow through the mind and focuses on certain aspects of learning such as attitudes and process, can be enhanced using transcription and the creation of supplementary learning on that transcript. Beyond this, the creation of content from scratch by AI models is on the horizon. This is similar to the creation of syndicated news, sports and financial articles by AI.

## References

Bailey, S (2019) Transcript: #167 – Henrietta Palmer, Learning Solutions, TUI Group on creating learning content with AI, The EdTech Podcast. Available at https://theedtechpodcast.com/transcript-167-henrietta-palmer-learning-solutions-tui-group-on-creating-learning-content-with-ai/ (archived at https://perma.cc/4TGB-QWSN)

Bjork, RA (1975) Retrieval as a memory solidifier: An interpretation of negative recency and related phenomena. In *Information Processing and Cognition*, ed RL Solso, pp 123–124, Erlbaum, Hillsdale, NJ

Bjork, RA (1994) Memory and metamemory considerations in the training of human beings. In *Metacognition: Knowing about knowing*, eds J Metcalfe and A Shimamura, pp 185–205, MIT Press, Cambridge, MA

Gates, AI (1917) Recitation as a factor in memorizing, *Archives of Psychology*, **40**, pp 1–104

Mayer, RE (1989) Systematic thinking fostered by illustrations in scientific text, *Journal of Educational Psychology*, **81**, pp 240–246

Mayer, RE (1996) Learning strategies for making sense out of expository text: The SOI model for guiding three cognitive processes in knowledge construction, *Educational Psychology Review*, **8** (4), pp 357–371

Mayer, RE, Bove, W, Bryman, A, Mars, R and Tapangco, L (1996) When less is more: Meaningful learning from visual and verbal summaries of science textbook lessons, *Journal of Educational Psychology*, **88** (1), p 64

Mayer, RE and Clark, R (2003) *E-learning and the Science of Instruction*, Pfeiffer, Hoboken, NJ (see p61 for multiple references)

McDaniel, MA, Agarwal, PK, Huelser, BJ, McDermott, KB and Roediger, HL (2011) Test-enhanced learning in a middle school science classroom: The effects of quiz frequency and placement, *Journal of Educational Psychology*, **103**, pp 399–414

Roediger, HL, Agarwal, PK, McDaniel, MA and McDermott, KB (2011) Test-enhanced learning in the classroom: Long-term improvements from quizzing, *Journal of Experimental Psychology: Applied*, **17**, pp 382–395

Spitzer, HF (1939) Studies in retention, *Journal of Educational Psychology*, **30**, pp 641–656

Wurman, RS (1990) *Information Anxiety: What to do when information doesn't tell you what you need to know*, Bantam, New York

# 09

# Video

## What can we learn from YouTube?

YouTube is the new television, the largest audio-visual channel in history and the second largest search engine, after Google. It has uncovered new ways of watching, patterns of attention and new ways of interacting with an audience. In short, it is a new learning platform that breaks many of the old rules around learning. We often forget that what powers YouTube is AI-driven search.

Unlike education, the web has a habit of producing pedagogic models that have massive user adoption. Short, instructive video is one such model. YouTube showed that short video clips have a serious contribution to play in learning. YouTube EDU puts lectures online, but if anything this was the old world porting its old bad practices into the new world. A bad one-hour lecture is not made better by putting it on YouTube. It is TED, Khan and the millions of other short instructional videos that have irreversibly changed the learning landscape. These are innovators who understand the use of video in learning and have adapted it to their audience's needs. Education will not be televised, it will be digitized.

YouTube is increasingly becoming the default search engine for young people and learners who want visual answers to questions. You name it, YouTube will show you how to do it. Its pedagogic power comes from the sheer size of the repository and range of content. Like Wikipedia, it is grow-ing exponentially and, as more serious content appears, teachers, trainers, lecturers and learners can use this content as a free resource.

YouTube has certainly influenced the way video appears and is shown on the web. Most of the clips have the pedagogic advantage of being short, avoiding overlong instructional content and therefore cognitive overload.

How long should an instructional video be? Only as long as it needs to be and no longer, ie short.

Creatively, YouTube has spawned lots of new genres of video instruction:

- *Khan blackboard and coloured chalk* – simple but effective, as the learner's mind is not cluttered with seeing Khan; it is the content that matters, not a talking head.
- *Thrun's hand and whiteboard* – again, it is not Thrun's head that matters but seeing worked problems and solutions.
- *RSA animations* – these are clever animations that end up as a single infographic.
- *TED talks* – show how lectures should be: short, with passionate experts, no notes, no reading, little PowerPoint.
- *Software demos* – show me the steps one by one.
- *Physical demos* – point the camera at the engine, radiator or whatever I need to fix and show me how to do it, with commentary.

Learning by doing has always suffered in the unreal world of the classroom and school. An important advance has been made through YouTube in vocational and practical learning, where real tasks are shown on video. These often involve the manipulation of real objects and the demonstration of processes. The pedagogy of learning by doing can be brought into the learning environment via YouTube.

YouTube has the potential to act as a vast education and training resource of free content, lowering costs for learning. More than this, it has introduced pedagogic changes around the use of video: its length, quality, format and breadth of uses. But beyond 'channels', YouTube does not give you context or structure. We have seen services indexing videos and using learner-led questions to find video answers, especially from a bank of experts. Khan has software that contextualizes maths in terms of prerequisites and so on. In other words, video often needs to be used in a blended context if the learning experience is to have breadth and depth.

## What can we learn from Netflix?

Netflix came from nowhere. Nobody saw it coming. Now a global channel, it has become a giant in the entertainment industry because it adopted a time-shifted, demand-driven solution in a world that was stuck in scheduled, supply-side delivery. Netflix is easy to use, time-shifted, searchable and personalized, extensively A/B tested, tiled and has an AI recommendation engine behind the interface. Technically it is streamed and multi-device. But what really makes it sing is the data-driven algorithmic delivery. This is why learning and video folk need to pay attention to technology, especially AI. That other behemoth, YouTube, the largest learning platform on the planet, is also searchable, personalized and time-shifted.

Could something similar happen in the learning world? Like movies and TV, learning experiences are delivered in roughly one-hour, scheduled chunks; in schools as periods, in higher education as one-hour lectures. Is it ripe for a player that produces the perfect storm of easy-to-use, personalized, AI and data-driven, streamed, time-shifted, low-cost delivery that Netflix created? But Netflix is entertainment, not learning content, so what more do we have to learn from cognitive science about what makes great learning video?

The first lesson is that we need to learn that technology matters in terms of delivery, data, recommendation engines, access, convenience and cost.

Netflix as we now know it was only possible when *cloud-based streaming* was possible at scale, and consumers had enough bandwidth to cope with streamed content. Cloud-based delivery is now becoming the norm for learning services. Content and management systems are moving to the cloud, as this is now a necessary condition for success. Large adaptive systems need to be cloud based as they are only scalable on that model, especially if they are tracking and delivering services in real time, to large numbers of learners in a personalized fashion.

Netflix outflanked both the TV and the movie business by being *consumer, not presenter, led*. It is addictive because you are in control and you have enough of a choice to fit your mood – movie, one episode, drama binge, comedy, documentary. *Time-shift* was the trick: watch when you want. Free yourself from the tyranny of time.

Far too much learning is delivered in real-time, synchronous learning. It is time we recognized that learning can largely be done asynchronously. This is what online learning offers. This is unlikely to happen in schools, where the physical care of pupils is essential. Even there, however, there is room for improvement. But there are ample opportunities in post-secondary, adult and corporate education. We need smart, scalable online delivery.

Netflix famously turbo-charged their *AI recommendation engine* with a $1 million prize. They did not actually use the winning algorithm but learned from it and used something simpler. It paid off in spades. It is this subtle recommendation engine that makes it more than a library of stuff. It turns it into a living, breathing, *personalized* service. That is exactly what learning delivery needs – a more personalized service, one that always knows what you as a learner need and delivers the right stuff at the right time. This has been a key feature of Google (essentially an algorithm service), Facebook (algorithm-driven ads), Amazon (algorithm-driven recommendation engine) and now Netflix. AI is the new UI. There is every reason to believe that this has efficacy in learning, where knowing what a learner knows, does not know and needs to know next is the key to delivering efficient learning. This is the Age of Algorithms and AI is the underpinning technology that will shape things for decades to come

It comes as a shock to people when they learn that Netflix gathers *data*, not only on what is popular, but cross-referencing actors with genres and sub-genres, as well as scene analysis. Netflix knows what you do not like, when people tend to lose interest and when they drop out. This data informs subsequent programme choices, even content commissioning and scene construction. Ted Sarandos, Netflix Head of Content, describes *House of Cards* as 'generated by algorithm' (Martinson, 2015). They calculated that the demographic that loved political thrillers also loved Kevin Spacey. This insightful content production is the result of a careful understanding of their audience.

According to Sarandos, decision-making at Netflix is 70 per cent data, 30 per cent human. Education and training operates at almost 100 per cent human decision-making, which is exactly why it is not improving fast enough. Learning has a lot to learn from this. We need to use *data* to build and improve content and delivery. This needs to happen in the creation and curation of content, as well as at the course and degree level. Everything needs to be seen as a system that improves with use. Education is a slow learner; let us make it learn fast. And listen up, learning folks – learners want services to work across the board, on all devices.

The Netflix user experience is slick, easy to use, easy to navigate, searchable and personalized. Compare this with most educational experiences. Most are curiously disjointed, complex and inconvenient. It takes a huge amount of effort to understand and navigate the system or even a course. We must make it easier to find things, study things, get help, get feedback and get assessed. This needs constant attention, lots of A/B testing and a relentless attitude towards the learning experience.

## Video and AI

Video, through YouTube, Vimeo, Netflix, Amazon Prime and other services, is the medium of the age and AI is the technology of the age. Combine the two and you have a potent mixture. But how do these two worlds interact? Well, AI has helped producers edit, colour balance, audio mix, caption, transcribe, translate, filter, search, personalize, analyse and predict.

In the creation of video, AI has already crept into video production tools. There are tools that allow you to edit video much faster and to higher quality. Different cameras shoot different colour balances? That can be fixed with AI. Same actor in different scenes with different skin tone? That can be fixed with facial recognition and skin tone matching – using AI. Need your music mixed down behind dialogue? Use AI. AI is increasingly used to fix, augment and enhance moving images.

Of course, easy editing with AI also means easy fakes. AI-generated avatars as TV presenters have appeared reading the news, using text-to-speech software. One can have Obama saying whatever you like from a voiceover artist mimicking his voice. Images of people morphing into famous actors is a common internet meme. Even more worrying is fake porn. Many famous actresses and actors have had their faces transposed to create 'deepfake' porn scenes.

Alibaba's *Aliwood* software uses AI to create 20-second product videos from a company's existing stills, identifying and selecting key images, close-ups and so on (Chou, 2018). The selected images are then edited together with AI and even change with musical shifts. They say it increases online purchases. Some video creation software goes further and also adds a text-to-speech narration, with edits at appropriate points. Many pop videos and films have been made using AI tools such as Deep Dream for image creation along with style capture and flow tools. There's even complete films made from AI-created scripts.

Once you have created a video, AI can also add captions. This type of software can even pick up on dog barks and other sounds and is now standard on TV, YouTube, Facebook, even Android phones, increasing accessibility. It is also useful in noisy environments. Language learners also commonly report captioning as having benefits in self-directed language learning. Although one must be careful here, as Mayer's research shows that narration and text together have an inhibitory effect on learning (Mayer and Johnson, 2008).

Speech to text is also useful in transcription, where a learner may want the actual transcription of a video as notes. Some tools take these transcriptions and use them to create online learning to supplement the video with effortful learning. The learner watches the video, which is good for attitudinal and affective learning, even process and procedures, but poor on semantic knowledge and detail. Adding an online treatment of the transcript, created and assessed by AI, can provide that extra dimension to the learning experience.

Once you have the transcribed text, translation is also possible. This has improved enormously from Google Translate to more sophisticated services. The technology promises to deliver speech-to-speech translation with an end-to-end translation model that can deliver accurate results with low latency. Advances like these will allow any video to be translated into multiple languages, allowing low-cost and quick global distribution of learning videos.

Ever thought why YouTube and other video services prevent porn and other undesirable material from appearing? AI filters identify offending videos through image recognition to search and then delete. Facebook claims that AI now identifies 96.8 per cent of prohibited content (Wiggers, 2019). It is not that AI does the whole job here. Removing 'dick pics' and beheadings relies on algorithms and image recognition, but there is also community flagging and real people sitting watching this stuff. Despite this, AI is increasingly used to protect us from undesirable content.

Want to know something or do something? Searching YouTube is increasingly the first option chosen by learners. YouTube is probably the most used learning platform on the planet. Yet we tend to forget that it is only functional with good search. AI search techniques are what gives YouTube its power. Note that YouTube search is different from Google search. Google uses authority, relevancy, site structure and organization; whereas YouTube, being in control of all its content, uses growth in viewing, patterns in viewing, view time, peak view times, and social media features such as shares, comments, likes and repeat views. Search is what makes YouTube such a convenient learning tool.

Video services such as YouTube, Vimeo and Netflix use AI to algorithmically present content. AI is the new UI, and most video content is served up in this personalized fashion. This is exactly what is happening in recommendation and adaptive learning systems, where individual and aggregated data is used to personalize and optimize the learning experience for each individual, so that everyone is educated uniquely.

Talking of Netflix, there is now a huge amount of data collected on global services that can inform future decision-making. Similarly in learning, analytics around usage, exits, and so on can inform decisions about the efficacy of the learning. We know from learning video data gathered from MOOCs that learners drop out in large numbers at around six minutes (Guo *et al*, 2014). It is down to 50 per cent at 9–12 minutes and 20 per cent beyond this. Evidence from other studies on attention, using eye-tracking, confirm this quite rapid drop in arousal (Risko *et al*, 2012). The recommendation is that we keep videos at six minutes or less – the less the better.

All of the above do and will affect the delivery of video in learning. Several are already *de facto* techniques. We can expect them all to develop in line with advances in AI, as well as learner demand. This is clearly an example of where the learning world has lots to learn and lots to gain from consumer services. Most of the above techniques are being built, honed and delivered on consumer platforms first then being used in a learning context.

## AI turns video into deep learning

With video in learning one can feel as though one is learning, as the medium holds your attention, but as you are hurtled forward that knowledge disappears. Like a shooting star, it looks and feels great, but the reality is that it burns up as it enters the atmosphere and rarely ever lands.

Let us start with the basics. What you are conscious of is what is in working memory limited in capacity to two to four elements of information at any time. We can only hold these conscious thoughts in memory for 20 seconds or so. So our minds move through a learning experience with limited capacity and duration. This is true of all experience, and with video it has some interesting consequences.

We also have a long-term memory, which has no known limits in capacity or duration, although lifespan is its obvious limit. We can transfer thoughts from long-term memory back into working memory quickly and effortlessly. This is why 'knowing' matters. In maths, it is useful to automatically know your times tables, to allow working memory to then manipulate recalled results more efficiently. We also use existing information to cope with and integrate novel information. The more you know, the easier it is to learn new information. Old, stored, processed information renders working memory enormous through effortless recall from long-term memory. All of this raises the question of how we can get video-based learning into long-term memory.

When learning meaningful information that is processed, for example in multiplication, you have two to four registers for the numbers being multiplied. The elements have to be manipulated within working memory and that adds extra load. *Element interactivity* is always extra load. Learning simply addition or subtraction has low element interactivity, but multiplication is more difficult. Learning vocabulary has low element interactivity. Learning how to put the words together into meaningful sentences is more difficult.

In video, element interactivity is very difficult, as the brain is coping with newly presented material and the pace is not under your control. This makes video a difficult medium for learning semantic information, as well as weak in the consolidation of learning through cognitive effort and deeper processing.

Quite simply, we engage in teaching, whether offline or online, to get things into long-term memory via working memory. You must take this learning theory into account when designing video content. When using video we tend to forget about working memory as a limitation and the absence of opportunity to move working memory experiences into long-term memory. We also tend to shove in material that is more suited to other media, semantic content such as facts, figures and conceptual manipulations. So video is often too long, shows points too quickly and is packed with inappropriate content.

There is also the distinction, in long-term memory, between *episodic* and *semantic* memory. Episodic memories are those experiences such as what you did last night, what you ate for supper, recalling your experience at a concert. They are, in a sense, like recalling short video sequences (albeit reconstructed). Semantic memory is the recall of facts, numbers, rules and language. They are different types of memory processed in different ways and places by the brain. When dealing with video in learning, it is important to know what you are targeting. Video appeals far more to episodic than semantic memory – the recall of scenes, events, procedures, places and people doing things.

We can recognize that video has some great learning affordances in that it can capture experiences that one may not be able to experience easily, for real: human interactions, processes, procedures, places and so on. Video can also enhance learning experiences, reveal the internal thoughts of people with voiceover and use techniques that compress, focus in and highlight points that need to be learned. When done well, it can also have an emotional or affective impact, making it good for attitudinal change. The good news is that video has had a century or so to develop a rich grammar of techniques designed to telescope, highlight and get points across. The range of techniques from talking heads to drama, with sophisticated editing techniques and the ability to play with time, people and place, makes it a potent and engaging medium.

Video is great at showing processes, procedures, real things moving in the real world, drama, even much-maligned talking heads, but it is poor on many other things, especially concepts, numbers and abstract meaning. The mistake is to see video as a learning medium *in itself*. Video is a great learning medium if things are paced and reinforced, but made greater if the learner has the opportunity to supplement the video experience with some effortful learning.

The danger is that, on its own, video can encourage the illusion of learning. This phenomenon was uncovered by Bjork and others, showing that learners are easily fooled into thinking that learning experiences have stuck, when they have actually decayed from memory, often within the first 20 minutes (Clark, 2018).

How do we make sure that video learning experience is not lost and forgotten? The evidence is clear: the learner needs some effortful learning; they need to supplement their video learning experience with deeper learning that allows them to move that experience from short- to long-term memory.

## Retrieval

One effective method is to engage in a form of deeper, effortful learning that involves retrieval and recall. An AI tool like WildFire does exactly this (WildFire Learning, nd).

When delivering WildFire-created content to nurses in the NHS, it was discovered that processes and procedures were recalled from video, but much of the detail was not. The knowledge that was not retained and recalled was often 'semantic' knowledge:

1 numbers (doses, measurements, statistical results, and so on);

2 names and concepts (concepts, drugs, pathogens, anatomy, and so on).

This is not surprising, as there is a real difference between *episodic* and *semantic* memory.

Episodic memory is all of those things remembered as experiences or events – you are an actor within these events. Semantic memory is facts, concepts, numbers, where meaning is independent of space and time, often thought of as words and symbols.

In healthcare, as in most professions, you need to know both. This is why video alone is rarely enough. One solution is to supplement video with learning that focuses on reinforcing the episodic and semantic knowledge, so that two plus two makes five.

The solution was to automatically grab the transcript (narration) of the videos. Some transcripts were already available, and for those that were not, one can use the automatic transcript service on YouTube or other tools. This transcript was put through the WildFire process, where AI was used to automatically produce online learning with open input questions to increase retention and recall. This allowed the learner to both watch the video (for process and procedure) and do the active learning, where they picked up the semantic knowledge, as well as reinforcing the processes and procedures.

In a nurse training video on allergy tests, where the nurse administers allergens into the skin of the patient and the reactions are recorded, the video shows the nurse as she gets the patient comfortable with a pillow under his arm. She then asks him some questions: 'Any lotions on your skin? Taken any antihistamines in the last four days?' Other important learning points are to blot (not rub), tell the patient not to scratch and so on.

Now the video did a great job on the procedure – pillow under the arm, lancets in sharps bin, blot not rub, and so on. Where the video failed was in the number of days within which the patient had taken antihistamines, the names of the allergens and the concept of a negative control. This was then covered by asking the learners to recall and type in their answers (not multiple-choice questions) in WildFire, items such as four days, names of allergens, negative control, and so on. In addition, if the learner didn't know, for example, what a negative control was, there were AI-created links to explanations, describing what a negative control is within a diagnostic test.

The learner gets the best of both worlds: the visual learning through video and the semantic learning through WildFire, all in the right order and context. It is important that the retrieval learning is very closely related to video content, which is why the transcript is used.

## Conclusion

How do you ensure that your learning is not lost and forgotten? Strangely enough it is by engaging in a learning experience that makes you recall what you think you have learned. WildFire grabs the transcript of the video, puts it into an AI engine that creates a supplementary learning experience, where you have to type in what you 'think' you know. This powerful form of retrieval learning not only gives you reinforcement through a second bite of the cherry, but also consolidates the learning.

Research has shown that recalling back into memory – literally looking away and thinking about what you know – is even more powerful than the original teaching experience or exposure. In addition, the AI creates links out to supplementary material (curates, if you wish) to further consolidate memory through deeper thought and processing.

Video is a fabulous learning medium – witness the popularity of YouTube and the success of video in learning – although there are some principles that make it better. When supplemented by AI-produced content, you get a double dividend: visual episodic learning and semantic knowledge.

## References

Chou, C (2018) Alibaba releases new AI video editor 'Aliwood', Alizila. Available at https://www.alizila.com/alibaba-releases-new-ai-video-editor-aliwood/ (archived at https://perma.cc/7MWV-Z3CF)

Clark, D (2018), Why almost everything we think about online learning may be wrong and what to do about it…, Donald Clark Plan B. Available at http://donaldclarkplanb.blogspot.com/2018/11/why-almost-everything-we-think-about.html (archived at https://perma.cc/ZM5Z-7YEC)

Guo, PJ, Kim, J and Robin, RLS (2014) How video production affects student engagement: An empirical study of MOOC videos, in *Proceedings of the First ACM Conference on Learning at Scale*, pp 41–50, ACM, New York

Martinson, J (2015) Netflix's Ted Sarandos: 'We like giving great storytellers big canvases', *Guardian*. Available at https://www.theguardian.com/media/2015/mar/15/netflix-ted-sarandos-house-of-cards (archived at https://perma.cc/Q3ZX-MWR5)

Mayer, RE and Johnson, CI (2008) Revising the redundancy principle in multimedia learning, *Journal of Educational Psychology*, **100** (2), p 380

Risko, EF, Anderson, N, Sarwal, A, Engelhardt, M and Kingstone, A (2012) Everyday attention: Variation in mind wandering and memory in a lecture, *Applied Cognitive Psychology*, **26** (2), pp 234–242

Wiggers, K (2019) Facebook says AI now identifies 96.8% of prohibited content, Venture Beat. Available at https://venturebeat.com/2019/05/23/facebook-says-ai-now-identifies-96-8-of-prohibited-content/ (archived at https://perma.cc/2TSG-E9NM)

WildFire Learning (nd) Available at http://www.wildfirelearning.co.uk/ (archived at https://perma.cc/8882-CGHR)

# 10

# Push learning

Behavioural psychology has much to teach us about why people procrastinate in learning. Understand learners and you understand why it is so difficult to get them to learn. Let us start with the metaphor of the elephant and its rider: the rider is the conscious, verbal, thinking brain; the elephant is the automatic, emotional, visceral brain. Jonathan Haidt created this metaphor in his book *The Happiness Hypothesis* (2006). The idea is that the more recently evolved rational rider part of your brain may want to learn, but more often than not the procrastinating, impulsive elephant takes over and decides to wallow in inaction. Academically this is similar to Kahneman's two systems, *fast* and *slow*, explained in *Thinking, Fast and Slow* (2011) and, in an alternative, more readable form, in *The Undoing Project* (2016) by Michael Lewis. If we can use technology and AI-driven systems to overcome our inner elephants, learning may flow more freely.

But there is a big problem. One elephantine, cognitive bias that hits learning hard is that of *hyperbolic discounting*, a well-researched feature in behavioural economics. Take two similar rewards: humans prefer the one that arrives sooner rather than later. We are therefore said to discount the value of the later reward and this discount increases with the length of the delay.

If the consequences of our learning are distant, we are likely to take it less seriously. Young smokers don't stop smoking just because you tell them it is dangerous, and there's no greater danger than death. In practice, smokers see the consequence of smoking as being some time off, many years if not decades, so they don't stop smoking just because you warn them of the consequence. So it is with learning. Rewards feel distant in learning, which is why students tend to leave study until the last moment and cram just prior to exams, or write essays on the last night. Similarly in organizations, they are not committed when it is likely that they won't use their newly acquired knowledge and skills for some time, if at all. No one watches printer problem videos until they have a printer problem, and no one really feels that compliance training is relevant as the implications seem so far off. So how do we get the learner to be a rider and not be stopped by the elephant?

## Peer learning

Reframe learning into a more social experience, online or offline, so that learners have their peer group to compare with. If you see that others are doing things on time, you are more likely to follow. Peer pressure is a powerful force. Starting with Harris and Baron-Cohen's brilliant work 'The nurture assumption' (1999) on peer pressure, then Eric Mazur's work at Harvard, explained in *Peer Instruction* (1999), it is clear that peer pressure can have a massive effect on behaviour. Future promises of promotion, even money, have less effect than near experiences of being part of a group doing things together or being encouraged, even peer-reviewed, as encouragement and feedback around this social pressure engenders action. This is good old-fashioned peer pressure.

Ivan Illich in *Deschooling Society* (1971) saw 'schooling' confuse teaching with learning, grades with education, diplomas with competence, attendance with attainment. Schools are separated, unworldly places that lead to psychological impotence and we become hooked on their role in society to the extent that other institutions are discouraged from assuming learning tasks. He described, well before the internet, the 'possible use of technology to create institutions which serve personal, creative and autonomous interaction'. He foresaw the power of technology in learning and saw an alternative to schooling through a network of services which gave each person the same opportunity to share their concern with others motivated by the same concern. His core idea was that education for all means education by all. He saw us as providing the learner with new links to the world instead of continuing to funnel all education through the teacher. In this sense, the inverse of school is possible, recommending four types of educational resource:

1  reference services to educational objects;
2  skill exchanges;
3  peer-matching;
4  reference services to educators-at-large.

This is starting to happen with the advent of the internet in learning, through AI-driven search, finding knowledge bases like Wikipedia, AI-driven search on YouTube, open educational resources and AI-driven social media.

Technology, driven by AI interfaces, personalized, has a role to play here, as it has in Tinder and chatbots that encourage messaging and finding mentors online. We can see the matching of learners with tutors and peers being aided by AI.

## Nudge learning

The psychological theory of nudge theory is laid out in the book *Nudge: Improving decisions about health, wealth and happiness* by Thaler and Sunstein (2009). They could well have added 'learning' to the title. Nudge is a nice little word, and some of their examples are quite catching. There's the now famous example of placing the image of a fly in airport men's urinals to reduce spillage and cleaning costs. Opting out of, rather than into, organ donation is another. Could nudging be used in learning?

Technology allows us to push motivating messages and opportunities to learners. We can *nudge* them into learning. Nudge theory has been used in everything from insects in urinals to reduce splashes to serious behavioural change. Differ is a learning chatbot that raises learner engagement by nudging and pushing students forward through timely reminders. We know that learners are lazy and leave things to the last minute, so why not nudge them into correcting that behaviour. Woebot is a counselling chatbot that simply pops up in the morning on Facebook Messenger. You can choose to ignore or reschedule. It has that drip-feed effect and, as the content is good and useful, you get used to doing just a few minutes every morning. Nudging can be accelerated by personalization, making it relevant and bringing it closer to your needs. Almost everything you do online – Google, Facebook, Twitter, Instagram, Amazon and Netflix – uses recommendation engines to personalize what the system thinks you need next. This is another way of making learning experiences relevant – personalizing nudges.

Another method of undermining hyperbolic discounting is to create habitual learning. This is difficult to embed, but once adopted is a powerful motivator. Good learners are in the habit of taking notes, always having a book in their bags, reading before going to sleep and so on. Choose your habit and force yourself to do it until it becomes natural, almost instinctive.

In Kahneman (2011) language, you must make sure that your System 2 has some of the features of what were once System 1.

Just-in-time training, performance support and workflow are all terms for delivering learning when it is needed. This closes the gap between need and execution, thereby eliminating hyperbolic discounting, as there is no delay. Having a solution to printer and other problems ready on tap, so that when the problems arise, solutions are at your fingertips, is exactly what is required.

A sense of immediacy can also be created by major events – a merger, reorganization, new product, new leader. All of these can engender a sense of imminence. Just as the new year may bring in resolutions, so new events may cause people to think about their future needs and development.

Or you can manufacture your own mini-event. Several companies have implemented 'phishing' training by sending fake phishing emails, seeing how people react and delivering the training on the back of that event.

A neat combination of events as catalysts, nudge learning and calls to action, used widely in marketing, was a project by Standard Life (Clark, 2018). They used an *event*, merger with another large organization, as a catalyst, short 90-second videos as *nudges* and *challenges* to do something in their own teams as calls to action. Use was tracked and produced great results. Calls to action are foundational in marketing, especially online marketing, where you are encouraged to contact, register, inquire or buy through a call or button. Have a look at Amazon, perhaps the most successful company in the world, built on the simple idea of nudges and calls to action.

Things move fast in organizations, and when Standard Life merged with Aberdeen Asset Management, an agile learning approach to changing behaviour in the new organization was implemented, a training intervention that is itself agile and resulted in actual behavioural change. A huge traditional course, whether face-to-face or online, based on a diet of knowledge, would have been counterproductive in this fast-moving, post-merger commercial environment and would have been seen as a bit old-school and non-agile. Whereas a series of short, sharp interventions that nudge people into applying agile in their own context and work environment was likely to work better. At least, that's what Peter Yarrow, Head of Learning, thought – and I think he's right. It was his brainchild.

Standard Life Aberdeen sent small, professionally shot videos, on average 90 seconds long, mainly talking heads from leaders and experts in the organization, out via email. In addition to the video, there was a 'challenge' to apply the lesson in their own working environment.

In their case it was general management techniques, but this agile technique could be applied in response to all sorts of needs. Each starts with a proposition, or problem, followed by a suggested solution and, finally and crucially, a call to action.

One nudge and challenge was a video on the importance of good communications. It is hard to be a high-performing team if colleagues don't know each other well. Without trust, mutual respect and goodwill, performance will most likely remain middle of the road. Exceptional performance is fuelled by positive working relationships. So the weekly challenge was to get to know your colleagues better.

Another was a nudge video on mentoring. Being mentored is a great way to develop and progress. But how do you get started? Begin by identifying someone you trust who has taken a career path you aspire to. So another week's challenge was to learn more about making mentoring relationships work.

These videos and challenges were sent out by email and usage tracked. The take-up across the organization surprised the training department and the feedback was very positive. People felt that it was integrated into their natural workflow (they were not too long and intrusive) and that it was made more relevant by virtue of nudging people towards action by them as individuals in their specific job.

Learning in the workflow could be hugely aided by contextual recognition, nudges through notifications on your smartphone when you are in a particular place as recognized by GPS, at a particular time doing something that needs performance support. Imagine arriving for your first day at work and your phone knows you are there so provides you with alerts as you go through the day depending on where you are in the building or part of the orientation process. As a manager, one may have to do some interviewing of candidates for a job and get an alert on basic interview techniques, enter an area in a factory and get a notification about that particular process.

Learning is one thing, getting people to learn is another. Psychologically, we're hard-wired to delay, procrastinate, not take learning seriously and see the rewards as too far down the line to matter. We have to fight these traits and do what we can to encourage authentic and effortful learning. Make it seem as though it really does matter through all sorts of nudges: social, autonomy, push, place in workflow, events as catalysts, recommendations, visual nudges, recommendations, calls to action and habits. Most of this is likely to be personalized and driven by recommendation engines, fuelled by AI.

## Campaigns

Great start, but rather than batch emails, one can use an algorithm to decide personal needs and take data from usage and get more precise in timing and targeting. This means harvesting more data, which one can do, even with internal email systems. Marketing professionals are used to seeing organizational tasks as campaigns, where multi-channel approaches are used to get people to do something. This is where the application of knowledge and skills matters – learning by doing or experiential learning.

On the challenges above, for example, one can use more of a pure marketing approach, a strong command verb at the start, really concise message, with reason and emotional pull. Give your audience a reason why they should take the desired action, maybe a bit of fear of missing out (FOMO), using social pressure, as mentioned earlier. Writing calls to action is both a science and an art and it is worth being a little creative.

Campaigns in learning can make projects fly. Few in marketing want to send out hours and hours of content – they think audience first, channels second and action third. Their whole way of thinking is around 'less is more'. This also happens to be exactly what the psychology of learning tells us about learning experiences. The limits of working memory, cognitive overload, forgetting and the need for transfer mean doing less but doing it better.

You need to create demand, as hyperbolic discounting tends to discount demand. If you have developed some great resources and really want to effect change through learning, you must get out there and get it to learners. Rather than create personas, which tend to average out and caricature target audiences, one can use data about each and every individual to get to the right people with the right message and content at the right time.

Branding, imagery and messaging are all important, as is the choice of channel. Marketing campaigns tend to be multi-channel and so should learning campaigns. Good timing is essential. This is where smart, AI-driven targeting and delivery can turbo-charge a campaign. It is all about targeting.

## Interleaving

Interleaving is counterintuitive and is rarely used as a learning strategy, yet it has a strong evidence base. The breakthrough research was Shea and Morgan (1979), who had students learn in a block or through randomized tasks. Randomized learning appeared to result in better long-term retention. This experiment was repeated by Simon and Bjork (2001), but this time they asked the learners at the end of the activities how they think they'll perform on day 2. Most thought that the blocked practice would be better for them. They were wrong.

Practising your handwriting by writing the same letter time after time is not as effective as mixing the letter practice up.

HHHHHHIIIIIIIIIIJJJJJJJJJ

is not as good as writing

HIJHIJHIJHIJHIJHIJHIJHIJHIJ

This also true in conceptual and verbal skills. Rohrer and Taylor (2007) showed that maths problems are better interleaved. Although it feels as though blocked is better, interleaving was three times better! The result in this paper was so shocking the editors of three major journals rejected the paper on first reading. The size effect was so great that it was hard to believe – so hard to believe, it would appear, that few try it!

Rohrer, Dedrick and Stershic (2015) took this a stage further and took unrelated topics in maths, to compare blocked with interleaved practice. Interleaved produced better performance in both the short and long term (30 days).

What about learning from examples, learning general skills from exposure to examples, like reading X-rays or inferring a painter's style by exposure to many paintings by specific painters? Kornell and Bjork (2008) did the painter test, 12 paintings by each of 6 artists, then showed learners 48 new paintings. The results showed that interleaving was twice as effective as blocked training. It has been replicated in the identification of butterflies, birds, objects, voices, statistics and other domains. Once again, learners were asked what sort of instruction they thought was best. They got it wrong. In young children (3-year-olds), Vlach and Sandhofer (2012) showed that learning interleaved with play produced better performance.

This is a strange thing. Interleaving, as opposed to blocked learning, feels wrong, feels disjointed, almost chaotic. Yet it is much more effective. It seems to fly in the face of your intuitions. Yet it is significantly more efficient as a learning strategy. But how often do we see interleaving in classrooms, homework or online learning? Hardly ever.

This is another technique that cognitive science has thrown our way, which can be implemented through AI-driven algorithmic technology.

The interleaving itself can be created, along with optimized interleaving using machine learning, to increase learning retention and recall.

## Spaced practice

Beyond these behavioural marketing techniques is another, more pedagogically sound technique that is known to increase retention and efficacy in learning – spaced practice.

Matthew Syed was Britain's no. 1 table tennis player for ten years. Not only that, the next five best players all lived within a few streets of him. How come? Well, they had a great coach, a club that was open 24 hours a day, they all had the keys, and the group practised, deliberately and mercilessly, to get to the top. It was nothing to do with natural 'talent' and everything to do with effort and practice. It is all in his excellent book *Bounce* (2010), where he explains not only his sporting journey but the psychology behind that journey, in particular his discovery of deliberate practice. Practice may make perfect, but that is not the whole story.

It is not simply a matter of repetition or following a predetermined pattern of exposure. Spaced practice is much more than this. At its simplest, it is the recall, rehearsal, revision, application or deliberate practice of knowledge or skills spaced over time to reinforce and consolidate them in long-term memory for automatic recall. Ultimately it is about performance, using evidence-based learning theory to apply the most effective techniques that lead to measurable performance. AI can help deliver this practice.

So, given that millions of teachers, lecturers, trainers, coaches and instructors are employed in the learning game, it is perhaps surprising that relatively little or no attention is paid to the idea of spaced practice. One could argue that without knowledge of this principle and its causes, those who teach are missing a key component in the process of learning. This a little unfair, since most traditional learning has been in fixed courses in training rooms, classrooms or lecture halls, and once the student has walked out the door, they have gone. All attempts at practice, revision and application are down to the learner. That shouldn't distract us, however, from making the effort to improve the situation, with or without technology – and with AI, technology can be smartly employed to personalize and deliver the solution.

In 1885 Ebbinghaus published *Uber Das Gedachtis (On Memory)* (published in English in 1913), a groundbreaking work which laid the foundations for the practical science of memory. He gave us the application of the scientific method to the measurement of memory and the famous *forgetting curve*, which even now has the ability to startle those who first encounter the precipitous nature of forgetting.

A solution to the problem of the failure to elaborate and shunt learned knowledge and skills from working memory to long-term memory is to repeat, review, revise, rehearse, recall and practise at spaced intervals in the future. Evidence suggests that the periodicity of these intervals matters, but it is also important that it involves active recall and not just the recognition of answers. The science suggests that this one technique can substantially increase productivity and performance in learning.

*Active recall*, pulling something out of memory, not just recognizing something from a list or multiple-choice questions, improves future performance, something we have known for a century (Gates, 1917). The act of active recall develops and strengthens memory. It also improves the process of recall in ways that *passive* recall – reading, listening and watching – does not. In practice, it is active recall that really matters in knowledge and skills, not recognition. An additional advantage is that if we learn in a way that mimics the conditions of future recall (rarely just recognition), recall is all the more certain (Morris *et al*, 1977).

We can take advantage in a formal, pushed system to push out cues and active recall on knowledge that users have shown they do not know, do not know well or do not feel confident about.

Although students often perform better immediately after '*massed practice*', a single bout of practice, they forget quicker and perform poorly in later tests than '*spaced practice*' students (Keppel, 1964). This is why much end-point assessment is often short term and short-sighted.

Forgetting is initially steep and shows that memories are lost very quickly, then more slowly. As forgetting is a curved descent, so methods that combat forgetting (remembering) need to be spaced across a curved ascent. But it is the combination of spaced practice with active recall (Landauer and Bjork, 1978), with repeated sessions as well as greater gaps, that leads to optimal retention and recall. The timing of this practice is important. We know that there is a point, soon after the learning experience, where it is essential to practise, but as decay slows over time, the practice sessions can be increasingly spaced out over time. This typically follows a minutes, hours, days, weeks, months pattern.

An additional feature of spaced practice is the self-awareness of the learner in relation to their confidence that they know something. However, simplistic metacognition, the students' knowledge of their own learning, is a double-edged sword. Self-perception of ability can both help and hinder learning. The bottom line is that one can study too little or too much (Nelson and Leonesio, 1988). This has led to spaced-practice systems that allow the learner to express a rating on their feeling of *confidence* about their ability.

Spaced practice can therefore be selective in that items that are clearly known can have less weight than items which the user is not confident about, had difficulty in learning or clearly does not know. Here spaced practice can involve algorithmic inferences that use performance data about each individual learner, then route that learner through a series of items, or network of knowledge, based on optimizing their learning and spaced practice.

## Technology and spaced practice

Spaced practice usually (not exclusively) requires technology and approaches that deliver spaced events to the learner. It is often push rather than pull. There are many ways to use technology to push and manage spaced practice, from the simple to complex. In all cases pedagogy is the driver, technology the accelerator.

Spaced-practice software tools deliver cued spaced practice for learning. Tools like this are a major breakthrough in learning technology. For smartphones the affordances are around quick, episodic events such as texting, photographs, looking things up, quick experiences, games or alerts. The average time someone spends on a mobile device is seconds, and it is getting shorter as texting on WhatsApp, or whatever, overtakes voice. As we use mobiles for short, episodic experiences, it follows that they can be used for short bouts of spaced practice.

Tools take the 'cues' from any course or learning experience and spaces them out in whatever frequency you determine after the course to an end date. It may be spaced out up to the start of a new job, an exam, a product launch, whatever. This can be delivered using algorithms that tailor delivery to individuals.

As AI technology develops, significant increases in retention and productivity could be realized. We can remind learners about tasks, activities and push snippets of learning topics to them at timed intervals. Systems like this can insert new life into previous learning with bite-size questions, tasks and activities to help refresh the learners' memory.

One problem with formal, pushed methods is *habituation*. This is seen in pop-up help or tip systems, where the user tires at being interrupted and starts to ignore the events that are pushed to them. This motivational problem can be solved by not being too aggressive with the push techniques, keeping them short, varying them and making them worthy of attention.

## Personalized spaced practice

One can categorize items as unknown, not confidently known and confidently known. Indeed, this categorization can be taken further with degrees of tested and subjectively assessed knowledge. However fine-grained the analysis, an adaptive system can deliver spaced-practice items based on a mathematical judgement (algorithms) that decides on the optimal delivery of those items. This optimum delivery schedule is based on what the science tells us, and data drawn from learner performance and learner perceptions.

Such systems deliver personalized spaced practice that is determined not by a preordained sequence but by identifying what the user can actually recall going forward. A useful technique is to gradually drop items that are well known. This selective presentation of items gradually drops items off the conveyer until no items remain. Like a satnav, it delivers the right corrective action depending on where it thinks you are. Sometimes it may deliver in a fairly predictable fashion as you are doing well; at other times it may deliver more items over a longer period if you're showing signs of poor recall or confidence.

An 80:20 ratio can be used here to distinguish between the bulk of the 'consolidation practice period' (80 per cent of the time) and its final 'fixing period' (20 per cent of the time). The consolidation period closes gaps, gradually drops items and increases recall. The fixing period simply increases speed of recall. You can see how technology, especially AI-driven, adaptive technology, is necessary to deliver this level of complexity.

By distributing workload over time, this method can contribute greatly to reducing worry and cognitive overload in students. Rather than procrastination leading to cramming, we have a balanced workload that consolidates and improves performance smoothly over time. Far from demotivating learners, spaced practice can motivate by raising self-confidence, meeting expectations and achieving goals.

Spaced practice is arguably the most powerful, yet most overlooked, benefit in learning and true performance. Implemented properly it is possible to have huge gains in productivity, namely the retention and recall of whatever has been learned. One could go further and say that without a spaced-practice strategy, there is no learning strategy.

## Conclusion

Cognitive science has given us many solid pieces of evidence-based learning strategies that can only now be delivered through technology, as we now have tools that are smart enough to do what is required on peers, nudges, campaigns, interleaving and spaced practice. As cognitive science continues to inform us about optimal learning strategies, these can be captured and baked into AI technology to deliver, in a personalized fashion, learning that greatly increases efficacy.

## References

Clark, D (2018), Why almost everything we think about online learning may be wrong and what to do about it…, Donald Clark Plan B. Available at http://donaldclarkplanb.blogspot.com/2018/11/why-almost-everything-we-think-about.html (archived at https://perma.cc/Q5WA-6AJH)

Ebbinghaus, H (1913) *Memory: A contribution to experimental psychology*, Teachers College, Columbia University, New York

Gates, AI (1917) *Recitation as a Factor in Memorizing (No. 40)*, Science Press, New York

Haidt, J (2006) *The Happiness Hypothesis: Putting ancient wisdom and philosophy to the test of modern science*, Arrow Books, Random House, London

Harris, JR and Baron-Cohen, S (1999) The nurture assumption: Why children turn out the way they do, *Nature*, **398** (6729), pp 675–676

Illich, I (1971) *Deschooling Society*, Marion Boyars Publishers Ltd, London

Kahneman, D (2011) *Thinking, Fast and Slow*, Penguin Books, London

Keppel, G (1964) Facilitation in short- and long-term retention of paired associates following distributed practice in learning, *Journal of Verbal Learning and Verbal Behavior*, **3** (2), pp 91–111

Kornell, N and Bjork, RA (2008) Learning concepts and categories: Is spacing the 'enemy of induction'?, *Psychological Science*, **19** (6), pp 585–592

Landauer, TK and Bjork, RA (1978) Optimum rehearsal patterns and name learning, in *Practical Aspects of Learning,* eds MM Gruneberg, PE Morris and RN Sykes, pp 625–632, Academic Press, New York

Lewis, M (2016) *The Undoing Project: A friendship that changed the world*, Penguin, London

Mazur, E (1999) *Peer Instruction: A user's manual*, Prentice-Hall, Upper Saddle River, NJ

Morris, CD, Brandsford, JD and Franks, JJ (1977) Levels of processing versus transfer-appropriate processing, *Journal of Verbal Learning and Verbal*

*Behavior*, **16**, pp 519–533

Nelson, TO and Leonesio, RJ (1988) Allocation of self-paced study time and the 'labor-in-vain effect', *Journal of Experimental Psychology: Learning, memory, and cognition*, **14** (4), pp 676–686

Rohrer, D and Taylor, K (2007) The shuffling of mathematics problems improves learning, *Instructional Science*, **35** (6), pp 481–498

Rohrer, D, Dedrick, RF and Stershic, S (2015) Interleaved practice improves mathematics learning, *Journal of Educational Psychology*, **107** (3), pp 900–908

Shea, JB and Morgan, RL (1979) Contextual interference effects on the acquisition, retention, and transfer of a motor skill, *Journal of Experimental Psychology: Human learning and memory*, **5** (2), pp 179–187

Simon, DA and Bjork, RA (2001) Metacognition in motor learning, *Journal of Experimental Psychology: Learning, memory, and cognition*, **27** (4), pp 907–912

Syed, M (2010) *Bounce*, Fourth Estate, London

Thaler, RH and Sunstein, CR (2009) *Nudge: Improving decisions about health, wealth, and happiness*, Penguin, New York

Vlach, HA and Sandhofer, CM (2012) Distributing learning over time: The spacing effect in children's acquisition and generalization of science concepts, *Child Development*, **83** (4), pp 1137–1144

# 11

# Adaptive learning

The human brain is arguably the most complex thing we know of in the universe. We all have one that is absolutely unique, that does not like impersonal, over-long, linear, flat experiences. Yet in learning we feed it exactly that – long lectures, flat pages of text, one-size-fits-all learning experiences.

Learning is a deeply personal experience and most learning theory, in terms of attention, deep processing, self-generation, practice and so on, points towards the need for sensitivity around individual needs. This is not always practical and there is nothing intrinsically wrong with direct instruction and whole-class teaching, as one may have limited resources. However, personalization is the one great gift that online learning, fuelled by AI, offers lecturers, trainers, teachers and learners. In classrooms teachers talk about differentiation, then struggle to differentiate with 30-plus students. In universities the mass that turns up to lectures, sometimes in the hundreds, is the opposite of personal learning. None of this can be described as 'personal' in any significant sense. But 'personal', when delivered online, can mean relevant, timely, self-determined, self-generated, targeted, private, even intimate. This is what AI through powerful search, new interfaces and recommendations can deliver for learning.

## Adaptive learning

Adaptive learning has been used in K12, higher education and corporate L&D, as all are looking for faster, more efficacious learning, to deliver the right learning, at the right time, to the right learner. Yet conventional e-learning has largely been one-size-fits-all, the same for everyone, with a focus on the presentation of content as media that generally ignores what is already known. Adaptive fits to the individual learner, as opposed to making the learner fit to the content, showing only what is necessary and what is right for that person, at that particular time. It is diagnostic and reacts to what the learner does, as its unique strength is its sensitivity to the actual learner's needs. Some systems do this through constant content curation at the point of need as the learner progresses through the learning experience. It can also correct misconceptions.

The linear approach to teaching is common in learning, uncommon in most other online experiences. Playing to a 'mean' or 'median' learner leads to increased failure for less competent learners and wasted time for the more competent. Some students learn faster with less support, and some learn more slowly and need more support. On the whole this tailoring process can save huge amounts of time. In a programme for a biopharmaceutical company, 500 learners, across four courses, took on average 2 hours 55 minutes using the Area9 adaptive system (Area9 Lyceum, nd), compared with an average of 5 hours and 14 minutes with traditional e-learning. This resulted in an extra 100 hours of productive time.

In addition, there is the engagement issue. One is not being subjected to learning one already knows or suffering from rejection and failure. It can build in pedagogic models, such as spaced practice, interleaving, deliberate difficulty and effortful learning. These systems also provide advanced analytics. This form of adaptive 'tutoring' can be delivered on *scale*.

One scalable system that supports one facet of personalized learning is 'adaptive' learning. This approach is sensitive to personal needs, potentially accelerating success and preventing failure. The personalization can depend on the individual, aggregated data and the algorithms used to determine such paths. In an advanced system, there is no linear course, only vectors through a domain of learning activities.

As we have seen, 'personalized' learning has a wide meaning around sensitivity to the individual learner and around differentiating learners. 'Adaptive' learning is more specific, where the online learning adapts to the learners' needs as they progress through a computer-based learning experience. Having said this, there is still a wide variety of adaptive approaches and methods, from simple pre-test assessment to full-blown algorithmic and machine learning adaption, with lots in between.

The most advanced systems adapt the online experience to the individual's needs as they learn, in the way a personal tutor would adapt. The aim is to provide what many teachers provide: a learning experience that is tailored to the needs of you as an individual learner.

Adaptive learning technology has received a lot of attention in recent years, much of which was seeded by the results of a now famous paper by Benjamin Bloom (best known for a taxonomy of learning) entitled 'The 2 sigma problem' (1984).

The paper described an experiment comparing the efficacy of lecture, lecture with feedback and one-to-one tuition. It formed a landmark motivation for the development and use of adaptive learning. Taking the 'straight lecture' as the mean, he found an 84 per cent increase in mastery above the mean for a 'formative feedback' approach to teaching and an astonishing 98 per cent increase in mastery for 'one-to-one tuition' (Bloom, 1984). In other words, the increase in efficacy for tailored one-to-one education, because of the increase in on-task learning, is huge.

Google's Peter Norvig famously said that if you only have to read one paper to support online learning, this is it (Norvig, 2007). This paper deserves to be read by anyone looking at improving the efficacy of learning, as it shows hugely significant improvements by simply altering the way teachers interact with learners. Online learning has to date mostly delivered fairly linear and non-adaptive experiences, whether through self-paced structured learning, scenario-based learning, simulations or informal learning. Recent progress in adaptive learning and AI means that we are closer to being able to deliver what Bloom called 'one-to-one learning', in the online sphere.

## Types of adaptation

Adaptation can be many things, but at the heart of the process is a decision to present something to the learner based on what the system knows about the learner and other elements, such as the instructional activity, the topic domain, the educational domain, the type of learning, the context and so on.

It is helpful to categorize different adaptive approaches. We can begin by creating categories for where in the educational or learning sequence the adaptivity occurs. If we think in terms of a standard school or college course (although this could also be applied to a module in a course or a chapter in a book):

- pre-course adaptive: a pre-course assessment or assignment of learners to a group;
- in-course adaptive: adaption occurs as the learner progresses through a course;

- post-course adaptive: adaption is used, eg, to reinforce memory;
- continuously adaptive: adaption occurs constantly through a learner's journey, with data and instructional activities shared across courses and programmes.

Within these categories of 'when' the adaption occurs, there are three further properties that are useful to describe:

1 what is being adapted;
2 the intention of the adaption;
3 the method used to achieve the adaption.

## Pre-course adaptive

In this category, data gathered prior to a learner taking a course is used to predefine the experience for them. Typical approaches include:

### MACRO ADAPTION OF LEARNING JOURNEY

Data about the student is used to define the learning journey at the macro level, recommending skills, courses, even careers based on individual needs. This is not easy, as these are high-stakes recommendations often made on limited data sets and using categories of skills that are far from agreed.

### PRE-ASSESSMENT OR INFERENCE OF LEARNING PROFILE

Normally, the learner takes a 'pre-test' to create a profile before starting the course, then the system adjusts the learning activities based on this. The adaptive software makes a decision based on the data specific to that individual that was gathered at the start of the process. This is a highly deterministic approach that has limited personalization and learning benefits but may prevent many from taking unnecessary courses.

It is also possible to start this process with personal data, such as educational background, competence in previous courses and so on, and infer a learning profile from this.

### PREFERENCE

In this case, the learner's learning style or media preference is determined in advance, and used to tailor the form of media or style of learning activity that they receive. This approach is not supported by research or modern theories of learning and cognition. Meta-studies have assessed research studies in this area and have not been able to identify a positive impact on student performance through adjusting learning activities based on the perceived style or preference of the learner. As a general rule, learning activities are best designed according to the nature of what is being learned and the context in which it will be used, rather than the perceived preferences of the learner. Having said this, learner preference should not be completely ruled out as a potential secondary effect, and is clearly important for learners with accessibility requirements. For the typical student, it is possible that advanced AI-based systems might learn to adjust to learner preferences in a sufficiently subtle way that may positively impact learning and that has not yet been achieved to date using crude-level preference categories.

Personality type is another potential form of learner preference, although one must be careful with poorly validated outputs from the likes of Myers-Briggs. The OCEAN model is much better validated (Ahmed, 2016). One can also use learner opinions, although this is also fraught with danger. Learners are often quite mistaken not only about what they have learned but also about optimal strategies for learning. So, it is possible to use all sorts of personal data to determine how and what someone should be taught, but one has to be very careful with these approaches.

## In-course adaptive

In this category, adaption occurs while the student works through a course, and is informed by data gathered throughout their progress. This is often referred to as a micro-adaptive course, which adjusts the learner's route frequently, or in real time. There is a spectrum of granularity of micro-adaptivity, ranging from the lesson level to the individual activity to within an activity.

In essence the software is adjusting a sequence of either predefined activities or algorithmically generated assessments. The fundamental idea is that most learning goes wrong when things are presented that the learner is not prepared for. If the system can help the learner to resolve issues with prior learning, the new learning will also be resolved.

A different perspective is that the system attempts to generate an ideal level of challenge. One can use the idea of desirable difficulty to determine a learning experience that is challenging enough to keep the learner driving forward, but not so challenging as to demotivate them.

Decisions can be based on a rule or set of rules – at its simplest a conditional *if… then…* decision, but often a sequence of rules or branched decision tree that determines the learner's path. These kinds of systems can be recognized by the fact that they respond to all learners in the same way. If two learners execute the same input to the system, the system will respond in the same way to them both.

It is worth introducing AI at this point. Adaptive learning is how the large tech companies deliver to your timeline on Facebook/Twitter, sell to you on Amazon, get you to watch stuff on Netflix. They use an array of techniques based on data they gather, statistics, data mining and AI techniques to improve the delivery of their service to you as an individual. Evidence that AI and adaptive techniques will work in learning, especially in adaption, is there on every device on almost every service we use online. Education is just a bit of a slow learner.

Decisions may be based simply on what the system thinks your level of capability is at that moment, based on formative assessment and other factors. The regular testing of learners not only improves retention, but it gathers useful data about what the system knows about the learner. Failure is not a problem here. Indeed, evidence suggests that making mistakes may be critical to good learning strategies.

Decisions within a course use an algorithm with complex data needs. This provides a much more powerful method for dynamic decision-making. At this more fine-grained level, every screen can be regarded as a fresh adaption at that specific point in the course.

AI techniques such as machine learning adaption can be used in systems that learn and improve as they go. Such systems are often trained using data at the start and then use data as they go to improve the system. The more learners use the system, the better it becomes.

Another measure, common in adaptive systems, is the measurement of confidence. You may be asked a question then also asked how confident you are of your answer.

Good learning theory can also be baked into the algorithms, such as retrieval, interleaving and spaced practice. Care can be taken over cognitive load and even personalized performance support provided, adapting to an individual's availability and schedule. Duolingo, for example, is sensitive to these needs and provides spaced practice, aware of the fact that you may have not done anything recently and forgotten stuff. Embodying good learning theory and practice may be what is needed to introduce often counter-intuitive methods into teaching, such as retrieval practice and spaced practice, that are resisted by human teachers.

## Post-course adaptive

### ADAPTIVE ASSESSMENT SYSTEMS

There is also adaptive assessment, where test items are presented based on your performance on previous questions. They often start with a mean test item then select harder or easier items as the learner progresses.

### MEMORY RETENTION SYSTEMS

Some adaptive systems focus on memory retrieval, retention and recall. They present content, often in a spaced-practice pattern, and repeat, remediate and retest to increase retention. These can be powerful systems for the consolidation of learning.

### PERFORMANCE SUPPORT ADAPTION

Moving beyond courses to performance support, delivering learning when you need it, is another form of adaptive delivery that can be sensitive to your individual needs as well as context. These have been delivered within the workflow, often embedded in social communications systems, sometimes as chatbots.

## Continuously adaptive

Adaptive software can be applied within a course, across a set of courses but also across an entire curriculum – as many learning experiences as you wish. The idea is that personalization becomes more targeted and personal the more you use the system. Aggregated data from a single learner's performance on a previous course can be used, as can aggregated data of all learners who have taken the course. One has to be careful here, as one cohort may have started at a different level of competence than another cohort. There may also be differences on other skills, such as reading comprehension, background knowledge, English as a second language and so on. Nevertheless, adaptive is now being applied to more than individual courses. Entire degree courses are being delivered using this technology.

---

### PERSONALIZED LEARNING AT ARIZONA STATE UNIVERSITY

Michael Crow has been the president of Arizona State University (ASU) since 2002. His goal, vision, even dream, was to create nothing less than the 'New American University', as described in his and William Dabars' 2015 book

*Designing the New American University.* Here they explain how they wanted to do the unthinkable: grow research at a blistering pace and, at the same time, raise the bar on teaching in terms of both access and quality. Any one of these would have been difficult, but doing all at the same time was tricky.

The key word for Crow is 'scale', a clever word on which to hang a vision. Scaling bums on seats is easy enough, but that is to focus on the wrong end of the learner. Quality, less dropout and attainment also have to be scaled. That is not easy. And it is here they have embraced an obvious truth: that scale must come through the smart use of technology. They take this as an assumed truth, as self-evident. If you can get increased numbers of students over that first-year undergraduate hurdle, in maths, writing and reasoning, you are well on your way to sustaining subsequent quality.

But here is the rub. Courses are almost universally felt to be owned by individual professors. They design, develop, deliver and assess their own courses. They are their babies and so implementing technology is like threatening to pull their offspring from their arms and shove them into some sort of uniform collective nursery.

That is why tech in higher education remains a cottage industry. It is stuck at the fragmented level of the individual. So when a VLE is rolled out, all of these professors create stuff, but they do not have the resources and skills to do it well, and we end up with lots of low-quality, repository resources.

The trick is to get a collegiate system going with all of the professors involved in the teaching of, say, maths. So you take a group of maths professors, explain to them the power of adaptive learning and personalization. Note that maths is a touchstone here as it is such a hurdle for many students. It also happens to be well defined with clear dependencies and therefore ideal for adaptive learning.

ASU managed to get a majority through developmental maths. The national standard for success is around 55–60 per cent. But there is likely to be a theoretical limit at around 95 per cent. That is smart, recognizing that success should be real and not too utopian. At the same time they have to move faculty towards a different sort of coaching and supporting role. That is the hard bit.

You have proved the technology has significant results on reducing dropout and increasing attainment. You have shown that groups of academics, working together, can leverage this technology on the scale that's needed. You now roll this out across other undergraduate courses and subjects. The cultural change is immense, but so are the benefits, namely losing fewer students. Once everyone is focused on that one problem, the solution becomes easier to implement.

The next step is to match student expectations on the quality of online courses. They all have smartphones, laptops and experience exemplary content on all of these devices when they access social media and other services. Education needs to meet those expectations. This is really hard. Learning is not entertainment and is often damaged when it becomes too glitzy. The stuff that's produced within VLEs looks like the stuff that was done on computers before these kids were born.

Michael Crow is not without his critics. He has, after all, challenged the nay-saying power of academics who want to keep control. He can't afford to let those attitudes win, as that is what keeps access low and costs high. What Crow rejects is that the system will always be built on scarcity and not abundance. He wants to scale out of scarcity into high-quality abundance through technology and adaptive technology, which personalizes the learning experience. They are redefining the university as a scalable organization serving the public good. You may not like his vision, but a vision it is.

## Adaptive results

AI in general, and adaptive learning systems in particular, will have enormous long-term effects on teaching, learner attainment and student dropout. This was confirmed by the results from courses at Arizona State University (initially in one course, Biology 100) delivered as blended learning. The students did the adaptive work on the CogBooks adaptive platform, then brought that knowledge to class, where group work and teaching took place – a flipped classroom model (Edsurge, 2015).

The aim of this technology-enhanced teaching system was to:

- increase attainment;
- reduce in dropout rates;
- maintain student motivation;
- increase teacher effectiveness.

It is not easy to juggle all of these at the same time, but ASU want these undergraduate courses to be a success on all fronts, as they are seen as the foundation for sustainable progress by students as they move through a full degree course.

## Higher attainment

It has been suggested that a less able, wealthy student is more likely to graduate from college than a smart, poor one (Kristof, 2016). So, increases in attainment are hugely significant, especially for students from low-income backgrounds, in high-enrolment courses. Many interventions in education show razor-thin improvements. So the results of ASU's programme – showing an increase in success rate from 76 per cent to 94 per cent – were significant, not just on overall attainment rates, but, just as importantly, the way this squeezes dropout rates (in the case of BIO 100, from 15 per cent to 1.5 per cent).

The impact on dropout is important. It can be catastrophic for students and – as funding often follows students – also for the institution. Given significant student dropout rates and student debt problems as well as the rising cost of higher education in many countries, adaptive learning may prove to be a significant solution to these problems.

It may lift many out of the idea that dropout is just collateral damage towards a system that pushes success for as many as possible.

If one can both increase attainment and lower dropout, especially in first-year courses, we have a chance to radically increase the efficacy of higher education. For introductory courses, where dropout can be catastrophic, adaptive learning provides the support that failing students need and this gives them the confidence to progress with their studies. The gains can be enormous.

## Results at ASU

This was confirmed by the results from courses run at Arizona State University (initially in one course, Biology 100) delivered as blended learning. The students did the adaptive work on the CogBooks adaptive platform, then brought that knowledge to class, where group work and teaching took place – a flipped classroom model (Edsurge, 2015).

ASU see adaptive learning as transformational, moving away from the traditional lecture-based degree format. In their School of Life Sciences they want personalized learning where delivery is dynamic rather than static, responding in real time, not to later feedback. An entire four-year degree uses an adaptive platform to support learning.

Jim Thompson, CEO of Cogbooks, believes that the adaptive approach builds on 'the importance of making connections when we are learning'

(Leander, 2019). If we struggle with new knowledge, it can be because we lack the prior knowledge to progress. Effective adaptive learning identifies these gaps or misconceptions and helps resolve them.

So they turned to life science majors, with more challenging content. Using adaptive courseware makes one see a degree not as a series of separate courses but as a single learning journey. It also means a realignment of the curriculum, more integration of content and a change in faculty role away from lecturing to leaders and teachers who intervene when students need that intervention. Faculty reported 'an ovation at the end of the junior-level major's course'.

## Content preparation

One of the difficulties in adaptive, AI-driven systems is the creation of usable content. By content, we mean content as a network, with non-linear structures, assessment items and so on. Most teachers are unfamiliar with the process of creating content that is not linear but a network, with dependencies, so most platforms have created suites of tools that allow instructors to create a network of content, working back from objectives. Editors, conversion of content, automatic help with layout, a defined process, roles, permissions, and even rights management are provided.

Beyond these results lies something even more promising. These systems throw off detailed and useful data on every student, as well as analyses of that data. Different dashboards give unprecedented insights, in real time, of student performance. This allows the instructor to help those in need. The promise here is of continuous improvement, badly needed in education. We could be looking at an approach that improves not only the performance of teachers but also of the system itself, the consequence being ongoing improvement in attainment, dropout and motivation in all students.

Underlying this approach is the idea that all learners are different and that one-size-fits-all, largely linear courses, delivered largely by lectures, do not deliver to this need. It is precisely this dimension, the real-time adjustment of the learning to the needs of the individual, that produce the results, as well as the increase in the teacher's ability to know and adjust their teaching to the class and individual student needs through real-time data.

It is already clear that this type of software can be, and has been, used across a wide range of subjects from US history to psychology, biology, anatomy and other subjects. As the software is content-agnostic and has been designed to run any course, it holds promise for adoption across entire institutions.

The success of this adaptive approach over a number of years has led ASU to launch a full BioSpine degree course, using this adaptive software. It uses data from individuals across the subjects taken as they proceed through the degree, as well as aggregated data from other students. This holistic approach across an entire degree benefits from the accumulation and cross-fertilization of data across students and courses.

## Medical and corporate learning

In healthcare, where ongoing learning and certification is absolutely necessary in a changing environment with new clinical approaches, medical technology, combined with an often ageing population and multiple chronic conditions, there is a real and practical need for efficient lifelong learning.

Medical students have used adaptive learning to prepare for board certification. The majority rated this approach as helpful, relevant and the content as good for test revision. Indeed, a significantly higher number passed on first attempt, compared with the national average (95 per cent versus 89 per cent) (Healy *et al*, 2018). Adaptive training has also been used for physicians, nurses and other clinicians for continuous education and the maintenance of certification. The training of sales and marketing representatives and medical affairs personnel, avoiding surplus information and tailored to their roles, has also been delivered adaptively.

Beyond healthcare, Hitachi have used adaptive learning for technical training (Area9 Lyceum/Hitachi, nd). Elsewhere, in the airline industry, it has been used for crew scheduling training, where three systems were collapsed into one and many had to 'unlearn' previous processes. The aim of reducing flight cancellations due to crew scheduling and reducing costs were met. Counter-terrorism training in terrorism threats, money laundering and terrorism finance have also been delivered adaptively (Area9 Lyceum/Home page, nd).

# Conclusion

Like a GPS in your car, an adaptive system can deal with millions of drivers simultaneously, all taking different routes towards different destinations. If any one of these drivers goes off course, the system immediately responds to get that driver back on course. The promise of adaptive learning is of autonomous systems that deliver massive amounts of high-quality learning at a very low cost per learner. Adaptive, personalized learning, when replicated across the system, may be the solution to the escalating costs in education, as it provides smart support at every point in the learning journey and is sensitive to the needs of a wide range of students – on scale.

# References

Ahmed, M (2016) Is Myers-Briggs up to the job?, *Financial Times Magazine*, 11 February. Available at https://www.ft.com/content/8790ef0a-d040-11e5-831d-09f7778e7377 (archived at https://perma.cc/CX79-RNL8)

Area9 Lyceum (nd) If you could design the ideal sales enablement approach, what would it be? Available at https://area9lyceum.com/use-cases/sales-enablement/ (archived at https://perma.cc/F7YA-76KK)

Area9 Lyceum/Hitachi (nd) Available at https://area9lyceum.com/cases/hitachi/ (archived at https://perma.cc/94PV-284Z)

Area9 Lyceum/Home page (nd) Available at https://area9lyceum.com/ (archived at https://perma.cc/7SD2-2CWF)

Bloom, BS (1984) The 2 sigma problem: The search for methods of group instruction as effective as one-to-one tutoring, *Educational Researcher*, **13** (6), pp 4–16

Crow, MM and Dabars, WB (2015) *Designing the New American University*, Johns Hopkins University Press, Baltimore, MD

Edsurge (2015) Case study. Available at https://www.edsurge.com/product-reviews/cogbooks/company-case-studies/arizona-state-university (archived at https://perma.cc/Z59M-ZJ2Y)

Healy, M, Petrusa, E, Axelsson, CG, Wongsirimeteekul, P, Hamnvik, OP, O'Rourke, M, *et al* (2018) An exploratory study of a novel adaptive e-learning board review product helping candidates prepare for certification examinations, *MedEdPublish*, **7** (3), 24

Kristof, N (2016) America's stacked deck, *New York Times*. Available at https://www.nytimes.com/2016/02/18/opinion/americas-stacked-deck.html?smid=tw-nytimes&smtyp=cur (archived at https://perma.cc/AY64-S7RS)

Leander, S (2019) ASU develops world's first adaptive-learning biology degree, ASU Now. Available at https://asunow.asu.edu/20190820-solutions-asu-develops-world-first-adaptive-learning-biology-degree (archived at https://perma.cc/B9FC-NJ8E)

Norvig, P (2007) Learning in an open world (transcript of keynote speech at the 2007 Association for Learning Technology Conference in Nottingham, England), 6 September. Available at https://www.alt.ac.uk/sites/default/files/assets_editor_uploads/documents/altc2007_peter_norvig_keynote_transcript.pdf (archived at https://perma.cc/H2FW-ASZH)

# 12

# Learning organizations

## What can we learn from Amazon?

When you use Amazon, the screen is actually a set of 'tiles', and what you see at any time is finely tuned to your personal needs. What you don't see is what lies beneath the surface, a powerful AI engine that decides what you are seeing. This invisible hand not only determines what you see; it plays a role in what you do. It nudges you, in real time, in one direction or another. This approach has much to recommend it in organizations that have to deliver learning.

Amazon make it easy to buy their product; they are also good at recommending what to buy and cross-selling other products. Their algorithms have been honed over many years taking inputs, such as what you have bought before, viewing history, repeat clicks, dwell time, your past search patterns, recently reviewed items, what is in your cart, what site you were referred from, demographic data (where you live and what type of person you're likely to be), user segmentation (if you bought books on photography it will try to sell you cameras and accessories) and so on. This is supplemented by aggregated data from other customers to produce different sets of recommendations, from other similar customers and so on to nudge you towards buying. Their conversion rate from website recommendations is very high.

This conversion rate is also applicable in learning, where you want to encourage people to learn. If you want people to learn in the workflow, a combination of push and pull techniques has to be employed and constantly fine-tuned.

Remember, also, they are the biggest online retailer in the world, so they have the biggest data sets. This gives them a real market advantage, as their algorithms have more to work with, can be tested on larger groups and use more aggregated data. One of the things that screws algorithms up is bad data. If the reviews are positive but they have been falsely placed by humans, this skews the recommendations. Publishers have been paying people to review by offering discount products, so Amazon has banned incentivized reviews. In learning, however, we may very well want to skew the recommendations towards pushed learning for a new product launch or emergency problem with compliance. That is why promotion and campaigns have a role to play in learning online.

In learning there is a balance to be struck between user-driven behaviour, pull, and what you want to push. It would be wrong to simply push all learning; the balance between this and human agency needs to be maintained and available.

One final point is that with machine learning, algorithms used to identify and deliver learning content and services simply get better and better. They are learning from their own generated data and can adapt to improve. This is much smarter than any human approach to recommended learning.

What can we learn about learning from all of this? First, recommendation algorithms will certainly play an increasing role in the learning game. They already have. Google is arguably the number one technology used by learners. We use it to search for things we want to know. That is a fundamental piece of pedagogic technology that has revolutionized the learning process, whether you are searching for knowledge, instruction on a process or skill on YouTube (owned by Google), or on Google Scholar for research.

We already have adaptive learning systems that use AI to navigate learners through courses. Learning is one area where significant advances are being made, and these advances promise to do what they have done for Amazon and others – offer a massively scalable solution to the problem of teaching and learning through real-time learning design, personalized recommendations, less linear teaching and better assessment. All of this, of course, is driven by machine learning, which makes these systems learn as they go.

Above all, what we can learn from Amazon is that you, the learner, are valued and that we must tailor our services to your actual needs, in real time. What education and training badly needs is this sensitive and personal approach to learning, not the blind, batch process we currently deploy. Let us not over-romanticize batched lectures to hundreds at a time in lecture halls or 30-plus kids struggling with the intricacies of maths or French in classrooms. There is plenty of room for improvement here, and some of the techniques have already been put to the test over decades with proven efficacy.

## AI and informal learning

Gloria Gery first talked about performance support in 1991. Jay Cross has been credited with inventing the term 'e-learning', was the pioneer in both the practice and theory of technology in learning, and pushed the idea that learning is not primarily about formal courses but informal learning.

After developing the first courses at the hugely successful University of Phoenix, Cross set up the Internet Time Group. A tireless thinker and presenter on learning, he pushed the learning world to think seriously about informal learning, and working smarter. For him, workflow learning ties learning into the actual workflow within an organization. According to Cross (2011), it takes us to support and on-demand services that are designed to exist within the real tasks we do in our everyday work. Out of this work on workflow learning came an even wider, and what he regarded as more important, set of reflections.

Averse to detailed semantic analysis, he compares the difference between formal and informal learning with the difference between taking a trip on a bus and driving your car. In the former, you are on a set route and not in the driving seat; in the latter you go where you want, when you want and on the route you choose. His reflections on the failure of training to really recognize informal learning are well represented in his oft-used 'spending paradox' (Figure 12.1).

Most learning is informal yet almost all the spend is on formal courses.

FIGURE 12.1   Formal and informal learning: source of the problem

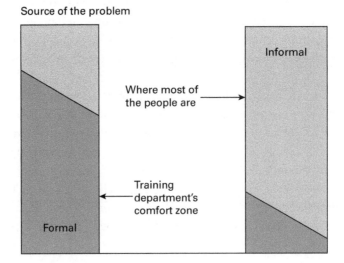

This is about seeing learning in a more naturalistic way, seeing learners as real people in real organizations, who use real tools in real networks, both offline and online. Informal learning is driven by conversations, communities of practice, context, reinforcement through practice and social media to optimize organizational performance. Blogs, podcasts, peer-to-peer sharing, aggregators, social media and personal knowledge management are all emergent phenomena, unlike the top–down tools and content that traditional online learning has provided. When we look at the internet, we see powerful tools and techniques emerge through genuine use. It is these, he believed, that point us towards success in learning.

Note that this does not imply the abandonment of formal learning, only that informal learning needs to be recognized and supported. There's still a need for underpinning learning with good content, from books to full courses, especially for novices and business-critical training such as compliance. You can't let people who don't know what they need to know drift, so there's a time and place for structured, formal learning. We simply need to also identify and use natural pathways, the unofficial, unscheduled events that take place in real contexts, underpinned by personal, intrinsic motivation. What matters is execution and performance, real business objectives and metrics. To see training as schooling is the mistake, often superficial, irrelevant and not reinforced by doing, that is often forgotten.

Rather than an unbalanced focus on top–down classes, tests and certificates, networked learning organizations need blends of workplace learning that include the experiential, unplanned and informal. This has to be done systematically and not left to chance. Informal learning is not some vague form of drift with chance encounters. You need to take control of your own learning and organizations need to inseminate and stimulate communities of practice. What has given workflow learning a boost has been the explosion of social media, which has provided communication through blogging, Facebooking and tweeting, as well as media sharing through YouTube, Vimeo and so on. It is fast, cheap and ubiquitous, so we see a pendulum shift towards the informal over the formal.

It is almost as if the language of learning is fading and development within the context of the workplace without the formal structures, labels, learning objectives and over-formality of courses. Far from decimating the training department, one can envisage development as a constant in organizations, not only inside the firewall but for all part-timers, freelancers and partners. The wall between company and customers is also crumbling, creating a new culture of customer education.

We need to reflect on the obvious, but shocking, fact that almost all of our attention (and spend) goes on the formal side, while the majority of the action is informal. This is not to abandon formal learning, but to consider the accelerating role of technology in informal learning, to move beyond the traditional LMS and content model to a newer, more naturalistic model of learning, based on real behaviour and contemporary technology. That contemporary technology has now come of age through more expansive technology involving AI, such as LXPs, LRSs and the specification, xAPI.

## Moments of need

Bob Mosher, who co-authored the '5 moments of need' model (Gottfredson and Mosher, 2012), has the same message: busy learning teams need to align themselves with real user behaviour and business needs. This means learning that is contextualized and designed to help learners. His moments of need are:

- Learn something for the first time.
- Learn more about a topic.
- Apply or remember something.
- Something has gone wrong.
- Something has changed.

The message from both Cross and Mosher is to embed the learning in the workflow and make it readily available at the moment of need. It helps to apply Occam's Razor to this problem and supply the minimum amount of effort to satisfy their goal. Contextualizing to specific roles and needs also oils the wheels. So how can one use AI, in practice, to achieve workflow learning?

## From LMS to LXP

In a more agile, flexible working, always-on, vying for attention, pressured workplace, something more than a warehouse for content, with scarcely any data or analysis, is needed. As old theories, such as learning styles and Kirkpatrick's evaluation, have waned and employees have become more networked and remote, the technology has matured. A consumer-level interface – mobile, personalization, chatbots, curation, all producing data – allows AI to flourish in more flexible learning ecosystems.

When the LMS starts to give way to the LXP, built around the individual and their learning experiences, it is then that AI can be used to help deliver learning. Agile learning is possible, with responsive, adaptive, personalized delivery. What we see is the collapse and breakup of the course as the cardinal delivery mechanism in training. Personalized means just that, not a one-size-fits-all experience. It means smaller units of learning, in line with good cognitive psychology, cognitive engagement and an understanding of behavioural psychology.

LMSs were designed for a world before personalized delivery, smart software and AI. Many are still written in old technology that cannot meet the demands of this new world, inflexible and failing to meet the agile needs of education and business. The world has moved on in terms of expectations, while the LMS and its online content model has remained flat, superficial and static, insensitive to new interfaces, personalized delivery and advanced analytics.

With learning experience platforms different learning needs are the engagement or touch points. For example, you may be recruitment interviewing for the first time and want a short introductory course outlining good practice, looking at deeper questioning techniques, reacting to a complaint about unfair process, looking at newer methods of recruitment or simply a quick brush-up before going into the interviews. These are different needs delivered according to context, sensitive to what you've done before, actually know and are about to do. This takes smart software.

LXPs are a response to what an AI-driven online world demands, namely technology that is more responsive to the needs of users, multiple systems and the real data needs of an organization. Learners need easier, more flexible, frictionless access with more personalized delivery. The learning world has learned from real delivery on the web, through Google, Facebook, Instagram, Twitter, Amazon and Netflix, and has seen that consumers expect a slick interface driven by underlying AI, access to content from a number of different sources, with advanced learning analytics, often including machine learning, that works on mobile. The traditional LMS comes far short of this.

One feature of this newer LXP world is xAPI, which allows one to track, in much more detail, from many different sources, learning experiences and content, even those outside of the LMS. It is much more holistic in its tracking of learning than its predecessor SCORM.

In parallel, we have seen the development of the LRS, which externalizes data, making it easier to use learning data as part of a bigger business data and integration effort. Learning can, by this route, become business savvy, directly responding to business needs and influencing business decisions.

As LXP platforms such as Degreed, EdCast, Pathgather and Headstream have emerged, they offer scope for more innovation around AI in learning. It is AI that is the global revolution in technology. What will make them different will be their use of smart software to deliver these better user interface experiences, personalized experiences and advanced use of data. AI will bear fruit on all three layers of an LXP:

- user interface experience layer (UX);
- learning experience layer (LX);
- data layer (DX).

## User interface experience layer (UX)

A great deal is being made of 'design thinking' here, but it is not clear that UX design is resulting in much improvement. Sure, clear navigation is important, as is getting rid of interface clutter, the use of conventions and so on. But if all it means is slicker access to the same old click-through stuff, with multiple-choice questions, drag and drop, or even worse, clicking on faces to see speech bubbles or pop-ups, nothing will have been gained. In fact, it is the underlying logic behind the UX that really matters – its ability to deliver from an AI system that recommends or re-sequences learning to suit the learner at that exact point.

LXP systems will have to differentiate themselves from the LMS by being smart through AI. If they simply window-dress an LMS, they will not be able to deliver the type of flexibility and personalization that almost every other web service delivers. It is all very well talking about learning experiences, but the evidence from the web itself is that this means AI-driven delivery.

When we learn, most of the processes going on in our brain are invisible, namely the deep processing involved in memory and recall. This activity, which lies beneath consciousness, is where most of the consolidation takes place. Similarly, it is sometimes difficult to see adaptive, algorithmic learning in practice, as most of the heavy lifting is done by algorithms that lie behind the interface and content. Like an iceberg, the hard work is done invisibly, below the level of visible content. Different students may proceed through different routes on their learning journey, some may finish faster, others get help more often and take longer. Overall, adaptive, algorithmic, recommendation systems, driving UX, promise to take learners through tailored learning journeys. This is important, as one of the major reasons for learner demotivation and dropout is difficulties with the course and linear, one size-fits-all courses that leave a large percentage of students behind when they get stuck or lost. Personalized learning, tailored to every individual student, has come of age and may be a solution to these problems.

Smart algorithms, in Google, Facebook, Instagram, Twitter, Spotify, Amazon and Netflix, can significantly enhance user experiences through recommenders, so how can they enhance the learners' experiences? It is often thought that data is the key factor in this process, but data is inert and only becomes useful as clean and relevant input to algorithms that interpret that data to produce useful actions and recommendations. The quality and quantity of data is important; the quality of the algorithms also count.

Smart software, formula-based algorithms, based on the science of learning, can be used to take inputs and make recommendations based on calculated probabilities. Multiple, combined algorithms can be even smarter. They may use knowledge of you as a learner, such as your past learning experiences and so on. Then, dynamically track how you are getting on through formative assessment, how long you're taking in a task, when you get stuck, keystroke patterns, sentiment analysis and so on. Add to this data gathered from other groups of similar learners and the system gets very smart – so smart that it can serve up optimized, learning experiences that fit your exact needs, rather than the next step in a linear course. It also learns as it goes to make it even smarter.

We must focus on 'learning experiences' not as 'experiences' in themselves, but as experiences delivered, behind the scenes, by smart AI. An LXP must also learn from its own experiences through machine learning. Without these experiences being AI-driven experiences, all we're delivering is the same old 'edu-tainment' that has been around for decades.

## Learning experience layer (LX)

There is much talk of revolutionizing the LX, but there is a danger that people focus on 'experiences' without the 'learning'. In the rush to push video, media and gamification, learning is often the first casualty. Purveyors of 'edu-tainment' and 'enter-trainers' are in danger of reviving an old myth – that learning is the same thing as fun. It is not. Of course we want to make memorable experiences. Attention is a necessary condition for learning, but there is a 'babies and bathwater' issue here. Experience is not a synonym for learning.

We have decades of research showing that learners are often delusional when it comes to deciding the best way to learn, so we should not think that giving them total responsibility for such choices is always wise. Software-guided delivery can be a sound strategy.

We also have oodles of research showing that making things 'easy' for learners, with passive and click-through experiences, results in poor retention. Research also shows that media-rich does not mean mind-rich. In the rush to talk about 'experiences', we are in danger of disengaging from real, effortful 'learning'.

The recognition of delivering learning within the workflow is one thing, a good thing, but it may mean that deeper, more considered experiences get sacrificed for fatuous learning.

An LXP tries to engage learners at various points of need with the minimum of effort from the learner. They provide chatbots, giving access to learning much like you would ask a colleague for help or advice. You can search content to directly deliver relevant content back to learners, integrated with whatever social system is most used in your organization. It is this workflow channel integration that gets the right learning to the right people at the right time.

It should also automatically surface quality recommendations to help your learners take action on their most important needs. They may also provide nudges.

Social is another, but if you are building a social system separate from slack, Microsoft teams or another existing social system that is already used within the organization, that could be a concern. The world is littered with failed social learning systems – unused and unloved.

## Data layer (DX)

As people learn from many different sources within an organization, and in order to know who is learning what, where and when, you will require a wider set of data. You will have to collect, store, analyse and use that data, from various sources, LMSs, mobile apps, portals, smart devices and other software.

One thing that an LXP does promise is that experiences will produce and sometimes depend on and be driven by data. When data is in the delivery loop, we can move beyond the limitations of SCORM, a 20-year-old stand-ard that became so entrenched that version 1.2 is still its most common use, not the later SCORM 2004. It excludes much of what we deliver these days: informal, mobile, social media simulations and so on. Hence the shift towards xAPI or other specifications for data-gathering and visualization. One of the problems with the rise of interest in gathering more data is the relative lack of real action taken on that data. It is pointless storing data if you have not decided what you want to do with it. It must be more than a mere storage system, as this is not about storage – it is about action and decisions.

The LMS and SCORM is about the packaging, delivery and management of content. The new specification, xAPI, is about learners and their behav-iour. It moves the focus from supply to demand and business needs. Now, in the data layer, with granular tracking using xAPI, along with a learning record store, learning data can be used and integrated into business data. With this data comes analysis, and correlations between training and sales, productivity or behaviour are suddenly possible, along with a much more powerful ability to analyse, predict and prescribe action.

A solid data storage solution helps you loosen up on learning, not seeing it as something only delivered from your LMS or in formal courses. It is the realization of the work done by Cross, Mosher and many others, that learn-ing takes place everywhere, has many touch points and needs to be seen in the context of an ecosystem. The question of how one uses data within that ecosystem is interesting. If one wants to use AI to describe, track, secure, visualize, analyse, recommend learning opportunities, play a role in adaptive learning, allow access to opinion and sentiment analysis and many other data-driven AI tools and techniques, one needs to manage data.

To manage data, one must sensibly store data. One of the problems that every organization has, in education or business, is how to gather, store and access their data. It most likely comes from multiple sources, in different formats and is stored in many places, making it difficult to exploit. So having *one source* for learning data can be advisable.

To implement AI solutions in your organization, an LRS can be used. It is a tool that consolidates and allows you to use learning analytics in your organization. An LRS can store not just learning analytics, but other evaluative and business data. This allows you to integrate learning into a fully integrated use of organizational data, which is valuable if you want to measure the role or impact of learning in reaching organizational goals. This alignment of learning and business, or learning and organizational goals, has long been the wish of learning professionals, but only now, through integrated data services, has this been possible.

First, it will help manage your data regulation, such as GDPR, which should be easier to implement if you have an LRS. It helps you identify, manage and report your data in ways that will satisfy your regulatory responsibilities, thus avoiding hefty fines.

Application programming interfaces (APIs) should be available, so that data can be collected from multiple sources, internal and external. This is where xAPI should be considered. xAPI is a specification designed to replace SCORM (first launched in 1999). It is a specification that allows you to literally track anything through triplets of information, namely noun–verb–object. For example, 'John read the book *AI for Learning.*'

It widens the scope of tracking, to recognize that learning takes place everywhere, not just on learning platforms. It broadens the horizon of learning to include especially informal learning. The aim is to replace SCORM with a more flexible specification that allows flexibility across an ecosystem of learning opportunities, not just LMS-delivered content.

This approach matches the emergence of complex learning ecosystems such as LXPs, as data from a wide range of integrated tools and technologies can be combined in a single source. If you are worried about the location of data, such systems can be in the cloud, enterprise-wide or on your premises.

An LRS should be able to store 'user' data, as this is essential for describing, analysing, predicting or prescribing action. Being able to attribute data to users, describe learning journeys, use recommendation engines or apply sentiment analysis, requires that your learners are clearly identifiable. Data dashboards can also be created to match different types of user – teachers, trainers, learners and managers. If you use a tool such as Tableau or PowerBI, data streams can be fed out to these tools.

It should allow you to track learner journeys across the organization, no matter what the activity. Some LRSs go much further and trigger actions, such as recommendations, personalized feedback and automated workflow. Data is dead and inert if it is not put to good use. An LRS enables this good use. Far from limiting learning, it frees you up to track and improve a plethora of learning opportunities.

Depending on the structure of your organization, you may want an LRS that can be multi-tenanted, so that you can have multiple data stores within the LRS for separate academic departments, divisions or different companies within a global group. That is up to you. The bottom line is that an LRS simply structures your activity to make it easier to harvest, store, access and use data in a way that suits your organization. It should be able to cope with any data that is thrown its way.

Automating push learning is an important use. If an employee does X, they may need Y – this can be a notification, nudge, reminder, contact, piece of advice. This is where AI comes in, as it can use algorithms to deliver push learning.

## Organizational learning

There is a much bigger AI idea around organizations as knowledge networks, where learning is leveraged and pushed in a just-in-time fashion. It centres around the idea that AI-powered enterprise software will unlock knowledge, insights and expertise within an organization so that it can power collective competence through sharing and learning.

Most organizational knowledge is locked away in repositories or in the heads of its people. Unlocking and sharing that knowledge is difficult because it is both structured and unstructured, in lots of different places among lots of different people. This last repository, the brains of your people, is the most difficult to unlock, as people are often inclined to keep things to themselves and not share.

Microsoft 'Cortex' now uses AI to deliver topic cards, just in time, that appear automatically, prompting you, in Word, Outlook and so on (Patton, 2019). They use AI to spring open stuff that is locked away in documents, PowerPoints, videos, meetings and chats, even third-party sources. They also include on these topic cards links to expertise, namely people. Only through AI can you really leverage structured and unstructured content, to identify topics, then reveal the relationships between these topics with content, just in time, inside the tools you use every day.

It is this integrated approach to knowledge that the learning community needs to see as its future. Isolating learning into a silo does not leverage the data and people one wishes to use in the wider sense of learning and development.

Cross was right to emphasize the plain fact that informal learning is by far the largest vehicle for actual learning in an organization. Only now, through AI, do we have the software that is smart and powerful enough not only to find the stuff we need, identify the relationships between content and people, when we need it, but also organize and distil it into meaningful information at our point of need.

This is not to say that the AI-driven provision of knowledge and people is enough. Novices will still need structured learning. Presentation alone is never enough, as little is learned on first exposure; most is learned from subsequent effort. This is why search is never enough and learning needs its own additional AI dynamic.

## Conclusion

Organizations need faster, more accessible and flexible systems to deliver learning. It was always the case that learning took place in an ecosystem with many points of contact. Those points of contact used to be classroom courses, manuals and, above all, learning from colleagues – all offline.

As points of contact went online to learning management systems, they tended to silo learning as separate from other sources and activities for learning. Yet internal knowledge bases, internal communications systems, external web resources, YouTube, social media and so on, through various devices, delivering learning, also have a role in learning. AI already plays a key role in search and social media and is now pivotal in the delivering of wider learning experiences through learning experience platforms. Ultimately organizations need to see themselves as learning organizations that leverage learning across everyone. This can only be done using AI.

## References

Cross, J (2011) *Informal Learning: Rediscovering the natural pathways that inspire innovation and performance*, John Wiley & Sons, Hoboken, NJ

Gery, GJ (1991) *Electronic Performance Support Systems: How and why to remake the workplace through the strategic application of technology*, Weingarten Publications, Inc, Boston

Gottfredson, C and Mosher, B (2012) Are you meeting all 5 moments of learner need?, *Learning Solutions Magazine*, June

Patton, S (2019) *Introducing Project Cortex*, Microsoft blog. Available at https://techcommunity.microsoft.com/t5/Microsoft-365-Blog/Introducing-Project-Cortex/ba-p/966091 (archived at https://perma.cc/2B2Z-VWYH)

# 13

# Assessment

Whether in educational institutions, candidate assessment in companies, or competence and professional assessment, high-stakes assessment is big business. Yet it can be an expensive, inefficient and slow business. Creating assessments, travelling to and from assessment centres, arranging invigilators, identifying candidates, preventing cheating, and marking, all make this a stressful and fraught business. AI has begun to have an effect on all of these to allow online assessment, improve ID checks, check for cheating, and marking. What were largely human roles are not being entirely replaced, but they are being automated in part. The increase in productivity should result in better, faster and cheaper assessment.

## Recruitment and assessment

Finding a job and finding and selecting candidates already involves AI for many. Social media, especially LinkedIn, has been instrumental in accelerating both processes online. As social media is itself mediated by AI, it is already embedded in the recruitment loop.

These methods can increase the volume of candidates, giving you a higher probability of finding the right candidate. Within this larger data set, you can be more precise in your targeting. Candidate engagement can also be increased through higher levels of automated and personalized contact. On process alone, efficiencies in time and money are clear. The process can be faster for both employer and candidates, reducing the frustration that is common among jobseekers who do not receive replies to applications.

Selecting CVs for consideration on the basis of your criteria, whether a personal or job specification, can certainly be aided by AI. Indeed, well-designed systems may be able to ignore the age-old human biases around names, gender, race and socio-economic group.

There is much debate around bias in recruitment assessment, but in weighing up the pros and cons, it is well known that much human recruitment is laden with bias. One must be careful that machine learning systems do not inadvertently introduce bias based on datasets that, for example, extrapolate from previous recruitment data that could be gender biased. If care is taken over data sets and the algorithms used with that data, AI can be improved through the pre- and post-processing of that data to ensure fairness. Another word of warning in using AI for recruitment and assessment is that machine learning techniques can make mistakes and may need data sets larger than you have at your disposal.

For actual candidate assessments, AI can provide uniquely generated test items that funnel down routes that one may want to explore with a candidate. Submitted video interviews can be more effective if the transcript is automatically created and AI applied again against selection criteria. Chatbot assessments can pose judgement tests and check decision-making prowess.

Lastly, one interesting criteria to consider is legal defensiveness. Can you defend your AI system against equality and diversity laws in recruitment and selection? This involves issues of transparency. Most AI-driven systems are used to aid the process, rather than automate it completely. This is sensible for all sorts of reasons, not only legal defensibility.

## Digital identification

In online exams, you can use face and document identification to verify that the candidate is indeed the right candidate. There have been cases of massive fraud in this area. Face and body analysis can also be used to check that the candidate is not cheating during the exam. Real-time face recognition is one way in which this will develop.

In language learning, assessing speaking and writing is necessary, in both formative and summative assessment. Some large accreditation companies have large data sets of graded and annotated scripts. These can be used to train AI systems that can determine the level of competence in the language tested.

It is important to remember that AI does not 'understand' the target language. It is competent without comprehension. Nevertheless, it is surprisingly good at using statistical techniques to grade proficiency based on actual use. Where it starts to struggle is at higher levels of proficiency, where people start to use metaphors, similes, analogies and humour. In spoken language this is not as easy, as audio quality, accents and intelligibility are practical problems that have to be overcome.

Most systems keep human assessors in the loop, in hybrid systems, where the workload for volume marking is reduced for assessors, so that they can focus on other tasks. The more such systems are used and developed, if they use machine learning, the more competent they will become at higher levels. For the moment they are used in either student feedback to submit, get feedback and improve writing and/or speaking, or in hybrid systems, where it gives a confident grade or, if the confidence rating is not high enough, refers the piece to a human assessor, who may want more evidence or may want to mark the piece.

AI has also been used to build assessment systems where open input test items are both created and marked by software. The test items are identified and removed from the text, and the candidate has to re-input those items, by either text or voice. AI has also been used to mark short-answer questions by using a variety of AI techniques to semantically analyse the free-text answer.

## Plagiarism and AI

It is odd that the only example of AI in learning to be found in higher education establishments is used to see whether students cheat. As the old adage goes, when students copy, it is plagiarism; academics call it research. This is a cat and mouse game, where predictable, often identical assignments, largely long-form essays, are set. Students procrastinate, share, cut and paste, only to wait for often sparse feedback and a solitary grade.

But the game is getting more complex as, on one side, institutions, teachers and academics are engaged in assessing through essays, while students cheat using essay mills, good comms, high tech and stealth. As long as institutions see this as a deficit problem – those pesky students and essay companies ruining our honest practice – nothing will change. This is a problem that needs smart solutions, not denial and mousetraps.

On one side, institutions and academics set predictable assignments. The format is the often lazy essay question. They often do not change for years. Why does this happen? Fossilized practice, teaching comes second to research, a dearth of assessment design skills, the institution encourages this singular form of assessment and the quality bodies are stuck in a model that has barely changed in decades.

On the other side, students use tech that makes it easier for them to play the game and win. They are on social media, making it easier to share. They have access to oodles of sources from which they can cut and paste. Beyond this they can buy relatively cheap, and undetectable, essays and dissertations online. To be fair, they often do not receive enough teaching and advice on how to do assignments with academic integrity. The psychology here is interesting. The assignment turns into a chore. They know that feedback will be light and that it is unpredictable when they will get the marked essay back. They start to see learning as a game.

Increasing numbers of students clearly results in more pressure to cheat. They or their parents have often had to outlay considerable sums of money, and failure is hard to take as it involves huge loss of face. On top of this is the reluctance of academics to do the necessary detection work, to follow up on cheating, which can be detailed and arduous. You need a lot of very sure evidence to pull this off and most do not want to start the process and climb that bureaucratic mountain. Another protective layer on top of this is the reluctance of the institution to admit it happens, as there is huge potential for reputation damage. This is a perfect storm, where students, teachers and institutions literally institutionalize cheating.

Essays are sometimes appropriate assignments if one wants long-form critical thought. But in many subjects shorter, more targeted assignments and testing would be better. There are a lot of formative assessment techniques out there and essays are just one of them. Short-answer questions, open-response, formative testing and adaptive testing are all appropriate. The truth is that education wants it easy, and essays are easy to set. They also have to accept that they are also now easy to cheat.

One other problem is the ready confusion between formative and summative assessment. There is perhaps far too much marking and summative assessment. If the assignment is a formative learning experience, why mark at all? It should be about the feedback. Black and Wiliam (2005), who have spent decades studying this issue, recommend *not* marking and instead focusing on feedback. Marking acts as an end point. High-performing students get 80 per cent then stop, assuming the other 20 per cent is not worth the effort; low-performing students get demotivated. What learners actually need is not a mark, but detailed and constructive feedback.

There is also the problem of what counts as plagiarism. One of the problems is that tools that check for plagiarism often count direct quotes as plagiarism, confusing the stats and sending false positives into the system. A second problem is what constitutes 'common knowledge', ie stuff that does not have to have citations. This is tricky.

But there is an even worse problem in assessment. To rely on the essay format or long-form prose answers is to encourage students to memorize essays and play roulette with the subject in their final exams. Students, the world over, play the game of final assessment by memorizing essays. There is a pretence that it is testing critical thought. It is not.

We know the scale of the problem. Compare the scanty number of cases actually reported by institutions against the number and size of the companies offering essay mill services. There is a massive gap – and this is just the tip of the iceberg, as most of it is in the grey economy, with even parents doing the cheating. Purchased essays and dissertations are now commonplace in universities. You could legislate against such companies but it would just shift abroad as it is online.

In truth, there are lots of alternatives to the long-form essay.

## Automatic essay assessment

One AI innovation – given the huge numbers and impossibility of providing real teacher grading and feedback – is automatic essay grading.

We need to start with some perspective on what this technology does. The trick here is not to see the AI as 'being human' and 'reading' the essay with real understanding. It does not. It has competence without comprehension. This is not about doing things exactly as humans do them.

Humans are good at many things; they are also bad at many things. Simple calculators can calculate faster than any human. Google's AI can search better than any human. Machines can outperform all humans in terms of mechanical precision, speed, strength and endurance – that is why they are commonplace in manufacturing.

The software is not perfect, but neither are humans. Human performance falls when marking large numbers of essays; they make mistakes, have biases based on names and gender, cognitive biases, as well as biases about what is acceptable in terms of critiques and creativity.

This is not about replacing teacher assessment; it is about automating some of that work to allow teachers to teach and provide more targeted, constructive feedback and support. It is about optimizing teachers' time.

The software takes lots of real essays, along with their human marked grades, and looks for features within those grades that distinguish them from the other grades. In this sense, the software is using human traits and outputs and tries to mimic them when presented with new cases. The features the software needs to pick up on vary but can include missing words/phrases and so on. So it is *not* the machine or algorithms on their own doing the work; it is a process of looking at what human experts did when they marked lots of essays.

Machine grading gives you a score, but it also gives you a probability, namely a confidence rating. This is important, as you can use this to retrain the algorithm on low-confidence scored essays. Automatic essay scoring also tries to give scores for each dimension in the scoring rubric; it is not just an overall grade.

This is a numbers game. It does not work in small classes, as you need hundreds, possibly many more, essays on that one topic to train the software. If you run a specific course, with obscure content, to relatively small numbers of students, this road is not for you. If, however, you are teaching a course where the cumulative number of students, year after year, is in the many hundreds, or across institutions to many thousands, or in MOOCs to hundreds of thousands, it starts to make sense. Sure it will make mistakes, but humans also make mistakes in essay grading. When researched, it is clear that they do. Machine marking even mimics the mistakes that the test human markers make when grading.

It is wrong to say that AI cannot spot good style or good writing. It is possible to measure all sorts of aspects of syntactic style, such as sentence length, identifying clichés, use of connectives, good phrases, relevant and subtle vocabulary and so on. If these have been identified by human graders, they can potentially be spotted by AI. That is not to say that it can do all of these tasks well, but it can do some of it well after getting a large amount of aggregated data from real, consistently graded essays by trained professionals. In a sense, style is already being checked in Word, as spelling is corrected, grammatical errors caught, common errors such as commonly confused homonyms highlighted and so on. But to be frank, style is not often a key learning objective, so let us not shoot the tennis player for being bad at golf.

It would be fair to say that machine grading systems do not mark for creativity, but this is a notoriously difficult term to define and human graders may well be hugely variable in making this judgement. If you are teaching a 'creative writing' course, fair enough – it is not going to help. But unless you're being explicit about being creative, whatever that means, it is unfair to blame the software for lacking creative judgement. Again, unless you as a human assessor know what 'creativity' means, and can define it to a level that gives AI a chance to spot it, do not blame the software.

To what problem(s) is this a solution? What do teachers see as their toughest chore? Marking. This frees up their time to teach, not mark. One problem it can address is overwork by teachers – the product of the massification of education, with ever greater numbers taking courses and stretched teachers.

This massification has also produced lots of students who submit thin, barely revised essays that may only meet the word count. These need to be cut off at the pass and immediate feedback given that the work is not yet fit to submit. This helps the student and does not waste the time of the teacher. For teachers, it can also be used as a 'first pass' tool – take some of the spade work out of assessing essays by letting the software pick up on the more obvious errors so that you can focus on your personalized input and more detailed feedback on specific points.

Students want instant feedback. They do not want to wait days, and in reality it is more likely to be weeks before getting back a grade and a few comments. Grading thus becomes feedback in the process of learning. We need to be clear that this improves learning. No teacher is ever going to go through half a dozen iterations for every student essay submitted. Machine marking will do this with ease.

This idea has been around for a long time and sees machine marking as a check on human assessment. It is like having another assessor at your side to check that you are being consistent and you're on your game. If the two differ, a second human grades the essay. Alternatively, the teacher can look at the essay again and consider a re-grading, or not.

A first-pass machine-marking run can allow teachers to focus more on students who need help, rather than on students who perform well and need less support.

Those who already use peer assessment are well up the ladder as machine assessment seems like a natural step. The trouble with peer grading and feedback is that it can be unreliable and suffers from grade inflation. If machine grading can lower this, we should take it seriously.

Students may feel short-changed with machine marking, but many already feel that way, with late, often barely commented feedback on essays submitted. Most students do not gain much by the common lines from real teachers, such as, 'Needs more detail…', 'Could be clearer…', and so on. They want specific, helpful and constructive feedback, not vague, well-worn phrases. This is why it is important to couch the feedback from machine learning with reasonable explanations about its supportive role in improving performance in essay writing. It is not there to replace teachers; it is there to help students do better.

We have to be careful here and be conscious of the sheer difficulty of interpreting 'meaning' from the written and spoken word.

One major issue arises when you reflect, in detail, on AI grading. Why do we rely so much on essays as a form of assessment? One has to conclude that, like lectures, they have become an easy default. They are easy to set, difficult to mark. It would surely be better to look at a range of appropriate assessment methods that are designed around the type of learning objectives and competences you want your students to acquire. This is not to say that essays should never be used, only that they are overused. It is institutionalized teaching, not optimal teaching or learning.

## Reference

Black, P and Wiliam, D (2005) *Inside the Black Box: Raising standards through classroom assessment*, Granada Learning, London

## PART FIVE

# Data

# 14

# Data analytics

Data is critical to the future of any organization. Or, more accurately, the analysis of data is critical to inform and shape the future of any organization. Learning data can reveal fascinating insights about that most important asset in an educational institution or business – its students or people. It allows you to adapt your learning strategy but also unlock insights that can power organizational decision-making.

## Sources of data

Data at all sorts of levels in learning reveals secrets we never imagined we could discover. It reveals things to teachers, trainers, learners and managers, and as we do more learning online, searching, reading, watching, communicating and socializing, we create more and more data that provides fuel for algorithms that improve with big numbers. The more you feed these algorithms, the more useful they become.

Online learning, by definition, can produce data – one of the great advantages of being online. For many years data has been gathered and used in online learning. SCORM emerged as the *de facto* specification, making this data interoperable. However, something new has happened – the awareness that the data produced by online learning is much more powerful than we ever imagined. It can be gathered and used to solve all sorts of difficult problems in learning, problems that have plagued education and training, such as take-up, formative assessment, dropout, course improvement, productivity, cost reduction and so on.

So how relevant is data to learning? We need to start with an admission: big data in learning is really just 'large data'. We are not dealing with the unimaginable amounts of relevant data that Google brings to bear when you search or translate. The datasets we are talking about come from individual learners, courses, individual institutions and sometimes, but rarely, from groups of institutions, national tests and examinations, and rarer still, from international tests or large complexes of institutions.

Nevertheless, data can be harvested at different levels, each increasing in terms of quantity, from:

- brains;
- learners;
- courses;
- across courses;
- organizations/institutions;
- groups of organizations/institutions;
- national;
- international;
- web.

Data is changing learning by providing a sound basis for learners, teachers, managers and policy-makers to improve their systems. Too much is hidden, so more and more open data is needed. Data must be open. Data must be searchable. Data must also be governed and managed. There is also the issue of visualization. Data is about decision-making by the learner or teacher, or at an organizational, national or international level, and must be understood through visualization.

## Data pitfalls

The old adage that 'on average humans have one testicle' is often used to show the dangers in drawing meaningless conclusions from sets of data. Averages can be dangerous, especially in the learning game. Complex algorithmic and machine learning approaches may turn out to be more expensive and far less reliable and verifiable than simple measures, like using a spreadsheet and Excel Analytics, or making what little data you have available in a visualized, digestible form to faculty or managers. Beyond this, traditional statistics are likely to prove more fruitful. Data analytics has taken on the gloss and allure of AI, yet much of it is actually plain old data science and statistics. So before you spend huge sums on learning analytics projects, consider the following.

They say that data is the new oil, but the danger may be that, in some cases, it turns out to be the new snake oil. It is often stored in odd formats and places, often old, messy, embarrassing, personal and even secret. To quote that old malapropism, 'data is a minefield of information'. Primitive analysis may even be massively misleading, as the testicle comment amusingly exposes.

The data problem can be even worse than mere messiness, as there is another problem – the paucity of data. Large tech companies use big data, but this is BIG data, not the trivial data sets that learning often produces, often on single courses or within single institutions. Institutions are not necessarily gushing wells of data. Data held by institutions on learners is often paltry. Universities, for example, rarely even know how many learners turn up for lectures, and the actual data, when collected, often paints a depressingly impoverished picture. So another problem with the use of data in learning is that we have so little of the stuff.

Old specifications such as SCORM, which has been around for 20-plus years, literally stopped the collection of data with its limited focus on course completion. This makes most data analytics projects, even in large organizations, rather difficult. This limited data is certainly not as large, clean and relevant as it needs to be to produce deep and genuine insights. Other data sources are often similarly flawed, as there is often little in the way of fine-grained data about actual performance. It is small data sets, often messy, poorly structured and not insightful.

Data is also often not as clean as you think it is, with much of it in odd data structures, odd formats, encrypted and different databases. Just getting a hold of the stuff is difficult. Then there is the problem of relevance and utility, as much of it is old, some of it useless and much of it messy. In fact, much of it could be deleted. Much of the stuff we simply haven't known what to do with, don't clean and don't know how to manage.

Problems can also arise around data that can be embarrassing, even dangerous. There may be very good reasons for not opening up historic data, such as emails and internal social communications. Trawling through social content may uncover things you wish you had not uncovered, as it may open up sizeable legal and other HR risks for organizations. Think of Wikileaks email dumps. Your data may turn out to be less like a barrel of oil and more like a can of worms.

In practice, even when those amazing (or not so amazing) insights come through, what do institutions actually do? Do they stop or record lectures because learners with English as a foreign language find some lecturers difficult and the psychology of learning screams at us to let learners have repeated access to resources? Do they tackle the issue of poor teaching by specific lecturers? Do they question the use of lectures? Do they radically reduce response times on feedback to learners? Do they drop the essay as a lazy and monolithic form of assessment? Or do they default to talking about improving the 'student experience' where nothing much changes?

The problem with spending all of your money on diagnosis – especially when the diagnosis is an obvious limited set of possible causes that was probably already known – is that the money is usually better spent on treatment. Look at improving student support, teaching and learning, not diagnosis.

## Types of data

It is also important to get a feel for the many types of data one might handle in AI for learning, the practical stages through which data must go before it is used and then how it is used.

In learning we can have 'personal' data, provided by the person or actions by that person with their full knowledge. This may be gender, age, educational background, job role, training objectives, courses completed, needs, stated goals and so on. Some also think that personality data is relevant, but there is a lot of controversy around the validity of Myers-Briggs. The OCEAN model has more support from research (Ahmed, 2016).

Then there is 'observed' data from the actions of the user, their start times, end times, how long they took on activities, choices, routes, clicks, dwell times, contributions to discussions, choices and answers. Who does what, where and when can be revealing, as it is raw, unpolluted data. It is like the flour in the baking of a cake – the base data.

You also have 'derived' data inferred from existing data to create new data. This is data that is computed from other data. We may have columns of scores on tests and derived data could be mean and median values from that data. This data can be used to good effect in adaptive learning, to decide on real-time personalized routes through courses.

At a higher level, 'analysed' data is data that has been inspected, cleaned, transformed and modelled to make it useful in decision-making.

In AI this can involve 'training' data used for training AI systems. This data, used to train a model, may be a large corpus of text, such as the United Nations translated content used for Google Translate. In learning it can be existing student data or previous queries from a social system used to train a chatbot.

Then there is 'production' data, the data used by the system after it is launched in the real world. This is where the surprises come, as this is often at odds with the training data, and can mean iterations of further development.

If you are serious about using AI and machine learning (they are not the same thing), be prepared for some tough times. It is difficult to get things working from structured data, let alone unstructured data, and you will need really good training and testing sets, of substantial size, to train and evaluate your system.

Given the problems stated above, it is not easy to get a suitable data set, which is clean and reliable for training your machine learning model. Then, when you launch the service or product, the new data may be subject to all sorts of unforeseen problems not uncovered in the training process. This is a rock on which many AI projects flounder.

Just when you thought it was getting clearer, you may also have to consider 'anonymized' data, free of attributes that may relate it to a specific source or individual. This is not easy to achieve as there are often techniques to reverse engineer attribution to individuals. Nevertheless, it is useful if regulations, laws and other ethical concerns are an issue.

Before entering these data analytics projects, ask yourself some serious questions about 'data'.

As mentioned previously, data is rarely clean in the sense of being ready for use, and cleaning data is a really important process in AI preparation. Many data scientists spend much of their time on this one task, as the quality of the data you put into algorithms really affects the quality of the output. Let us take numerical scores on a course. Cleaning means identifying and removing outliers (someone started but left the window open on their laptop), getting rid of duplicates, normalizing data to make the data similar and usable (putting scores onto the same scale). In large data sets, because you have so much data, you can ignore missing data; whereas with small data sets you can use numerical methods such as using the median or some predictive algorithms to fill in the missing points and still make use of as much of the data as possible.

Data size by itself is important and size still matters – whether $n$ = tens, hundreds, thousands, millions, the Law of Small Numbers still matters. But getting the right data may be even more important. Do not jump in until you are clear about how much relevant and useful data you have, where it is, how clean it is, in what databases and what you want to do with it.

## Learners and data

Let us look at learners and data. Learners may not care that much and, if truth be told, there may not be a great deal to worry about. Most of the fuss may be from administrators who get paranoid about 'privacy'. Nevertheless, it is worth asking a few questions about the issue and the law.

To what problem is transparency on data a solution? Are learners queuing round the block for their data? Learners are not that interested, as they are generally brought up in a world where they know that letting people hold and use your data is the price you pay for free stuff. That is not to say it is not an issue or that it will not become an issue in organizations, but there is no need for panic here.

Should we promise all data on demand? If learners demand it, should an institution promise to give them all data? Not really. In the UK, we have the Data Protection Act. However, this is not a blanket rule and there are lots of exemptions, as well as practical issues. So there is no reason, practically or legally, to promise the world on data, as you may neither need, nor be able to, deliver on that promise. An important point that is often missed is that, if they have not asked, you do not have to provide the data. Even if asked for, it is likely that in its raw form the data would be meaningless. Data is rarely useful unless it is analysed and then visualized.

What about predictive models using analytics and adaptive learning? Should learning institutions provide that data? First, you only have to provide 'stored' data, not data used on the fly, which is common in these adaptive systems. You also have the argument that much of this is not stored data but algorithms with inputs and outputs. It is not so much isolated data as statistical inference or probability that is the object of curiosity.

There are also exemptions. You do not have to provide data where there have been infringements of IP by learners, data to do with a crime/investigation or third-party data provision.

Remember, also, that if you're thinking of loosening up on data, making it available to learners, you also have to be very careful with access. Learners are smart, savvy and skilled. Many have the ability look for access to change, say, grades!

Data, in itself, is only useful if it is the right data, of usable size and can be used to solve the problem you want it to solve. An important point to remember about data in relation to AI is that it is not a trivial task to clean, train AI models and have the certainty you may wish to have over outputs. Nevertheless, it is clear that AI provides the means to use data to solve problems that have plagued the world of learning. Learning analytics are now part of the learning technology landscape.

## Learning analytics

Many now regard 'learning analytics' and data collection in 'learning record stores' as a strategy that opens up the use of AI for learning. On the whole, this is admirable, but the danger is in spending this time and effort without asking 'Why?' Many talk about analytics, but few are talking about how to show that this will actually help increase the efficacy of the organization. Some are switched on and know exactly what they want to explore and implement; others are like those that never throw anything out and just fill up their home with stuff, as they feel it may be useful at some time in the future.

Another problem is that people want to shift from first to fifth gear without doing much in between. The online learning industry has been stuck with the traditional LMS/VLE and SCORM for so long, along with a few pie charts and histograms, that it has not really developed the mindset or skills to make this analytics leap. This, therefore, is an opportunity to look at using learning analytics and AI as a tool for genuine improvement.

In the end this is all about *decision-making*. What decisions are you going to make on the back of insights from your data? Storing learning data for present and future use may not be the best use of data. Perhaps the best use of data is directly in teaching and learning, to create courses, provide feedback, adapt learning, text to speech for podcasts and so on. Use AI in a precise fashion to solve specific learning problems, rather than analysis and the paralysis by analysis that often follows. If your goal is to harvest data and use it to gain insights and improve the learning and outcomes for the organization, be clear about those goals. The least efficient use of data may be to store it in a huge pot, boil it up and hope that something, as yet undefined, emerges.

Learning analytics uses data to improve learning. It has become clear that data can and will be used to help inform and shape learning. This means understanding what data is, what it can do and how you can use it.

Let us start with a good, basic schema for learning analytics. It is almost pointless to gather data if it remains unloved and unused. There must be purpose to the endeavour, in the sense of goals and uncovering evidence-based insights. These goals can be to:

- describe;
- analyse;
- predict;
- prescribe.

This provides a rough escalator of functionality where you can consider what you want to do with your data. Each of these steps gets progressively more difficult, so we must be realistic about our ambitions, resources and the certainty of the output.

## Level 1 – describe

What does the learning data tell us about *what things* are happening?

This can include who learned what, where and when. Dashboards can visualize such data to capture and expose actual behaviours for individuals and/or groups of learners. To record, track and report on activity, data can be used to do this without involving too much complexity.

### Tracking

The traditional LMS/VLE uses SCORM to track users and their completion stats, but it is an old, data-poor, tracking tool. Many organizations now want far more detail on their online and other learning activities. In addition to completion, there is a need to track time taken to complete, average completion times and time taken on different tasks and more fine-grained data on specific parts of the learning experience. There is also the tracking of where, when and why people drop out.

One may also want to track use of what were seen as non-learning resources within and from outside the organization, external resources such as YouTube and so on. At a more basic level, browsers used, operating systems and locations may have to be tracked, especially if one is interested in decisions around mobile use or browser policy. Tracking is the key to hunting down problems and solutions to those problems.

## Visualization

Data needs to be accessible and visible if it is to be useful. One visualizes data for a purpose – in order to understand its meaning. Yet visualization is not an end in itself. Many feel happy that visualized data is the end point, once seen and understood – job done. What is actually needed is action upon that visualized data, a feed into decision-making. Tools such as Tableau, even Excel, can do wondrous things in terms of visualization, but there must be a clear purpose, so work back from the business or organizational purpose. Visualized data can then be used in reports and fuel business progress. Visualization gives life to data and aids decision-making.

However, one must be careful about thinking that this alone encourages agency or positive outcomes in self-directed learning. Visualization through, for example, dashboards, may not be as useful as one imagines. In 'A systematic review of empirical studies on learning analytics dashboards: A self-regulated learning perspective' (Matcha *et al*, 2019), dashboards were rarely grounded in learning theory and did not support metacognition. Neither did they offer any information about effective learning tactics and strategies. In short, they had significant limitations.

## Security and privacy

Data is contentious. To manage it properly an organization should make sure that it is stored securely, with privacy maintained, in line with regulation and legislation, such as the GDPR. Data is easier to manage if it is in one place. An LRS allows one to store, manage and report from one place. In fact, it can be a key part of your stated GDPR policy, which is largely about the correct management of data. It may also allow you to comply with data storage requirements that demand data to be stored within a country or geographical border. In the long term, it also allows you to react easily and quickly to any future legislation and regulation around data. Having established a base camp for storage, one that is integrated into all of the necessary systems, one can then consider possible uses.

## Level 2 – analyse

What does the learning data tell us about *why* things are happening?

Analysis allows you to drill down and look for causes of either good or bad behaviour and outcomes. Correlations with other data sets (such as sales, productivity, complaints, absenteeism and so on) may also be useful. Analysed data allows one to take data and subject it to computational analysis to report more useful findings and look for insights that can inform decision-making.

### Evaluation

Analysis of data can expose weaknesses in the learning experience. This requires a mindset that accepts failure, where the whole point is to uncover weaknesses in design and delivery. At a simple level, learners who, for example, get one or two questions consistently wrong may expose either poorly constructed questions or a consistent knowledge gap. Both are possible diagnoses. The same data can have different causes. At another level, more serious questions can be asked. Are the videos too long? Are users clicking through content without actually reading or watching it?

Analysis of data also allows you to move beyond the limitations of that rather dated form of evaluation in organizational learning – the Kirkpatrick model. Kirkpatrick has for decades been the only game in town in the evaluation of corporate training, although hardly known in education. In his early 'Techniques for evaluation training programs' (1959) and *Evaluating Training Programs: The four levels* (Kirkpatrick and Kirkpatrick, 2006), he proposed a standard approach to the evaluation of training that became a *de facto* standard. It is a simple and sensible schema – focusing on the four levels of reaction, learning, behaviour and results – but has not stood the test of time.

First, Kirkpatrick is the first to admit that there is no research or scientific background to his theory. This is not quite true, as it is clearly steeped in the behaviourism that was current when it was written. It is summative, ignores context and ignores methods of delivery. Some therefore think Kirkpatrick asks all the wrong questions – the task is to create the motivation and context for good learning and knowledge-sharing, not to treat learning as an auditable commodity. It is also totally inappropriate for informal learning.

Senior managers rarely want all four levels of Kirkpatrick data. They want more convincing business arguments. It is the training community that tell senior management that they need Kirkpatrick, not the other way round. In this sense it is over-engineered. The four linear levels are too much. All the evidence shows that Levels 3 and 4 are rarely attempted, as all of the effort and resource focuses on the easier-to-collect Levels 1 and 2. Given the time and resources needed, and demand from the organization for relevant data, it is surely better to go straight to Level 4. In practice, Level 4 is rarely reached, as fear, disinterest, time, cost, disruption and low skills in statistics mitigate against this type of analysis.

The Kirkpatrick model can therefore be seen as often irrelevant, costly, long-winded, and statistically weak. It rarely involves sampling, and both the collection and analysis of the data is crude and often not significant. As an over-engineered, 60-year-old theory, it is badly in need of an overhaul.

You can adopt a much more business-congruent evaluation of your learning if you have an adequate amount of data that exposes actual learning through to business impact and avoid the lower-level evaluations, involving happy sheets and short-term memory tests in often primitive forms of assessment. Harvest and analyse real data and you get more than just opinions. In practice, analysis of learning analytics can revolutionize your approach to evaluation.

## Business performance

Looking for correlations between, say, increases in sales and completed training gives us a powerful rationale for future strategies in learning. It need not be just sales. Whatever outcomes the organization has in its strategy need to be supported by learning and development. This may lift us out of the constraints of Kirkpatrick, cutting to the quick, which is business or organizational impact. We could at last free learning from the shackles of course delivery and deliver what the business really wants – results.

One can deliver learning that aims to improve business performance, KPIs, goals, tactics or strategy. This may be sales, profitability, customer care improvements, a reduction in legal cases and so on. For example, AI-generated content for TUI plc led to a 36 per cent increase in sales (Clark, 2018a). To do this properly one has to look for correlations between the training and consequential increases in sales, being wary of other causes, in what may be a multifactorial context. The advantage of having your data in one place is that one can, at least, look for such correlations with actual performance.

Beyond correlations, one may want to really investigate whether people actually remember what they need to know. Implementing contemporary pedagogies such as effortful learning, interleaving and spaced practice many need validation. The transfer of learning may also need investigation.

## Improve ROI

Online learning is now at the sharp end of education and training, but the problem lies in convincing the powers that be. The intellectual capital of a business, especially in its people, is being increasingly recognized as a vital asset, with learning becoming a key business activity. The ability to predict, calculate, measure and report on the financial and other business benefits of learning is therefore becoming a key skill. Companies are increasingly demanding evidence that training makes a measurable difference to the performance and profitability of a business. A return on investment (ROI) has to be more than just a defence against cutbacks in the budget. It is, after all, the very rationale for investing in learning in the first place. If you wish to make a strong case for online learning within your organization, you will need evidence. In the case of business, this needs to be financial as well as reasoned, quantitative as well as qualitative. A return on investment in training is often assumed and expected; whether it happens is another matter. Evaluation often stops with a happy sheet at the end of a course. Even when the expected ROI has been calculated, as a reason for investing in learning, it is rarely followed through and measured in terms of real business performance. The good news is that, given a sizeable target audience and a company-wide intranet, the ROI on online learning solutions can be huge and the benefits measurable. Online learning makes an ROI easier to measure as usage, efficiency and effectiveness data can be gathered across a network by virtue of being online. The ROI cycle is the wheel that keeps the investment in learning going. It is therefore a primary tool in the management of learning. Learn from your mistakes and successes. An ROI is far more likely to shine the spotlight of success on managers. If you can prove that your work has led to considerable increases in performance and profitability, it will be seen as a success.

## Determine how people learn

One could look for learning insights into 'how' people learn. However, it is hard to see how this trumps actual research. Recording what people just 'do' is not that revealing in click-through courses, without much cognitive effort. Just showing them video, animation, text and graphics, no matter how dazzling, is almost irrelevant if they have learned little. This is a classic garbage in, garbage out (GIGO) problem. Some imagine that insights are buried in there and that they will magically reveal themselves – think again. If you want insights into how people actually learn, set some time aside and look at the existing research in cognitive science. You will do better looking at what the research actually says and then redesigning your online learning around that science. Remember that these scientific findings have already gone through a process of controlled studies, with a methodology that statistically attempts to get clean data on specific variables. This is what science does – it is usually more than a match for your own harvested data set.

# Level 3 – predict

What does the learning data tell us that is *likely to happen*?

Predictive analytics allows one to anticipate what will happen in the future. This helps with decision-making, through forecasts and foresight. Note that this forecasting can be for the benefit of the teacher, system and/ or learner. Predictive analytics can be used to look forward in time and spot probable events, both positive and negative. For example, you can use predictive analytics to spot potential failures and dropouts.

## Predict performance

You may want to predict grades and outcomes so that instructors can target resources and action to learners based on their real needs, especially those who are likely to have problems. At-risk students can be specifically helped, attainment gaps closed, completions increased and overall attainment raised. Increasing attainment by predicting problems can also help with progression from one stage of the educational journey to the next.

## Predict dropout

Learners may be at risk of dropping out, so predicting those at risk can help instructors and institutions prevent this catastrophic outcome. Dropout can be catastrophic, not only for the learner but also the institution. Data is often drawn from student record systems as well as VLEs to train the prediction model. Some data, with known outcomes, can also be used to check the accuracy of the predictive model. There can be hundreds of fields, including: current grade, year of study, part-time/full-time, entry grade, age, course size, average grades, financial status, interactions, total length of interactions, and many others.

Whatever the prediction, it is important to look at the problem holistically. Academic performance may also be affected by external causes, some very private. Here, pointing students towards student services and sources of help other than academic can be useful.

## Level 4 – prescribe

What does the learning data tell us that *should happen*?

Prescriptive analytics may prescribe training needs for an organization, a personalized learning plan, the sequence of learning events presented to learners individually in real time or a timetable that has no clashes. It determines and prescribes action within an organization. When data is used to prescribe action, it is forcing action in a deterministic fashion.

### Recommendation engines

Recommendation engines can recommend new skills, routes through courses, routes through databases of micro-learning right through to complex adaptive learning and personalized systems where data can be used, often in real time, to deliver sequenced personalized content to learners through courses, on scale, based on data that exists and is gathered as one does the course or learning. It may even use aggregated data about you from across the whole curriculum or learning experience within your organization, or use aggregated data from all learners that have completed that course.

This is not easy. It is difficult to get a recommendation engine to work on relatively small data sets (not really big data) that are less than reliable. You may come to the decision that personal learning plans are actually best constructed using simpler software techniques from spreadsheet levels of data. However, in cases where data is good and substantial, recommendations may be possible.

One use of AI-driven recommendation engines is in LXPs, which are designed to move beyond what is perceived as the rather passive 'management' only functions of the traditional LMS or VLE. The new focus is to increase employee engagement, enhance the end-user experience and offer more choice to give employees the ability to select what and when to learn. The idea is to present learning less as courses, more in the workflow. An LRS provides the data which allows a more flexible delivery of searchability, content, curation and learning services, based not on supply but demand. The ability to push learning through notifications and nudge techniques will arguably give learning more purchase, making it more relevant, but there is also the use of recommendation engines to recommend or determine routes through learning experiences.

Many of these do not use AI at all and are simply determined by an often rather crude model; others attempt to prescribe routes that are often felt by employees to be quite simply wrong, not quite relevant and rather restrictive. We have lessons to learn from how AI is used in Google, YouTube and notification services from other services like Spotify. A more dynamic, open, algorithmic system that takes into account new knowledge and skills may be more useful.

## Chatbot data

Many chatbots have to be trained with data sets. Saving sets of queries and responses from whatever social system is used in an organization can be useful, as it can be used to 'train' the designed chatbot. The successful Georgia Tech teacher support chatbot from Chapter 6 used 40,000 email inquiries to train their chatbot. Chatbots can be used for learner engagement, learner support, delivery of learning, assessment and well-being. If they are to be part of your learning strategy, they need data, not only to be trained, but, if they involve machine learning, also to improve over time. Seeing what questions learners ask chatbots is fascinating and a rich source of insights about the organization and the learning. With the introduction of sophisticated dialogue software, such as Google Duplex, we may find that social data is as important as other forms of data. So saving such data may be wise.

## A/B testing

Another source of data, not often used in learning, is A/B testing, where a series of quick adaptions could be tested with real users, but few have the bandwidth and skills to make this happen. The promise may be way ahead of what is perceived and actually possible to deliver.

One of the benefits of the data revolution is that new data techniques can be used to give insights into what works and what does not work in learning. A/B testing is one such technique. It is widely used in digital marketing and something that the world's largest tech companies routinely use – Google, Facebook, Twitter, Amazon, Netflix and so on. You try two things, wait, measure the results and choose the winner. It only works when you have large numbers of users, and therefore data points, but provides quick comparative testing and evaluation. We are now seeing this being used in education and one of the first results was surprising.

Benjamin Jones, at Northwestern University, wanted to know what lesson plans were more successful than others, so he randomly implemented different lesson plans in a series of A/B tests and waited on the results (Chatterji and Jones, 2016). His EDUSTAR platform delivered the plans and harvested the results of short tests, to see which lesson plans got better results. One of his first A/B tests was on the teaching of fractions using gamification versus non-gamification lesson plans. One group did a straight 'dividing fractions' lesson, the other a 'basketball dividing fractions' lesson. This was an exciting experiment, as many thought that gamification was literally a game changer, a technique that could significantly raise the efficacy of teaching, especially in maths. So what happened? The gamification lesson plan fared worse than non-gamified lesson plans. There are many possible reasons for this: extra cognitive load required for the mechanics of the game, loss of focus on the actual learning, time wasted and so on. Interestingly, the kids spent more time in the gamified lesson (on average 4.5 minutes longer) but learned less, suggesting that interest may be trumped by poorer deep processing and learning. But all we need to know at this point is that gamification fared badly when compared with more straightforward teaching methods. Interesting.

A/B testing may be the one saviour here, in that educational techniques may be individually tested, quickly and cheaply. Traditional research takes ages and is costly. Schools, universities and organizations need to be contacted, learners selected, administration completed – this all takes time – lots of time. The experiments are also often costly and time-consuming, whereas randomized A/B tests can be quick and cheap. Online learning has lots to gain here, as A/B testing can improve interface design and lower cognitive load, but it can also quickly identify efficacious interventions. Adding the button 'Learn More' increased sign-ups to Obama's campaign. This was identified through A/B testing (Siroker, 2010).

## Learning analytics and organizational change

On an organizational level, one may wish to use learning analytics to drive much larger business goals. Chris Brannigan is the CEO of Caspian Learning and is unusual in that his background is in neuroscience. This, along with his technical and financial skills, has allowed him and his team to build a platform that brings the power of flight simulations to business.

He uses learning analytics to investigate, diagnose and treat business problems within organizations. This can be compliance issues, risk or performance of any kind. The aim is to do a complete health check, using 3D simulated scenarios, sophisticated behavioural analysis right through to predictive analysis and recommendations for process, human and other types of change. The ambition is breath-taking.

Financial institutions nearly took us all down in 2008. Some are still being fined billions of dollars for regular breaches on risk, processes and mis-selling. We know that existing compliance training rarely works; it is often a tick-box exercise. So how do you know that your tens or hundreds of thousands of employees perform under high risk? You do not. The problem is that the risk is asymmetric. A few bad apples can incur the wrath of the regulators. You really do need to know what they do, why they do it and what you need to do to change things for the better.

They have run sophisticated simulation training, used data analysis and AI to identify insights, then make decisions to change things. So they put the employees of a global bank through simulation training on loan risk analysis and found that the problems were not what they had imagined – handing out risky loans. In fact, in certain countries, they were rejecting 'safe' loans – being too risk-averse. This deep insight into business process and skills weaknesses is invaluable. But you need to run sophisticated training, not click-through online learning. It has to expose weaknesses in actual performance.

Brannigan's system learns from experts, so that there is an ideal model, then employees go through scenario training which subtly gathers data over 20 or so scenarios, with lots of different flavours. It then diagnoses the problems in terms of decision-making, reasoning and investigation. A diagnosis, along with a financial impact analysis, is delivered to senior executives and line managers, with specific actions. All of this is done using AI techniques that include machine learning and other forms of algorithmic and data analysis to improve the business. It is one very smart solution.

Note that the goal is not to improve training but to improve the business. The data, intelligence and predictive analytics all move towards decisions, actions and change. The diagnosis will identify geographic areas, cultural problems, specific processes, system weaknesses – all moving towards solutions that may be more training, investment decisions, system changes or personnel changes. All of this is based on modelling business outcomes. The point is to identify an optimum way forward that always increases productivity, while solving other problems.

This ticks all the boxes. It draws on the behaviour of real people, and uses simulation and scenario-based data-gathering to focus on actual performance. AI and machine learning is then used to deliver concrete recommendations that can be used in decision-making. Not stuck in the training rut of course delivery, it has direct business impact, gets better the more it is used and is ambitious.

Learning and development (L&D) talk a lot about business alignment but often do not get very far down that track. This model moves beyond L&D into other business units. What Brannigan gathers for an organization is a unique data set, combined with a unique AI platform that really does deliver recommendations for change. It is light years ahead of happy sheets and Kirkpatrick. What is more interesting is that it lies way beyond much of what is being done at present, with low-key, non-interventionist training.

## Conclusion

There is a danger that organizations are being pulled in the wrong direction with their obsession with learning analytics, at the expense of more fruitful uses of AI in learning. Sure it has some efficacy, but the money being spent may be disproportionate. Much of what is being paid for here may be exercises that only bring obvious results. What insights are being uncovered here? That dropout is being caused by poor teaching and poor student support? That students with English as a second language struggle? Ask yourself whether these insights really are insights or whether they are something everyone knew in the first place.

The problem here is the paucity of data. Most educational establishments do not know that much about their learners. Few know how many students attend lectures because few record attendance. That is the first problem – poor data. Other data sources may be similarly flawed, as there is little in the way of fine-grained feedback, especially on learning. It is small data sets, often messy, poorly structured and not well understood.

So much of this seems like playing around with the problem, rather than facing up to solving the problem. That is not to say you should ignore its uses – just do not get sucked into data and learning analytics projects that promise lots but deliver little. There are a lot of promised efficiencies through learning analytics in higher education, mostly around preventing dropout, yet little in the way of verifiable analysis that it works. It is far better to focus on the use of data in adaptive learning or small-scale teaching and learning projects where relatively small amounts of data can be put to good use. AI is many things, and a far better use of AI in learning would be to improve teaching through engagement, support, personalized, adaptive learning, better feedback, student support, active learning, content creation and assessment. All of these are available right now. They address the real problem – teaching and learning.

# References

Ahmed, M (2016) Is Myers-Briggs up to the job?, *Financial Times Magazine,* 11 February. Available at https://www.ft.com/content/8790ef0a-d040-11e5-831d-09f7778e7377 (archived at https://perma.cc/TND2-GT4R)

Chatterji, AK and Jones, BF (2016) *Learning what works in educational technology with a case study of EDUSTAR.* Available at https://www.hamiltonproject.org/assets/files/learning_what_works_in_ed_tech_pm.pdf (archived at https://perma.cc/JY3B-N8W8)

Clark, D (2018) Wildfire wins 'Best Learning Technologies Project'. Available at http://www.wildfirelearning.co.uk/wildfire-wins-best-learning-technologies-project/ (archived at https://perma.cc/RJ4V-F98Q)

Kirkpatrick, DL (1959) Techniques for evaluation training programs, *Journal of the American Society of Training Directors,* **13,** pp 21–26

Kirkpatrick, DL and Kirkpatrick, J (2006) *Evaluating Training Programs: The four levels,* Berrett-Koehler Publishers, San Francisco, CA

Matcha, W, Gasevic, D and Pardo, A (2019) A systematic review of empirical studies on learning analytics dashboards: A self-regulated learning perspective, *IEEE Transactions on Learning Technologies*. Available at https://doi.org/10.1109/TLT.2019.2916802 (archived at https://perma.cc/Z6TW-PJ47)

Siroker, D (2010) How Obama raised $60 million by running a simple experiment, Optimizely Blog, 29 November. Available at https://blog.optimizely.com/2010/11/29/how-obama-raised-60-million-by-running-a-simple-experiment/ (archived at https://perma.cc/9YVA-754M)

# 15

# Sentiment analysis

*The Square and the Tower* by Niall Ferguson (2019) takes the public square in Sienna and the tall tower that looms above as a metaphor for flat, open networks and their accompanying hierarchical structures. Julian Stodd, the social learning expert, makes a similar distinction between open, flat networks and formal, hierarchical structures, although both are networks, as a hierarchy is just one form of network (2014). Networks tend to be more creative and innovative; hierarchies are more restricted. In most contexts you need both.

Ferguson's point is that history shows that both have been around for a very long time. Indeed, he tries to rewrite history in terms of these two opposing forces. He sees history through the lens of networks, the main distinction being between *disruptive networks*, often fuelled by technology, such as tool-making, language, writing, alphabets, paper, printing, transport, radio, telegraph, television and the internet; then *institutional hierarchies* such as families, political parties, companies and so on. Networks come in all shapes and sizes. In terms of communities, we have criminal networks, terrorist networks, jihadi networks, intelligence networks, and so on. In terms of technology, social networks, telephone networks, radio networks, electricity networks. History understates the role of networks. We now even have cyberwars between networks. This is the age of networks.

We can trace this back to the fact that we are a species that has evolved to 'network'. Our brains are adapted towards social interaction and groups. We, the co-operative ape, have distributed cognition and this has increased massively as technology has allowed us to network more widely. Technologies have been the primary catalysts for this networking. Nevertheless, much human behaviour has been tempered with chiefs, kings, lords, emperors and so on… hierarchical structures that lead and control. Even the web is now spun by hierarchical and rapacious spiders – the giant tech companies. Europe's failure is interesting here, as we have Apple, Google, Facebook, Amazon, Microsoft and Netflix in the US, and Baidu, Alibaba and TenCent in China. Europe merely regulates. These oligopolies dominate the networks.

## Social learning

Learning is a complex and subjective thing. The problem learning professionals face is that cognitive diagnosis – knowing what is going on in the minds of learners – is a problem. Teachers are mostly working blind. This results in some crude teaching methods and often a mismatch between teachers and learners. Many teachers bemoan the fact that their students don't ask questions or speak up in class. Academics complain about the lack of critical thinking and inquiry among their students in tutorials. But this is a teacher, not a learner, problem.

The old 'hands-up anyone' is the hand-me-down practice that typifies the nature of the problem. There are good reasons for getting rid of this practice. The people who put their hands up usually know the answer. Asking these learners to provide an answer does nothing to improve their learning – they know it already. The converse is that this technique destroys the confidence and self-esteem of those who are not sure or do not know the answer. It also excludes those who are introverts, as it is an invitation for extrovert behaviour.

It can also expose learners to ridicule; if the answer is way off-piste, it encourages peer-pressure, in the sense of exposing learners to their class colleagues. Worst of all, it conditions learners to see the learning process as one of providing correct answers to questions. It does *not* encourage students to *ask* the questions or engage in critical thinking themselves. If the practice of 'hands-up anyone...' is thought by teachers to command attention, it actually instils in learners the fear of being exposed – that is why most keep their heads down and do not put their hands up.

Another rationale is that this allows the teacher to do whole-class assessment, to know who knows and who does not know. First, it does not do this at all – many with their hands down are simply scared to answer. And if this is the reason, as we've seen above, it does more harm than good. This is not active, collaborative or constructivist learning. It is an insidious way to reinforce weak teaching and to get learners, not to think for themselves, but to fear authority.

You can see these problems also arise at large and expensive conferences, where participants are just too embarrassed to stand up and ask a question or engage in debate, so it is an extrovert-only environment.

In educational institutions and organizations, there is usually a tension between teaching and management hierarchies (the tower) and social networks (the square). In learning this manifests itself as formal versus informal learning, the LMS versus other forms of networked exchange of learning or even direct subversion.

We also have to recognize that social learning both helps and inhibits performance. Open networks often collapse into powerful tribes of belief and power. Social activity is messy, soaked in biases, and can be negative in output. Some of these tribes may be good and useful, where they generate innovation and get things done, but there are also the crippling effects of the mob and its tribes that generate and consolidate groupthink and false beliefs. Gangs form but gangs are not often good.

Social interaction is an important dimension in learning, yet we rarely really know what anyone else is thinking. What we mostly do is infer what they are thinking and feeling from language, spoken or written. This is why the Turing test has been seen as the litmus test for AI. It is felt that language, not faces, gestures or behaviour, is the window to the mind and that social intelligence and language is what really marks us out as human.

A solution to this dilemma is to interrogate networks, harvest the language data, objectify the process and analyse it to exclude mess and bias. One can also look for insights, innovations and valid ideas, to separate the social wheat from the chaff. AI can come to the rescue here.

## Sentiment analysis

Typical techniques we use to diagnose learners are through formative and summative assessments, but these are crude measurements and rarely tell us what problems learners have and what people actually feel about their learning journey. Rather than rely just on the visual identification of hands in the air or contributions in assessments and tutorials, we can add to our tools by looking at online social contributions.

One area of AI that has progressed rapidly is NLP. We can see this in search, translation, voice recognition and speech generation. None of these services comprehend language in the way we do. They are competent with-out actual comprehension, but competent to the level of being incredibly useful. NLP can also be used to analyse social data from which thoughts and opinions can be identified and summarized, giving us access to the social dimension of learners and learning. In fact, AI can help create a fairer, deeper and broader solution to this problem.

The AI technique that helps us do this is *sentiment analysis*.

Sentiment analysis measures subjective thoughts. It attempts to identify and bring to the surface internal thoughts and feelings, as expressed in online conversations. This is not easy, as the data is often unstructured and messy. Nevertheless, techniques exist to cope with this type of data and we can move beyond the simple identification of polar views, such as whether a learning experience is liked or disliked, towards deeper insights. The use of AI to identify insights in unstructured data is giving us richer identification and analysis.

One should note at the outset that simply identifying a learner's opinions may not be the end in itself. Research has shown that learners are often delusional in their judgements of learning strategies and may love things that do them little good and loathe those that are most efficient in learning. They can also be delusional about what they think they have learned.

Sentiment analysis can work on several levels. It can work on the sentence, paragraph, document or multi-document levels. This can be anything from the interpretation of whether there are discrete positive, neutral or negative ratings to measures on a continuous scale. Further analysis can get more fine-grained where we look at specific aspects within the text. This is not easy as, although God is in the detail, details can be misleading. To take an example, colloquial terms such as 'not bad' do not mean good or bad, but neutral! Colloquialisms such as these are a feature of language that sentiment analysis has to deal with.

Sentiment analysis is usually done on a binary rating of positive or negative, for example in categorizing learner feedback. Was the learner's feedback positive or negative? So we analyse any piece of text, let us say views of the course, conversations in social learning, questions asked and answers to questions, to identify positive, neutral or negative sentiment. This is useful and is often represented in RAG reports (Red = negative, Amber = neutral, and Green = positive). These could also be done on a continuous scale, let's say 1–10. Sentiment analysis in learners' responses and evaluations can typically identify categories such as anger, fear, joy, sadness and surprise. Joy and surprise could be taken as positive polarities. Anger, fear and sadness could be negative polarities.

Different flavours of sentiment analysis can be used in learning, depending on what sorts of insights you are after and data that is available. It is a strand of AI that is maturing quickly. Here are some of the current techniques used:

- *Aspect-based sentiment analysis* tries to identify aspects within the text, for example, learners having difficulty with a topic may say that the worked example was 'too complex for me'. The aspect is 'worked example' and the sentiment would show they have a negative polarity towards the 'worked example'.

- *Sentiment classification with user information* is similar to standard sentiment analysis. However, we are also given information on the user who has expressed thoughts on, for example, the course and information about the course. These two extra pieces of information are used in conjunction with sentiment analysis to give deeper insights.

- *Subjectivity analysis* is related to sentiment analysis and has the goal of distinguishing between subjective and objective opinions. This can be powerful in the context of learning, as we can start to draw a line between criticism and actual virtues and vices in a course.

Here is a real example. Let us say we have a dataset of learners' experiences from a MOOC. We are trying to mine all of this data to provide insights into what things in their learning experiences were good or bad. This can be broken down into three steps:

1 Identify sections of text related to *aspects* of the learners' experience, such as length, delivery times, levels and so on.

2 For each of these aspects we're looking for learners' opinions or *sentiments*; we want to look for positives and negatives, as neutral may be of little interest.

3 The information gleaned from steps 1 and 2 can be used to *summarize* and provide information on what aspects can be improved on the course.

Sentiment analysis is a relatively new tool and is already being used by organizations to identify and improve what they do. It is largely used in marketing and it may well be that your organization or institution is already using sentiment analysis to measure opinions and attitudes towards your brand and learning offers. Brands matter in education and learning. Some, like universities, have been around for centuries, but in this day and age they are more fragile and susceptible to pressures that mean their brands and reputations can rise or wane.

Sentiment analysis has more precise applications in learning. Learners are notoriously silent about their learning. Many suffer in silence, or the louder voices win out. Listening to what learners actually say by examining their actual voices while engaging in the learning process can give us bigger sets of data in a more natural setting, where people are far more likely to express opinions and thoughts than in a face-to-face social group or on happy sheets and questionnaires.

They could be views about levels of difficulty, lack or presence of engagement, lack or presence of learner support, views of assessments, finding the learning difficult, complaints, suggestions, expressions of personal failure, even psychological problems.

This is not to say that sentiment analysis is flawless. There will still be a skew in those who choose to express themselves in online forums or social media. This can be much fewer than many imagine and may represent a skewed sample of your audience. There is also the problem that people tend to only go to a forum or message board if they have a polarized view, good or bad. People rarely express neutral views. This is why sentiment analysis should be used in conjunction with other tools and sources. Nevertheless, it is still a valuable vein to mine.

Another problem these techniques face is noise. Much communication may be full of irrelevant spam, idle chat and other irrelevant noise, so it has to be cleaned and filtered. Sentiment analysis is essentially a statistical method that attempts to get to unadulterated opinions, even objectivity. It tries to get to the unalloyed truth, avoiding the weaknesses of traditional instruments such as happy sheets or surveys, which have many statistical and practical problems.

It is important to be clear about what you want to find out here. What are your primary problems? Dropout? Low attainment? Teaching quality? Well-being? Deeper, meaningful insights may also be things you have not thought of. We don't know what we don't know.

## Digging deeper

One danger in analysis is small samples, the Law of Small Numbers, and intrinsic bias. People lie, but in large data sets lies the truth. In *Everybody Lies: Big data, new data, and what the internet can tell us about who we really are*, Seth Stephens-Davidowitz (2017) shows how data from online sources such as Google searches, Facebook, Twitter, Amazon and even pornography sites can give us unique insights into what people actually think and do, rather than what they tell us they think. These large data sets can be full of surprises, some counterintuitive.

Google Trends uses AI to uncover word and phrase frequency across time. It shows the relative frequency but can be supplemented by other anonymous data sources, such as Google AdWords, to uncover the trace lines of our views and opinions.

If we are to do sentiment analysis, it must be for some purpose. Descriptive sentiment data can be used to tell us *what* people are thinking. This can tell us what individuals or groups are saying about the organization, institution, teaching or course. It may also describe difficulties, problems and frustrations, things that could be done better. This can be made available through dashboards. Analysis of sentiment data can ask *why* things are happening and identify insights that may be known but need confirmation or uncover insights that are unknown. Correlations with other data such as absenteeism, socio-economic groups, being taught in a second language and so on may also help improve student retention and learning outcomes. Predictive data analysis with sentiment analysis can predict whether students are likely to drop out or fail. This can allow formal interventions to prevent such failure. Prescriptive data analysis with sentiment analysis can be used to mandate or prescribe action, contributing to the sequence of learning events presented to learners individually in real time. One can see that moving forward through these levels is progressively more difficult and dangerous.

We should also recognize that such AI software can be used for surveillance. There are genuine concerns about surveillance software in schools. Such software has been driven by worries about inappropriate internet content, worries over mental health and radicalization. The problem comes when that technology is being used as an extension of the surveillance society, described by Shoshana Zuboff in *The Age of Surveillance Capitalism* (2019). It is technology used to police other technology.

Monitoring screens for activity around learning and the results of that learning seems sensible, as is monitoring to prevent access to inappropriate material like porn, but the use of sentiment analysis to constantly snoop on thinking is another thing entirely. The problem is more severe in the US, fuelled by the fear of school shootings. One can see the sense in monitoring official school, college, university and workplace email and social systems for signs of bullying, self-harm, mental health and plans for a school shooting. Problems arise when such software is placed on private devices to monitor private communications. Schools are stuck on the horns of a dilemma here.

They have legal responsibilities to care for young people, but how far that extends is open to debate. It is a fine line between monitoring and snooping, and we should have some concerns in terms of privacy.

## Conclusion

Most teachers, trainers and lecturers would like to know what their learners think, either of their teaching performance or what they actually teach. It is especially important for those who teach to know whether the content is appropriate and that learners are not confused and finding things so difficult that they are likely to fail. Feedback can also be used to improve design and delivery. Sentiment analysis can uncover boredom, difficulty, frustration, anxiety, and even bullying, self-harm and mental health problems. It allows us to get into the minds of students using their honest expressions, but the degree to which we should be allowed to get into the minds of students is a moral issue that needs careful consideration.

## References

Ferguson, N (2019) *The Square and the Tower: Networks and power, from the freemasons to Facebook*, Penguin Books, London

Stephens-Davidowitz, S (2017) *Everybody Lies: Big data, new data, and what the internet can tell us about who we really are*, HarperCollins, New York

Stodd, J (2014) *The Social Leadership Handbook*, Sea Salt Publishing, UK

Zuboff, S (2019) *The Age of Surveillance Capitalism: The fight for a human future at the new frontier of power*, Profile Books, London

## PART SIX

# Future

# 16

# Future skills

AI is the single most important shift in technology in our age, as it changes why, what and how we learn. It will, inevitably, have a huge impact on the knowledge and skills needed by those involved in online learning design, technology and procurement.

Organizations struggling to find talent now look towards developing a strong learning and development culture to keep competitive. As employees start to work alongside AI and automation in a hybrid fashion, the World Economic Forum (2018) estimates that each employee will need 101 days of learning by 2022.

AI will also reshape the nature of work. McKinsey Global Institute estimates that 30 per cent of activities across 60 per cent of occupations are likely to be automated over the next decade (Manyika and Sneader, 2018). This is why it is essential for HR and L&D to open their eyes to the nature of AI, its place at the heart of business growth and its place in learning. Those in the learning world need to be more tech-savvy around AI in general and AI for learning in particular.

This means smarter procurement from companies that can deliver technology that is smarter than the old flat, rather inert, technology. Most find themselves with old LMS technology that is data light, so they have a paucity of data or data that does little more than record activity. This, coupled with low internal skills around data analytics, means that little progress is made.

AI for learning also brings learning professionals up to speed with the rest of the organization. You become more credible by being faster, more responsive and data-led. There is little doubt that most organizations are using AI in many different contexts. The organization's needs will also be better met by educators and L&D being faster, cheaper and better through AI.

This brings us to the skills we need to handle a future where AI is used for learning. Most interactive designers are skilled people, sensitive to the needs of learners, but we must always be willing to 'learn', for that is our vocation. New skills and techniques come into their own with AI for learning. We will see a shift in skills and therefore also a shift in the nature of teams, methods, procurement and production. They will also have to shift towards personalization, adaptivity, chatbots, dialogue, voice, open input and curation. Teams will have to become more technology-savvy, as AI is more complex and varied in what it can deliver than traditional software techniques. Methods of production will become more agile as fast iterations with tight timescales emerge. Finally, procurement in terms of outsourcing/insourcing will have to cope with a very different set of needs and requirements.

AI will change, relentlessly, the traditional skills that have been in play for decades. The old, core skillset that included writing, interactive design, media production and assessment will have to adapt and add newer skills associated with smarter software that delivers more adaptive and personalized software, using technology that is far more powerful and complex.

## AI and learning design

Online learning companies now see a shift towards AI services and products and are having to identify individuals with the skills and attitudes to deal with this new demand. This means understanding the new technology (not trivial), learning how to write for chatbots and dealing more with AI-aided design and curation, rather than doing this for themselves.

In another context, using AI tools and services means not using, or at least supplementing, the skills of traditional interactive designers, as the software either does some of this job or changes it dramatically. For example, we have seen how AI can identify the learning points, automatically create the interactions, find the curated links and assess using free-text input, formatively and summatively. It can create content in minutes, not months. This is the way online learning is going.

The gear shift in skills is already here and accelerating. Although still uncertain, Table 16.1 shows some suggestions based on the concrete experience of making and observing this shift in real online learning production companies.

Taking these one by one, we can see that a greater awareness of the technology is needed and with this comes the need for a greater understanding

TABLE 16.1  New skills for learning design

| Old | New |
| --- | --- |
| One size fits all | Personalization |
| Learning techniques | Learning science |
| Media production | Chatbots |
| Monologue | Dialogue |
| Typing | Voice |
| Multiple choice | Open input |
| Linear | Complex |
| Branching | AI/adaptive |
| Content | Curation |
| Communications | Communicate expectations |
| Creation | Automation |

of cognitive psychology, as the technology has to deliver what could be described as cognitive ergonomics. To deal with this different type of smart, learning technology, which itself learns, you need to be aware of both the technical and cognitive ergonomics of the different areas of AI. AI needs to capture pedagogy if it is to work well.

*Personalization.* Most online learning has no or limited personalization, unlike most search, social media, Amazon or Netflix; it does not respond much to your own learning needs, apart from simple remediation or rule-based branching. AI changes this dramatically. Learning experiences will be delivered to individuals based on complex algorithms in real time, especially in adaptive learning. Personalized chatbots may also have to be considered. In sophisticated adaptive learning companies, this software is complex and the sequencing has to be handled by software, not designers – that's what makes personalization on scale possible. This loss of fixed delivery means that one's mindset has to be around systems that deliver recommended options and content adaptively based on data and algorithmic identification of need, often in real time. The process of personalization must be understood.

*Learning science.* As AI requires pedagogic design to guide its execution, this must capture and deliver sound pedagogy. We have already seen an increase in AI and algorithmic design to deliver good cognitive-science-based pedagogy, such as retrieval, interleaving, spaced practice and personalization. As one must build in these techniques and use data to train and determine sequencing of content, a knowledge of cognitive science will be necessary. Few interactive designers can name many researchers or identify key pieces of research on, say, the optimal number of options in an MCQ (3), retrieval practice, length of video, effects of redundancy, spaced-practice theory, even the rudiments of how memory works (episodic versus semantic). This is elementary stuff, but it is rarely taken seriously. With the implementation of AI, the AI has to embody good pedagogic practice. This is interesting, as we can build good, well-researched learning practice into the software, such as effortful learning, open input, retrieval and spaced practice. To build in pedagogy, one has to know that pedagogy in the first place.

*Chatbots.* As online learning became trapped in 'media production', most of the effort and budget went into the production of graphics (often illustrative and not meaningfully instructive), animation (often overworked) and video (not enough in itself). Media-rich is not necessarily mind-rich, and the research from Reeves and Nass (1996) shows that the excessive use of media can inhibit learning. Unfortunately, much of this research is ignored. We will see this change as the balance shifts towards effortful and more efficient learning. There will still be the need for good media production, but it will lessen as AI can produce text from audio, create text and dialogue. Chatbots are complex and require thinking beyond the linear narratives and storytelling of traditional online learning. With chatbots, where we've been designing everything from invisible LMS bots to tutorbots, the whole form of interaction changes and you need to see how they fit into workflow through existing collaborative tools such as Slack or Microsoft Teams.

With chatbots, for example, it is all too easy to set too high an expectation on performance. You will need to know where these lines are in terms of what you have to do as a chatbot designer and writer. What are the limitations of the natural language interface? What scope can be delivered given the limitations of the 'training' of the model? What does one do if it cannot answer?

*Dialogue.* Writing dialogue requires very specific skills. Most existing online content is monologue or straight description or narration. Chatbots need dialogue writers, who understand the vagaries of conversation and sequencing of questions within a complex, branching structure. To write for chatbots one must really know what the technology can and cannot do, and also write natural dialogue (actually a rare skill). That's why the US tech giants hire screenwriters for these tasks.

*Voice.* There is also voice interaction to consider. There will be entire learning experiences where all navigation and interaction is voice-driven.

This needs some extra skills in terms of managing expectations and dealing with the vagaries of speech-recognition software.

*Open input.* We are likely to see a reduction in the formulaic multiple-choice question (MCQ) production. MCQs are difficult to write and often flawed (Clark, 2017). Then there's the often vicariously used 'drag and drop' and hideously patronizing, 'Let's see what Philip, Alisha and Sue think of this...'. You click on a face and get a speech bubble of text. This will be an area of huge change as the limited forms of MCQ start to be replaced by open input – of words, numbers and short text answers. NLP also allows us to interpret this open-input text. Writing assessment items may change dramatically once one is freed from the constraints of MCQs.

*Complex.* With AI, what you see is not what you get. When you use Google or other AI-mediated services online, most of the mechanics are invisible but bring a massive amount of real-time analysis and decision-making to bear at that single moment of need. The complexity of this invisible process has to be understood.

*AI/adaptive.* Rather than seeing branching, or even gamification or other exiting entertainment genres, as the solution to successful learning, adaptive learning will come to the fore, where the software, rather than the designer, decides what is sequenced for the learner. This will be done in real time on the basis of individual or aggregated data, to optimize learning for individuals. The aim is to educate everyone uniquely. This means understanding the nature of the adaptivity and designing content loose enough to be re-sequenced on scale.

*Curation.* Curation strategies are also important. We often produce content that is already there, but AI helps automatically link to content or provides tools for curating content. Curation, aided by AI, may mean more autonomous searches for content in a changing online environment. In other words, curation may not be the curation of fixed options but for ongoing crawled content.

*Communicate expectations.* Communications with the client and SMEs on AI can be difficult. Some of the output is AI-generated, and as AI is not remotely human (not conscious or cognitive), it can produce mistakes. You learn to deal with this when you work in this field – overfitting, false positives and so on. But this is often not easy for clients to understand, as they will be used to design document, scripts and traditional QA techniques. We had AI once automatically produce a link for the word 'blow', a technique nurses ask of young patients when they're using sharps or needles. The AI linked to the Wikipedia page for 'blow' – which was cocaine – easily remedied but worrying!

*Automation.* AI is here. We are, at last, emerging from a 30-year paradigm of media production and multiple-choice questions, in largely flat and linear learning experiences, towards agile, smart, intelligent online learning. AI solutions often behave more like a good teacher, where you are taught as an individual with a personalized experience, challenged and – rather than endlessly choosing from lists – engaged in effortful learning, using dialogue, even voice. As a learning designer, learning experience designer, learning engineer, interactive designer, project manager, graphic artist, video producer, whatever the title, you will have to adapt to a world where some of the tasks completed by learning designers will be automated.

AI can reduce iterations with SMEs, the cause of much of the high cost of online learning. If the AI is identifying learning points and curated content, using already approved documents, PowerPoints and videos, the need for SME input is lessened. As AI tools produce content very quickly, the clients and SME can test and approve the actual content, not from scripts but in the form of the learning experience itself. This saves a ton of time. What is needed is a change in mindset, as well as tools and skills. It may be difficult to adapt to this new AI world, where many aspects of design will be automated.

## AI and technology design

Technical understanding will, of course, be different and more demanding. AI-created content is very different and has a sort of 'life of its own', especially when it uses machine learning. At the very least get to know what the major areas of AI are, how they work and feel comfortable with the vocabulary.

This is not to say that you need to be able to code or have highly technical AI or data science skills. It does mean that you will have to know, in detail, how the software works. If it uses specific AI techniques, one will have to make the effort to understand the approach, especially its weaknesses and strengths (see Table 16.2).

*Integrated team.* Communications between designers and AI developers and data scientists is a challenge. Designers know a lot about communications, learning and goals, but are often unfamiliar with this new technology. Technologists know a lot about the software but often little about learning and the goals. There is a need for a much closer understanding of each other's worlds and the onus is on both to accept that this needs close teamwork.

TABLE 16.2 New skills for technology design

| Old | New |
| --- | --- |
| Silos of skills | Integrated team |
| Learning system | Learning ecosystem |
| Fixed delivery | Dynamic delivery |
| Fixed text | Natural language processing |
| Fixed content | Machine learning |

*Learning ecosystems.* Learning ecosystems bring with them levels of complexity way beyond the traditional LMS. They get more complex as the front-end user-experience layer becomes more dynamic and personalized. The content layer also becomes more complex, with LXPs that work with LRSs operating through xAPI, along with multiple content sources, social learning capability, curation, secure data transfer and storage. This may all need to be understood along with integration into existing HR or talent management systems, even offline course delivery and external education establishments. Finally, the data and analytics layer that takes data from all of these sources needs to be fed back into personalized dashboards, adaptive learning or chatbots, some of which may use machine learning.

Interactive or experience designers, whatever they are called now or in the future, will need to know far more about what the software does, its functionality, strengths and weaknesses, than they did in the past. A knowledge of how the actual AI techniques work and are applied, such as NLP, machine learning, adaptive learning and data analytics, will be a necessary skill to match the technology with the pedagogic aims across more complex ecosystems. Those with some technical understanding will fare better here as they can understand both the potential and limitations of AI for learning.

*Dynamic delivery.* With traditional online learning, the software largely delivers static pages with no real adaptability, optimization or self-learning. Content and services will no longer be served up as static, fixed pages, but in forms of dynamic delivery. It can change in real time to the needs of learners, delivering different screens and elements to different learners depending on their needs at that particular time. It can also change across time, improving as more learners use the system and aggregated data is used to improve the performance of the overall software. The software is, in a sense, a growing, learning entity that changes over time. One must understand that this requires a different approach to design, documentation and testing. The designed entity is no longer a fixed script with linear and simply branched events, but a complex system based on data and probabilities. Testing, for example, requires a deep understanding of the inputs and outputs.

*Natural language processing.* Text remains the core medium in online learning. It remains the core medium in online activity generally. We have seen the pendulum swing towards video, graphics and audio, but text will remain a strong medium, as we read faster than we listen, and it is editable and searchable. That's why much social media and messaging is still text at heart. Literacy tests have been used for interactive designers before they started, no matter what qualifications they had. It proved to be a good predictor, as writing is not just about turn of phrase and style; it is really about communications, purpose, order, logic and structure. However, the sort of writing one has to do in the new world of AI has more to do with being sensitive to what NLP does and dialogue. For example, systems may automatically produce audio using text to speech, and that needs to be written in a certain way. Beyond this, coping with synonyms, lemming and the vagaries of natural language processing needs an understanding of all sorts of NLP software techniques.

*Machine learning.* Algorithmic delivery, especially machine learning, can be complex, even opaque. It is useful to become familiar with the basics of neural networks and other forms of machine learning and the way they interact with data. There are already learning systems that use machine learning in chatbots, recommendation engines and social intelligence, and there will be many future applications. It is important to understand how these work, as these learning systems, in a sense, have some autonomy going off into the future.

## AI and data design

As learning ecosystems deliver smarter, multiple, integrated solutions, data can be pulled together to measure, improve, feed and recommend better learning. Just as a car benefits from data that is fed from sensors to computers to improve the performance of your car, either directly or indirectly to you as the driver, so data will be used directly or indirectly in dynamic

TABLE 16.3  New skills for data design

| Old | New |
| --- | --- |
| Scores and completion | Data analytics |
| Social activity | Social analysis |
| SCORM | xAPI |
| Learning | Learning record stores |
| Testing | A/B testing |

learning systems. In general, we will see a shift towards more data analysis and the use of data within systems as well as the reporting data. An understanding of the differences in data types and what can be done with learning analytics is essential, as this lies at the heart of many AI techniques in learning (see Table 16.3).

*Data analytics.* Data in itself is a complex subject, with data preparation and cleansing being important, along with training data sets, quite separate from the data used in the delivered product. Learning analytics will also become more complex, as this lies at the heart of LXPs which use LRSs. You will have to know what data you want to gather and for what purposes.

First, one may require data from HR and similar systems to identify learners and their profiles. Activity data then has to be harvested from all online and offline activities. The visualization of completion and other performance data needs to be available. There's also the data needed for recommendation engines or adaptive learning.

SCORM looks increasingly like a crippling limit on online learning, incompatible with AI in learning. Completion is useful, but rarely enough. It is important to supplement SCORM with far more detailed data on user behaviours. But even when data is plentiful, it needs to be turned into information, visualized to make it useful. That is one set of skills that is useful – knowing how to visualize data. Information then has to be turned into knowledge and insights. This is where skills are often lacking. First you have to know the many different types of data in learning, how data sets are cleaned, then the techniques used to extract useful insights, often machine learning. You need to distinguish between data as the new oil and data as the new snake oil.

We take data, clean it, process it, then look for insights – clusters and other statistically significant techniques to find patterns and correlations. For example, do course completions correlate with an increase in sales in those retail outlets that complete the training? Training can then be seen as part of a business process where AI not only creates the learning but does the analysis – and that is all in a virtual and virtuous loop that informs and improves the business. It is not that you require deep data scientist skills, but you need to become aware of the possibilities of data production, the danger of GIGO and the techniques used in this area.

*Social analysis.* Rather than just provide social systems that supplement learning experiences with social learning experiences, social activity will be subject to detailed analysis. This may be semantic analysis of topic the being discussed, but also opinion and sentiment analysis to determine views on specific topics. We can expect to see social data as something that can be usefully mined and analysed, using AI, to provide useful insights for both teachers and learners. Familiarizing yourself with these techniques will be essential.

*xAPI.* As SCORM recedes and new standards, such as xAPI, allow learning ecosystems to take advantage of systems other than the LMS, the learning designer will have to become more aware of the dynamics of integrated systems and the data that needs to be gathered from these different sources. Once you use an ecosystem which deals with multiple suppliers, and you have to deal with secure authenticated inbound and outbound web services (APIs) with secure data transfer methods, encryption of data, preferably via web services (API) over HTTPS (CSV via SFTP as a minimum) and therefore xAPI, there has to be a way of coping with this complexity in all three layers of the system – learning experience, content and data. An LRS, like Learning Locker, will natively collect xAPI data from a variety of sources. It can also gather other non-xAPI-compliant sources of data by changing non-xAPI data streams into the xAPI format by acting as a single source of data for the ecosystem. Integration with other business data systems and tools is possible and desirable.

*Learning record stores.* To analyse the many different sources of data, xAPI compliance ensures that all data can be stored in an LRS and used to inform business decision-making. xAPI statement data can be used now or later to fuel recommendations, adaptive learning systems, nudge learning and other targeted initiatives. It can also feed different dashboards – for learners, teachers, trainers and lecturers, or at the departmental level.

## AI as agile production

We have seen how the promise of AI to increase productivity and produce new forms of pedagogy in online learning is real. We have also seen how the skillset will change, as AI enters the world of learning. This brings us to the idea that AI can act as a catalyst for *agile* content production.

The TUI example was a ground-breaking project, delivered without a single face-to-face meeting (Clark, 2018a). It shows what can be achieved when a training department is innovative and brave. We must get past the model that says it takes months to produce content at prohibitive costs. Agile production needs agile tools, agile production methods and, above all, agility of thought and mindset. Organizations have traditionally moved much faster than training delivery. That means we're often out of phase with the business. An agile mindset and production attitude allows us to transcend that historical gap. Once we become responsive to the business, they will respect us more as we become more aligned with the actual speed of the business.

In the TUI project, as the tool did most of the design and build, using AI techniques, an agile approach to production and project management was intrinsic. No instructional design scripts were necessary, as the software built the content so quickly that quality assurance could be done on the actual modules. Despite there being no interactive 'designer', 95 per cent rated the design and approach as good or very good and 62 per cent confirmed they could identify a specific sale based on knowledge gained. Their knowledge of the countries, locations, attractions, currencies, airport codes, and so on, was reported time and time again by front-line staff as having helped them sell holidays and flights. Remember – this is a location-driven business. If you want to sell holidays and cruises, you have to know the destinations and attractions.

This next example shows how far one can push the agile approach to production.

So you walk into a hotel, you're in the queue, and it is taking ages to check in. Or at breakfast, there's no milk on the table... it's all those little things that matter in the hospitality trade. In the age of TripAdvisor, it matters. A hotel chain took this seriously by training their staff to a set of defined, exacting standards.

This meant agile training using content produced by AI – relentless attention to training and the behaviour of customer-facing staff. By agile we mean the use of AI to create training quickly – training that really does deliver high-retention training to front-line staff on any device. WildFire, the AI online content creation tool, quickly turned a set of 209 standards into 6 online learning modules on general standards, front office, breakfast, restaurant, bar and room service. Each module focused on essential knowledge – what staff needed to know to do their jobs well (Clark, 2018b).

An essential ingredient in this project was an agile project manager. In both the projects outlined, there wasn't a single face-to-face meeting. It was all quick decisions, problems solved on the spot and process change to get things done. The project managers never saw problems, only issues to be solved – quickly.

It was made easier by the fact that AI was used to produce content in minutes, not months. That meant the quality control was on real content, not paper documents. And as approved documents, PowerPoints and videos were used, there was no real need for intensive subject matter expert input, which is the main brake on agile production.

AI is now being used to create content and add curated resources at the click of a button. Want an audio podcast or audio introduction to the course? It takes seconds using AI to do text to speech. The time savings are enormous, as well as cost savings. AI is used not only to identify learning points; it also creates audio, constructs the questions, recognizes speech input, assesses open input (words or full short answer) and locates links to external resources for further learning.

One important lesson in being agile is the 'garbage in, garbage out' rule. When you use an agile production process, you need agile preparation. An intensive look at the input material pays dividends. Eliminate all of that extraneous material and text, cut until it bleeds and cut again, catch those pesky spelling and punctuation errors, make sure things are consistent. The source material needs to be edited down to the essential 'need to know' content.

The six modules in the hotel chain course were created in a day, as the AI created the content by identifying the relevant learning points and automatically creating the learning experiences. The look and feel, logo, images and palette numbers for screen features were quickly agreed. This superfast production process meant that quality assurance could be done on the real modules, without the need for design documents and scripts. There was no need for multiple iterations by SMEs, as the original document contained all the necessary knowledge. Everything from brief to final delivery was done through Skype. Not a single face-to-face meeting was necessary.

Every module has an AI-generated audio introduction (text to speech) that explains what you have to do – and tells you to relax about getting things wrong, as it is fine to make mistakes while learning. Staff then read the standards and, rather than click on multiple-choice questions, have to bring to mind and 'type in' the behavioural standards. This 'effortful' learning was again justified by the recent research in learning that shows recall, with open input, is superior for retention when compared with simply recognizing answers from a list.

Agile is as much a state of mind as process. Yet learning and development still works to an old model of months, not minutes. We procure slowly, prepare slowly, produce slowly and deliver slowly. Despite relentless calls to align with the business and respond to business needs, we are too slow. L&D needs things in days, yet we deliver in months. This is what needs to change.

In response, online learning has traditionally been rather slow in design and production, but we can now use AI to create content quickly, to produce agile learning and data that allows us to adapt to new circumstances. 'Agile' captures, in a word, what is now necessary. The days of seeing online learning production as some sort of feature film project with matching budgets and timescales – months – should be re-examined. Of course, some high-end content may need this approach, but much can be automated and done at a fraction of the cost, in a fraction of the time.

You will find that the quality assurance process is very different, with quick access to the actual content, allowing for immediate testing. In fact, AI tends to produce fewer mistakes in my experience, as there is less human input – always a source of spelling, punctuation and other errors. The advantage of using AI-generated content is that all sides can share produced content to solve residual problems on the actual content, as seen by the learner.

## AI and procurement

One major issue that arises as a result of all of the above is your organization's position and skills on procurement. There are many options here depending on your ambition, direction of travel and resources.

The main choices are:

- in-house development;
- learning technology companies;
- large tech companies.

## In-house

In-house development has the advantage of keeping control with costs low and predictable. However, it is clear that AI talent and skills are not easy to find and are expensive. You may want to build things in-house, but the task can be daunting. There is a strong argument for prototyping or piloting some AI for learning projects, but many (not all), for the foreseeable future, are likely to be outsourced.

## Learning technology companies

Some learning technology companies have made the leap into AI for learning. They are sensitive to the learning game and have people who understand that this is about learning and who have experience with technical integration. The advantage of using this type of company is that they have a balanced approach to learning and technology. The downside may be lock-in to a supplier, their lack of breadth and depth, and costs. If, however, you choose a system that is sensitive to xAPI and can draw upon a variety of services from different sources, AI may actually free you from the single supplier trap.

## Large tech companies

Large tech and outsourcing companies will emerge in this area. They have the advantage of breadth and depth, with good support, but tend to be one-size-fits-all, expensive and insensitive to your learning culture and needs. Tech giants like Google, IBM, Microsoft and Amazon already offer a mixture of open source tools and metered usage services for AI applications. Your IT department may already be aligned with one of these companies, and this AI-on-tap approach has some appeal as they provide well-tested and trained models. However, they don't do well in handling learning issues, detailed integration and service. They also have a habit of changing their generic services, sometimes with little or no warning.

This is not an easy landscape to navigate. As a technology transition, like no other, it not only delivers; it delivers in a way that changes what humans do, augmenting our ability to personalize, deliver the right stuff at the right time in the right place and also make delivery more responsive. AI for learning learns alongside your learners. The more it is used, the better it gets. In general, data lies at the heart of the process. Skills in procurement, contracts, pricing and support needs will be essential in this more complex world.

# Conclusion

The shifts outlined here are not trivial; they are challenging. Yet we know that the AI revolution is here. It is everywhere in almost all online services, from Google to Netflix. It will also be a key technology in learning.

New skills have always been required as technology changes. These have, largely, been front-end skills around presentation, look and feel, limited interactions and media. But AI is more to do with back-end technology, where the software itself does much of the work. This does not negate front-end skills but adds to them.

In that sense it is more technically demanding but also exciting in that one can do so much more in terms of learning. This means shifts in skills on design technology and data. Beyond this lies a shift in mindset towards smarter systems with more autonomy and a greater awareness of the issues around procurement.

# References

Clark, D (2017) 7 reasons to abandon multiple-choice questions, Donald Clark Plan B, 1 November. Available at https://donaldclarkplanb.blogspot.com/search?q=7+reasons+to+abandon+multiple-choice+questions (archived at https://perma.cc/4DJH-YB9Q)

Clark, D (2018a) Wildfire wins 'Best Learning Technologies Project'. Available at http://www.wildfirelearning.co.uk/wildfire-wins-best-learning-technologies-project/ (archived at https://perma.cc/RT9F-Z264)

Clark, D (2018b), Agile training at Jurys Inn – used AI to produce in minutes not months, Donald Clark Plan B. Available at http://donaldclarkplanb.blogspot.com/2018/10/agile-training-at-jurys-inn-in-minutes.html (archived at https://perma.cc/6UMN-NF7S)

Manyika, J and Sneader, K (2018) *AI, Automation and the Future of Work: Ten things to solve for*, McKinsey Global Institute, New York

Reeves, B and Nass, CI (1996) *The Media Equation: How people treat computers, television, and new media like real people and places*, Cambridge University Press, Cambridge

World Economic Forum (2018) *The Future of Jobs Report 2018*, World Economic Forum, Geneva

# 17

# Ethics and bias

No other area of technology than AI has been subjected to so much ethical scrutiny by so many hastily convened 'committees'. For some in the learning game, the mere mention of the words 'artificial intelligence' induces irrational fears about bias, surveillance and privacy. They want to keep it out at all costs. For others, it is the saviour that will accelerate the longed-for personalized learning, eliminate the harmful effects of human bias and make learning much more open, efficient, personal and productive. As usual, the truth lies somewhere in between.

The confusion is caused by not really understanding the full range of AI used in learning. But there are also a number of general dangers that lurk in the world of AI and algorithms, so it is important that the debate is open and that we do not close down opportunities by being naive about what AI is, how it works and what it can and cannot do for us.

The proliferation of literally hundreds of AI ethics working groups, panels, councils and boards is largely overkill, largely noise. The danger is that the noise crowds out, even halts, actual innovation in learning. What matters are the top-end, trusted organizations with the expertise and influence, such as the Institute of Electrical and Electronics Engineers, Association for the Advancement of Artificial Intelligence, and Partnership for AI, which include the majority of the tech giants. Government bodies, such as the EU's High Level Expert Group, are also important. One hopes that they will see AI technology realistically, as being a force for both good and bad, and that the good will triumph if we use it for learning. This not an 'us' versus 'them' issue; it will need all of us to be positive but vigilant.

An immediate problem is that 'artificial' intelligence sounds a little pejorative. 'Artificial' suggests something not real, in direct opposition to what is real. It suggests something unnatural, a mere imitation. This pejoration almost debases the concept and lies behind many of the dystopian attitudes many have towards AI. Rather like artificial grass or artificial limbs, AI successes, no matter how astonishing in learning, feel as though they are second-rate and inferior.

An even stronger pejorative suggestion is the idea that AI is fake or counterfeit, the 'artificial' as something feigned or bogus. As the word explicitly compares the abilities of mind and machine, brains and computers, anthropomorphic judgements tend to sneak in. It defines the field as simply copying what humans or human brains do, whereas in practice AI tends to do things that are very different. The human brain may not be the benchmark here. Humans may not be the measurement of the machine.

## Brains and AI

When AI is mentioned, it is often only a matter of time before the word 'bias' is heard. They seem to go hand in hand, like ping and pong, especially in debates around AI in education. Yet the discussions are often quite shallow in terms of understanding what AI is, with a heavy dose of anthropomorphism. There is often little analysis behind the claims that AI programmers are largely white males – patriarchal and racist – or the commonly uttered phrase that all algorithms are biased. In practice, you see the same few examples being brought up time and time again: racist face recognition, recruitment and reoffender software. Most examples have their origin in contrarian texts such as *Algorithms of Oppression* by Safiya Umoja Noble (2018) or Cathy O'Neil's *Weapons of Math Destruction* (2016). More of this later.

To be fair, AI is, for most, an invisible force, that part of the iceberg that lies below the surface. AI is many things, can be opaque technically and true causality can be difficult to trace. But it may be wise to start with the baseline against which AI can be compared – our own brain.

First, let us examine the baseline – us humans. It is true that *all* brains are biased, as shown by Nobel Prize-winning psychologist Daniel Kahneman (2011) and his colleague Amos Tversky, who exposed a whole pantheon of biases that we are largely born with and that are difficult to shift, even through education and training.

Teaching is soaked in bias. There is socio-economic bias in policy, as it is often made by those who favour a certain type of education. Education can be bought privately, introducing inequalities. Gender, race and socio-economic bias is often found in the act of teaching itself. We know that gender bias is present in subtly directing girls away from STEM subjects and we know that children from lower socio-economic groups are treated differently. Even so-called objective assessment is biased, often influenced by all sorts of cognitive factors – content bias, context bias, marking bias and so on.

The tragedy of teaching is that our cognitive apparatus, especially our brain, has evolved for purposes different from its modern needs. Evolved brains are impressive but they are stuck in our skulls and limited in size, as women would not be able to give birth if they were bigger. There are also evolutionary limits in terms of what can be supported on the top of our bodies along with heat and energy requirements. This makes things very difficult for teachers and trainers. Our role as teachers is to improve the performance of that one organ and effect lasting change in the long-term memory of the brain, yet it remains stubbornly resistant to learning.

It takes around 16 years of intensive *nurturing* and *parenting* to turn brains into adults who can function autonomously. Years of parenting are at times fraught with conflict – the teenage brain, as brilliantly observed by Judith Harris (2011), is obsessed with peer groups. This nurturing needs to be supplemented by around 13 years of sitting in classrooms being taught by other brains – a process that is painful for all involved – pupils, parents and teachers. Increasingly, this is followed by several years, getting longer, in college or university, to prepare the brain for an increasingly complex world.

You do not have to be a teacher or parent for long to realize how *inattentive* and easily distracted brains can be. Attention is a necessary condition for learning, yet they are easily distracted. You are also doomed to *forget* almost everything written in this book, as our memories are not only limited by the narrow channel that is working memory but the massive failure to shunt what we learn from working to long-term memory. And even when memories get into long-term memory, they are subject to further forgetting, even reconfiguration into false memories. Every recalled memory is an act of recreation and reconstitution, and therefore fallible. Without reinforcement, we retain and recall very little. This makes brains very difficult to teach.

Our brains *sleep* eight hours a day – that is a third of life gone, down the drain. Cut back on this and we learn less, get more stressed, even ill. Keep the brain awake, as torturers will attest, and you will drive it to madness. Even when awake, it is prone to daydreaming. This is not an organ that takes easily to being on task.

Technically, brains cannot *upload* and *download*. You cannot pass your knowledge and skills to me without a huge amount of motivated and mediated teaching and learning. AI can do this in an instant. Brains can't *network* and our attempts at collective learning are still clumsy, yet collective learning and intelligence is a feature of modern AI.

As it ages the brain's performance falls and problems such as dementia and Alzheimer's occur. This degeneration varies in speed and is unpredictable. And in the end, that single, fatal objection – it *dies*. Death is a problem, as the brain cannot download its inherent and acquired knowledge or skills before death. Memories literally disappear. The way we deal with this is through technology that archives such acquired experience in technical media, such as print, images and now data.

Brains, for all of the reasons above, just do not scale. Limited though online teaching and learning seems, it does scale. It scales as it frees us from the tyranny of time and location. Now that AI, smart software, is enabling and driving online teaching and learning, we can see that AI can scale, not in a linear but in an exponential fashion, as it holds the promise of self-improvement. It learns to get better.

Harari in *Homo Deus* (2016) proposes an argument that eliminates the artificiality of AI. *Homo sapiens* is, like all other living beings, an evolved entity, shaped by natural selection, which is profoundly algorithmic. These algorithms exist separately from the substrate in which they reside. $2 + 2 = 4$ is the same, whether it is calculated in our brain, on wooden blocks, the plastic beads of an abacus or the metal circuits of a calculator. It does not matter that algorithms reside in one form or another. We should conclude that there is no reason to suppose that our organic abilities will not be replicated, even in many cases surpassed. In other words, algorithmic power resides in the power of the maths to solve problems and come up with solutions, not how accurately they mimic human abilities.

An even stronger argument is that there is every reason to suppose that other substrates will be better. The brain has evolved for an environment that it no longer operates in. It has severe limitations, suited to survival in a place and time with very different needs.

## Human bias and AI

One thing we do have in our favour is the fact that our brains have almost certainly evolved in tandem with our use of technology. The extraordinary explosion of activity around 40,000 years ago suggests a key role of tools and technology helping shape our brains.

However, there is one fascinating downside. The brain is inherently *biased*, not only sexist and racist; it has many cognitive biases, such as groupthink, confirmation and many other types of dangerous biases, that shape and limit thought. More than this, it has severe weaknesses, not only inherent tendencies, such as motion sickness, overeating, jet lag, phobias, social anxieties, violent tendencies, addiction, delusions and psychosis.

Another bias is at work here – *neophobia* (fear of the new) – antipathy towards new technology. Neophobia is not new. From Socrates – who thought that writing was an ill-advised invention – to the present day, people have reacted with predictable horror to every piece of new technology that hits the street. It happened with writing, parchments, books, printing, newspapers, coffee houses, letters, telegraph, telephone, radio, film, TV, railways, cars, jazz, rock n' roll, rap, computers, the internet, social media and now artificial intelligence. The idea that some new invention rots the mind, devalues the culture, even destroys civilization is an age-old phenomenon.

Neophobia is the product of a superficial reaction about cognition that conflates content with process. The mind, and human nature, is not that malleable and obviously not subject to any real evolutionary change in such a short period of time. Yes, the mind is plastic, but it is not a blank slate waiting to be filled with content from the web. It is far more likely that the neophobes themselves are unthinking victims of the familiar destructive syndrome of neophobia.

Interestingly, the medical evidence suggests that neophobia, as a medical condition, is common in the very young, especially with new foods. It fades throughout childhood and flips in adolescence, when the new is seen as risky and exciting. Then it gradually returns, especially during parenthood, and into our old age, when we develop deeply established habits or expectations that we may see as being under threat. This mimics the demographic attitudes towards technology. Teenagers take readily to new technology; adults tend to be suspicious, even shun it.

There are several other human biases behind our thinking about AI. *Anthropomorphic bias* is arguably the most common, so common that some AI in learning techniques, such as chatbots, rely on its existence. Reading 'bias' into software is sometimes the result of this over-anthropomorphizing.

*Availability bias* arises when we frame thoughts on what is available, rather than pure reason. So crude images of robot teachers enter the mind as characterizing AI, as opposed to software or mathematics, which is not, for most, easy to call to mind or visualize. This skews our view of what AI is and its dangers, often producing dystopian 'Hollywood' perspectives, rather than objective judgement.

Then there's *negativity bias*, where the negative has more impact than the positive, so the 'rise of the robots' and other dystopian visions come to mind more readily than positive examples such as cost savings or raising attainment.

Most of all we have *confirmation bias*, which leaps into action whenever we hear of something that seems like a threat and we want to confirm our view of it as ethically wrong. When we are used to classroom, lecture hall and training room models, it is hard to see alternatives.

Indeed, the accusation that all algorithms are biased is often (not always) a combination of ignorance about what algorithms are and four human biases – anthropomorphism, availability, negativity and confirmation bias. It is often a sign of bias in the objector, who wants to confirm their own deficit-based view and apply a universal, dystopian interpretation to AI with a healthy dose of neophobia.

## Common charges

First, there is the charge that the root cause of gender and racial bias are male, white coders and that AI lacks transparency.

The main problem here may not be the very real issue of eliminating bias from software, which is what we must strive to do, but the clickbait contrarianism behind much of the debate. *Weapons of Math Destruction* by Cathy O'Neil (2016) is typical of the contrarian literature. An unfortunate title, as O'Neil's supposed that algorithms are as bad as Saddam Hussein's mythical WMDs – the evidence similarly weak, sexed up and cherry picked. This is the go-to book for those who want to stick it to AI by reading a pot-boiler. But rather than taking an honest look at the subject, O'Neil takes the 'Weapons of Math Destruction' line far too literally, and unwittingly reuses a term that has come to mean exaggeration and untruths.

### Racism

The racial mix in the AI coding community is more healthily multicultural than many imagine. AI programmers these days are as likely to be from

China, the Far East or the Indian subcontinent, as white. One would struggle to find a white programmer in those powerhouses of AI – India and China. AI is a global phenomenon, not confined to the Western world. The Chinese government has invested a great deal in these skills through Artificial Intelligence 2.0. The 13th Five-Year Plan (2016–2020), the Made in China 2025 programme, Robotics Industry Development Plan and Three-Year Guidance for Internet Plus Artificial Intelligence Plan (2016–2018) are all contributing to boosting AI skills, research and development. India has an education system that sees 'engineering' and 'programming' as admirable careers and a huge outsourcing software industry with a $150 billion IT export business. Even in Silicon Valley the presence of many Chinese and Indian programmers is so prevalent that they feature in every sitcom on the subject. The current CEOs of Google and Microsoft were both born and educated in India. Even if you do not accept this argument, the idea that coders infect AI with sexist and racist code is far-fetched. One would not deny the presence of some bias, but the idea that it is common or omnipresent tends to betray bias in itself.

Take PredPol, the predictive policing software. Yes, it has its glitches, but the advantages vastly outweigh the disadvantages – and the system and its use has evolved over time, with pre-processing techniques used to eliminate the problems of bias. The main problem here is a form of bias or one-sidedness in the analysis. Most technology has a downside. We drive cars, despite the fact that well over a million people die gruesome and painful deaths every year in car accidents. Rather than tease out the complexity, even comparing upsides with downsides, we are given one side only. The proposition that all algorithms are biased is as foolish as the idea that all algorithms are free from bias. This is a complex area that needs careful thought, and the real truth lies, as usual, somewhere in between. Technology often has this cost–benefit feature. To focus on just one side is quite simply a mathematical distortion.

The temptation to anthropomorphize technology is always there. We must resist the temptation to think this is anything but bias. When an algorithm, for example, correlates a black face with a gorilla, it is not that it is biased in the human sense of being a racist, namely a racist agent. The AI knows nothing of itself; it is an artefact, just software. Indeed, it is merely an attempt to execute code, and this sort of error is often how machine learning actually learns. Indeed, this repeated attempt at statistical optimization lies at the very heart of what AI is. Failure is what makes it tick. The good news is that repeated failure results in improvement in machine learning, reinforcement learning, adversarial techniques and so on. It is often absolutely necessary to learn from mistakes to make progress. We need to applaud failure, not jump on the bias bandwagon.

When Google was found to stick the label of gorilla on black faces in 2015, there was no doubt that it was racist in the sense of causing offence, rather than someone being racist in Google, or having a piece of maths that is racist in any intentional sense; this was a systems failure. The problem was spotted and Google responded within the hour. We need to recognize that technology is rarely foolproof; neither are humans. Failures will occur. Machines do not have the cognitive checks and balances that humans have on such cultural issues, but they can be changed and improved to avoid them. We need to see this as a process and not just block progress on the back of outliers. We need to accept that these are mistakes and learn from these mistakes. If mistakes are made, call them out, eliminate the errors and move on. FAIL in this case means First Attempt In Learning. The correct response is not to define and dismiss AI because of these failures, but see them as opportunities for success.

## Sexism

True, there is a gender differential, and this will continue, as there are gender differences when it comes to focused, attention-to-detail coding in the area of AI programming. We know that there is a genetic component in autism, a constellation (not spectrum) of cognitive traits, and that this is heavily weighted towards males. For this reason alone there is likely to be a gender difference in high-performance coding teams for the foreseeable future. In addition, the idea that these coders are unconsciously or, worse, consciously creating racist and sexist algorithms is an exaggeration. One has to work quite hard to create sexist and racist code, and to suggest that *all* algorithms are written in this way is wrong. Some may be, but most are not. It is not as if armies of young men are deliberately writing sexist decision-making into their code.

You are likely in your first lesson on algorithms to be taught some sorting mechanisms (there are many). Now it is difficult to see how sorting a set of random numbers into ascending order can be either sexist or racist. The point is that most algorithms are benign, doing a mechanical job and free from bias. They can improve performance in terms of strength, precision and performance over time (robots in factories), compressing and decompressing comms, encryption algorithms, computational strategies in games (chess, GO, Poker and so on), diagnosis–investigation–treatment in healthcare and reduced fraud in finance. Most algorithms, embedded in most contexts, are benign and free from bias.

It is not true to say that all algorithms and/or data sets are biased, unless one resorts to the idea that everything is socially constructed and therefore subject to bias. As Popper (2012) showed, this is an all-embracing theory to which there is no possible objection, as even the objections are interpreted as being part of the problem. This is, in effect, a sociological dead-end.

## Transparency

When it comes to decisions that affect the lives of humans, we must, of course, be careful with the introduction of bias into algorithms and data. With algorithms, one can insist on transparency, but even the definition in GDPR Article 14 – 'meaningful information about the logic involved' – is a fudge.

There is a danger that the AI becomes black box, esoteric maths that will become increasingly opaque. Few could read the maths that constitute modern algorithmic and machine learning. It is a variety of complex techniques that is readable by a minority. Nevertheless, this is not as completely opaque as one imagines. A lot of this maths is open source, from Google and others, as is the maths itself, in the AI community. Of course, proprietary systems abound, but it is not 'all' locked up in black boxes. One could argue that this is also true of most 'teaching', and the process (algorithms) and knowledge (data) lies in the brains and practices of teachers, lecturers and trainers, much of it totally inaccessible and opaque.

The inner workings of AI can be opaque, especially machine learning using neural networks. But compare this with another social good – medicine. We know it works but we don't know how. As Jon Clardy, a professor of biological chemistry and molecular pharmacology at Harvard Medical School, says, 'the idea that drugs are the result of a clean, logical search for molecules that work is a "fairytale"' (Johnson, 2015). Many drugs work but we have no idea why they work. Medicine tends to throw possible solutions at problems, then observe if they work or not. Now most AI is not like this, but some is.

We will need more work on explainability and transparency. Remember that this is not always possible, even in human decision-making, so when we get AI right, it should have the edge. This is not to say that all bias will be eliminated. A further check may need to be honest and compulsory admissions about bias, where the service is cleared by regulators as being unbiased or biased and to what degree it could potentially be biased.

Of course, we need to be careful about bias, but in many cases, especially in education, we have a far greater chance of tackling these problems using AI than by sticking to good, old-fashioned bias in human teaching. The imperative for transparency may also kill the very things we value. If you demand total transparency in algorithms, Google and Google Scholar may have to be banned in your institution. Does that seem like a proportionate reaction? A sense of balance is needed between solving problems and transparency.

## AI as statistics

AI is not conscious or aware of its purpose. It is just software and as such is not 'biased' in the way we attribute that word to 'humans'. The biases in humans have evolved over millions of years with additional cultural input. AI is maths and we must be careful about anthropomorphizing the problem.

Much AI and data analysis is statistical analysis and pattern-matching. We are at the zenith of two millennia of maths, probability, and statistical thinking, much of it wholly concerned with the elimination of error and bias. The degree to which findings in science are possibly erroneous is often fundamental to the reporting of the methodology and mathematics used in research. In fact, unlike human bias, as AI is largely a set of statistical techniques, the whole rationale is to work towards the elimination of bias or the identification of possible false outcomes. We so often forget that bias in AI is real but different, as it is mathematical or statistical bias. In fact, there is a definition of 'bias' in statistics, which is not a pejorative term, but precisely defined as the difference between an expected value and the true value of a parameter. If the value is zero, it is called unbiased. This is not so much bias as a precise recognition of difference.

The statistical approach at least recognizes these biases and adopts scientific and mathematical methods to try to eliminate such biases. This is a key point – human bias often goes unchecked; statistical and mathematical bias is subjected to rigorous checks. That is not to say that it is flawless, but error rates and attempts to quantify statistical and mathematical bias have been developed over a long time, to counter human bias. That is the essence of the scientific method.

One must also distinguish between algorithms and data. Data is where most of the problems arise. One example is poor sampling: too small a sample, under-representations or over-representations. Data collection can also have bias due to faulty data-gathering in the instruments themselves. Selection bias in data occurs when it is gathered selectively and not randomly, and this is most likely to occur in the human part of the process.

So in discussions of bias in AI, and in AI for learning, humans – and all teachers are humans – are by definition full of bias. So the false comparison between virtuous, unbiased teachers and vicious, biased AI is a false dichotomy.

## Avoiding bias

In learning, the glass always seems to remain half empty, even when the data suggests it is close to the brim. But it is important to be neither too utopian nor too dystopian when discussing AI in learning. We must resist the temptation to have either pessimism or optimism as our starting point. Realism should be our watchword.

### Fairness

Bias in AI can, of course, damage the reputation of systems, companies and AI in general. The danger is that people are dealt with unfairly in employment, legal, health, finance and education if the AI decision-making is inherently biased. If the decision-making is faulty, it can have serious consequences for those on the end of that decision-making.

The danger is also that bias is not only baked into AI but also massively scaled. The problem, oddly, is that the bias in the AI datasets is likely to have been produced by humans, namely words in text that show a gender bias or bad sampling that unfairly targets on race. These problems are real and the scaling issue is real, as the problem may indeed be exacerbated and amplified by AI.

Bias, in practice, is far more likely to be found in the data and even then it usually draws upon established and pre-existent bias in society. Garbage in, garbage out is a general problem in software, but arguably more dangerous in AI. Race, age, gender, socio-economic and other biases can be introduced through the data used by AI and/or the algorithmic model that uses the data. The aim is obviously to avoid discrimination by identifying the many biases that are possible, whether they are in the data or algorithmic models, and eliminate them or at least quantify them. One of the arguments used for transparency in algorithmic models is the need to identify such bias.

The scrutiny of bias in AI is actually more likely to inform us about human bias, bringing the problem of bias to the surface. AI can clearly do much to eliminate or at least reduce human bias. It has already made us more aware of bias as the ever-present human phenomenon in decision-making. Human bias is relatively fixed and very difficult to train out of our brains, whereas AI bias is a set of problems that can be solved. AI in this sense raises the bar for us all.

To be fair, a huge effort is being made to introduce fairness into algorithms. To be actionable, we need concrete ideas that can either prevent or at least significantly reduce bias. Methods have been developed that protect attributes such as race and gender, so that outputs are not biased. There are also pre- and post-processing techniques that can be applied to minimize that carryover of human bias. These pre-processing techniques have been tested on datasets such as the ProPublica COMPAS prison recidivism dataset, criticized for being racist. Pre-processing can construct counterfactuals or apply fairness criteria. Post-processing techniques have also been used that transform predictions to avoid bias. This is the way in which bias is most likely to be reduced, using data techniques that identify, reduce and try to eliminate the inputs.

There is a good argument for being cautious here, proceeding carefully without halting what could be beneficial decision-making, optimizing the delivery of social goods.

## Pedagogic concerns

There are also some ethical considerations that are specific to learning – that it may do more harm than good. These issues also have to be surfaced.

### Too deterministic

One danger, some claim, in the algorithmic age is that it may start, without us realizing, to funnel us towards groupthink in learning. We get fed the same newsfeeds, sold the same popular stuff, hear the same music, buy the same books, get trapped in our bubbles. This debate is alive in learning, where adaptive, AI-driven platforms can deliver personalized learning but, if we are not careful, may also constrict the nature of learning. We need to be careful that the learner retains the curiosity and critical thinking necessary to become an autonomous learner. The danger is that AI could deliver narrow, deterministic, prescribed pathways, not allowing the learner to breathe and expand their horizons, and apply critical thought. On the other hand, many argue, it may expand our horizons.

This is really a design issue, as sometimes a narrowing of focus is necessary and desirable – when diagnosing misconceptions and teaching tight but difficult concepts and processes, such as maths and science; and sometimes it is not, when a more critical approach is needed.

AI does not always make the learning narrower or more deterministic. That is because many of these systems still leave lots open, indeed suggest open options, to the learner. One can allow the learner as much freedom as you wish by making the course porous and curating content. One tool that automatically creates online learning content does this by using AI to create links out to further exposition, explanation and exploration. It deliberately suggests lots of links to the student to content on the web, based on what they look at and their performance. This is the sort of thing they are likely to receive from a teacher or lecturer, but with AI it is personalized. It tracks what you do and predicts what it thinks you may need to supplement your knowledge. Far from closing you down, it opens up the mind to other sources and possibilities. The degree to which human agency is included in AI-driven systems is a design issue. Learning is about giving learners the teaching and tools to support them in their learning, not just leaving people to flounder around on their own without support.

## Makes it too easy

There is an argument that says you cannot make learners' lives too easy. They need to make the effort, overcome problems, even struggle. There is a real piece of psychology that backs this up: Bjork's concept of 'deliberate difficulty' (Bjork and Bjork, 2011). However, this is no excuse for leaving students to drown and fail, with light feedback. Dropout and failure are not desirable. In fact, AI-driven systems can be finely tuned to make levels of difficulty fit that of the individual student, to get that balance of achievement and challenge. You have a far greater chance of delivering deliberate difficulty through AI than through one-size-fits-all courses.

## Surveillance

Picture this for a moment. You are a teacher in a classroom. All of your students are wearing headsets, but each has a coloured light on their forehead – red means full-on focused, yellow focused, and blue calm. This is not science fiction. It has already happened and raises all sorts of questions about learning and ethics (Ye, 2019). Once we know what people are thinking and feeling, there is no privacy. Consciousness itself is open to scrutiny and can be accessed, not only by teachers but also the unscrupulous. There is literally nowhere to hide one's thoughts. Having an open mind is one thing; literally opening up minds with technology is another.

## Overpromising

Another danger with reliance on AI and machine learning models is that there are lots of them, and people get attached to the one they know best. This is not always best for the actual output. More specifically, 'overfitting' problems may lead to putting too much confidence into models and data sets that do not actually bring home the predictive bacon. The good news is that these are problems that can be solved. AI and machine learning are making lots of little leaps that all add up to fast, at times very fast, progress. As long as we recognize that these systems can overlearn and not produce the results we expect, we will get somewhere. To imagine that they will solve all teaching and learning problems immediately, or even soon, is hopelessly optimistic. To imagine that they have and will continue to have a major role in supporting teachers, administrators and learners in the world of learning is realistic.

# Doomsday is hot

'Doomsday is hot,' claims Stephen Pinker (2018a). What he means is that it is all too easy to get fashionably apocalyptic. This could make matters worse in learning: seeing AI as perpetually dystopian risks ruling it out as a solution to major problems, such as education, health and climate change. Catastrophism is not new. As he explains in *Enlightenment Now* (2018b), end-of-days scenarios have been around for a long time, including recent scares around overpopulation, running out of resources and, in technology, the false belief in Y2K. He also points towards the false belief that Iraq had weapons of mass destruction as an example of a dystopian scenario that led to a catastrophic war and the deaths of thousands of innocent people. This, as we shall see, is sadly mirrored in one of the most popular AI contrarian tracts, *Weapons of Math Destruction* by Cathy O'Neil (2016).

The real danger, he argues, is to think of AI as dangerous, thereby avoiding it as a solution, albeit partial, to the real catastrophes we are trying to avoid. We only have so much bandwidth to deal with global problems, and unnecessary doom-mongering about relatively small, remote and distant risks may distract us from the risks we know we face here and now. As a psychologist, he puts this type of thinking down to our inability to deal with risk, seeing all risks as equal, rather than calculating their actual probabilities. Then there are availability and negativity biases. We pay attention to what we regularly see on the news, the zeitgeist issues, and have a bias towards the negative.

The threat of runaway AI as an existential threat is slim, if not negligible, in that we create and engineer this technology, so we will be able to test and control its application. Catastrophic autonomy is not, Pinker (2010) thinks, a probable outcome. AI is not a threat on par with the problems created by humans. We live with our imperfect evolved biases and traits. There is every reason to suppose that we will design AI that is largely free from those traits and destructive objectives. AI is not pulling us towards an imminent and cataclysmic end; it may well be the very thing that saves us from more pressing problems. Learning is one of those pressing problems.

Another calming consideration comes from Daniel Dennett in *From Bacteria to Bach and Back* (2017), where he sees a fusion of human evolution and AI, with consequences for the ethics of AI. He takes a holistic and forgiving view of AI. As he rightly says, we make children without actually understanding the entirety of the process – similarly with new, generative technology. We already trust systems that are way more competent than we humans, and so we should.

Almost all AI has been parasitic on human achievements; corpuses of text, images, music, translated content, maths and other mother lodes of data. Rightly sceptical about strong AI, master algorithms and super-intelligent agents, Dennett's call is for us to keep an eye on the boundaries between mind and machine, as we have a tendency to overestimate the comprehension of the machines, way beyond their actual competence, anthropomorphizing comprehension. We see this with even the most casual encounters with chatbots and devices such as Alexa or Google Home. We all too readily read intentionality, comprehension, even consciousness into technology when it is completely absent.

By adopting regulatory rules around false claims of anthropomorphism, especially in advertising and marketing, we can steer ourselves through the ethical concerns around AI. Overreach and concealing anthropomorphism and false claims should be illegal, just as exaggeration and side effects are regulated in the pharmaceutical industry. Tests, such as variations of Turing's test, can be used to test their upper limits. Dennett is no fan of the demands for full transparency, which he thinks are utopian. Many use Google Scholar, Google and other tools without knowing how they work, and competence without comprehension is not that unusual.

More than this, in learning Dennett really does think that AI has the potential to overcome the brakes on learning in the current system. He sees AI as helping us solve problems in partnership, all the time keeping a close eye on the dangers that come with autonomy.

Education is another case in point. We have the late, great Douglas Adams (2002) to thank for this sensible set of observations:

1) Everything that's already in the world when you're born is just normal;

2) Anything that gets invented between then and before you turn 30 is incredibly exciting and creative and with any luck you can make a career out of it;

3) Anything that gets invented after you're 30 is against the natural order of things and the beginning of the end of civilization as we know it, until it's been around for about 10 years when it gradually turns out to be alright really.

## Conclusion

AI is the wonder of our age – something so exciting that it tends to produce extreme reactions in commentators. This is fine, but we must not fall into either dystopian or utopian visions. We must be realistic. That is not to say we should be complacent. We have already seen the power of AI to transform online services, automate factories and seriously impact employment. We must therefore be vigilant on regulation and its political consequences.

With some technology, the dangers may be too great – nuclear, chemical weapons, autonomous weapons and so on. But most technology has downsides. Cars kill and we still drive cars. It is a calculus where we accept technology when the benefits outweigh the cons. Yes, as technology has become more virtual, it may be harder to spot, combat and regulate. Technology is always ahead of the sociology, and older politicians and regulators find it hard to understand the pace and consequences, often rushing to throw both baby and bath out with the bathwater. But these AI opportunities must be taken at the flood, with one eye on the dangers, the other on the benefits.

# References

Adams, D (2002) *The Salmon of Doubt: Hitchhiking the universe one last time*, Vol 3, Random House, New York

Bjork, EL and Bjork, RA (2011) Making things hard on yourself, but in a good way: Creating desirable difficulties to enhance learning, *Psychology and the Real World: Essays illustrating fundamental contributions to society*, **2**, pp 59–68

Dennett, DC (2017) *From Bacteria to Bach and Back: The evolution of minds*, WW Norton & Company, New York

Harari, YN (2016) *Homo Deus: A brief history of tomorrow*, Random House, London

Harris, JR (2011) *The Nurture Assumption: Why children turn out the way they do*, Simon & Schuster, New York

Johnson, CY (2015) One big myth about medicine: We know how drugs work, *Washington Post*. Available at https://www.washingtonpost.com/gdpr-consent/?destination=%2fnews%2fwonk%2fwp%2f2015%2f07%2f23%2fone-big-myth-about-medicine-we-know-how-drugs-work%2f%3f (archived at https://perma.cc/G6YJ-RYLD)

Kahneman, D (2011) *Thinking, Fast and Slow*, Penguin, London

Noble, SU (2018) *Algorithms of Oppression: How search engines reinforce racism*, New York University Press, New York

O'Neil, C (2016) *Weapons of Math Destruction: How big data increases inequality and threatens democracy*, Broadway Books, New York

Pinker, S (2010) How is the internet changing the way you think?, Edge. Available at https://www.edge.org/response-detail/11247 (archived at https://perma.cc/T5TK-7FPY)

Pinker, S (2018a) The dangers of worrying about doomsday, *The Globe and Mail*. Available at https://www.theglobeandmail.com/opinion/the-dangers-of-worrying-about-doomsday/article38062215/?utm_medium=Referrer:+Social+Network+/+Media&amp;utm_campaign=Shared+Web+Article+Links (archived at https://perma.cc/5CTY-FJK7)

Pinker, S (2018b) *Enlightenment Now: The case for reason, science, humanism, and progress*, Penguin, London

Popper, K (2012) *The Open Society and Its Enemies*, Routledge, London

Ye, Y (2019) Brain-reading headsets trialled on 10,000 schoolchildren in China, *New Scientist*, 14 January. Available at https://www.newscientist.com/article/2190670-brain-reading-headsets-trialled-on-10000-schoolchildren-in-china/ (archived at https://perma.cc/45Z2-9J67)

# 18

# Employment

It is vital that learning professionals in education and training take an interest in the impact of AI on society and employment, or under-employment or unemployment, as some believe. AI is likely to change things for better or worse, but certainly forever. As the landscape of work and life will be changed by AI, so will the learning landscape. So let us look at its impact on work and the professions, including learning. We have created the network we call the internet, but that network is now being increasingly managed by AI. This has some profound consequences.

Machines led to workers moving from fields to factories, then, with robots in manufacturing, from factories to offices and services, to produce long-term, structural, blue-collar under-employment and unemployment. We may now also be seeing the start of white-collar under- and unemployment, as AI becomes capable of doing at least some of what even well-educated workers and graduates could do in the past. Each technological revolution tends to bring in job losses as well as new opportunities. Let us also not imagine for one moment that the learning field is immune from such economic shifts. We have already seen its effect on reducing the number of librarians, trainers and other learning professionals. There is, undoubtedly, more to come.

John Maynard Keynes introduced technical unemployment into economics in the 1930s (1930/2010), and as AI has hit the streets, there has been a flood of texts such as *The Rise of the Robots* (Ford, 2015) and *The Future of the Professions* (Susskind and Susskind, 2015). What we do see is what Brynjolfsson and McAfee in *The Second Machine Age* (2014) called the 'great decoupling' of productivity (profits) and wages. Wage stagnation is real and is causing political turmoil and social unrest. In truth, we face an uncertain future but one where we will have to adjust and adapt to finding meaning in life, not work. It seems clear that 'learning' to adjust, adapt and find meaning in life is essential. This is why AI in learning may be a necessary condition for the future happiness of our species.


## 47 per cent of jobs will be automated...

This turned into a meme in newspapers, articles and conference slides. It is from a 2013 paper by Frey and Osborne. First, it refers only to the US, and only states that such jobs are under threat. Dig a little deeper and you find that it is a rather speculative piece of work.

They looked at 702 job types, then, interestingly, used AI itself (machine learning), which they trained with 70 jobs judged by humans as being at risk of automation or not. They then trained a 'classifier' or software program with this data, to predict the probability of the other 632 jobs being automated. You can already see the weaknesses. First, the human-trained data set: get this wrong and it sweeps through the much larger AI-generated conclusions. Second, the classifier: even if out by a little, it can make wildly wrong conclusions. The study itself, largely automated by AI, rather than being a credible forecast, is more useful as a study of what can go wrong in AI. Many other similar reports in the market parrot these results. To be fair, some are more fine-grained than the Frey and Osborne paper, but most suffer from the same basic flaws. We are now many years on, with record levels of employment in places like the US, where AI is at its most active.

The fact that 47 per cent of jobs may be automated makes a great headline, but it is a lousy piece of analysis. Change does not happen this way. In many jobs, the context or culture means that complete automation will not happen quickly. There are human fears and expectations that demand the presence of humans in the workplace. We can automate cars, even airplanes, but it will be a long time before airplanes will fly across the Atlantic with several hundred passengers and no pilot. Self-driving cars are also likely to take longer. There are human perceptions that, even if irrational, have to be overcome. We may have automated waiters that trolley food to your table, but the expectation that a real person will deliver the food and engage with you is all too real. Similarly in medicine, it is unlikely that AI will replace doctors, although it will automate parts of their work, like investigative radiography.

Organizations grow around people and are run by people. These people build systems, processes, budget plans and funding processes that do not necessarily quickly lead to productivity gains through automation. They often protect people, products and processes that put a brake on automation. Most organizations have an ecosystem that makes change difficult – poor forecasting, no room for innovation, arcane procurement and sclerotic regulations. This all mitigates against innovative change. Even when faced with something that saves a huge amount of time and cost, there is a tendency to stick to existing practice. As Upton Sinclair (1994) said, 'It is difficult to get a man to understand something, when his salary depends on his not understanding it.'

Another flaw is the hyperbole around 'robots'. Most AI does not need to be embedded in a humanoid form. As Toby Walsh (2018) rightly says when he eviscerates certain parts of the Frey and Osborne report, there is no way robots will be cutting your hair or serving your food by weaving through busy restaurants with several plates of food any time soon. The vast majority of robots, AI-driven machines that perform a useful function, do not look like humans; many are online and almost invisible. This imagining of robots in homes, offices and workplaces is largely illusory.

AI, as we saw, is an *idiot savant*. It is incredibly smart at specific things in specific domains, but profoundly stupid at flexible and general tasks. This is why entire jobs are rarely eliminated through automation, except for very narrow, routine jobs, like warehouse picking and packaging, spray painting a car and so on. Most automation is partial, as the general worker still outfoxes AI.

This common flaw, as Walsh rightly spotted, was that the training data in the Frey and Osborne paper was either a 0 or 1 probability of automation, but the outputs were between 0 and 1. This is an example of not so much garbage in, garbage out, as binary in, range out. You can see this manifest itself in some absurd predictions around jobs that are unlikely to be automated, like hairdressers, waiters and cleaners. Beware of AI-generated predictions around employment.

The process of automation in employment is a messy business with many variables. Heuristics can help here. Some categorize jobs as:

- cognitive versus manual:
    o cognitive routine;
    o cognitive non-routine;
    o manual routine;
    o manual non-routine.

But even the distinction between manual and cognitive is not mutually exclusive. Few manual jobs require no knowledge, planning or problem-solving. These can be useful rules of thumb, but the world rarely falls neatly into these binary or four-way categories. Yet they often lie at the heart of predictive analysis. Beware of simplistic heuristics.

Bias in analysis is also all too common. Take just one example – the analysis of education. The people doing the analysis are often academics or people who have an academic bent. The Frey and Osborne paper conflates education into one group, as if kindergarten work was the same as academic research. The routine aspects of education – the fact that most teachers, trainers and lecturers do a lot of administrative work that is actually routine and repetitive – is conveniently ignored. Google, Wikipedia and online management and learning have already eaten into the employment of librarians and teachers. It is a displacement industry. As the task of finding things became super-fast, the process of learning, research and teaching became quicker. Library footfall falls, as we no longer have to troop off to the library to get the information. Amazon has commoditized the purchase of books. Commoditization is what technology is good at and what Marx recognized as a driving force in market economies (Marx and Engels, 1867/1883). Educators do not like to hear this, but they have a lot to gain here. Teaching is a means to an end, not an end in itself. It has been and will continue to be automated, not by robots, but by smart, personalized, online learning.

In truth most jobs will be partially and not completely automated. This has been going on for centuries with technological advances. Sure, horse grooms and carriage drivers no longer exist, but car mechanics and taxi drivers do. Typesetters have been replaced by web designers. ATMs have simply changed the nature of bank tellers, not completely automated the process. Indeed, in many professions the shift has been towards more customer service and less mechanical service. What matters is not necessarily the crude measure of 'jobs' being automated, but rather 'activities' – specific tasks, competences and skills – being automated.

What is also often forgotten in such analyses is the business case and labour supply context. Automation will not happen where the investment cost is higher than hiring human labour, and is less likely to occur where labour supply is high and wages low. We see this in countries where the population is high and growing, or labour costs low through immigration, making the business case for innovation and automation low. Many jobs could be automated, but the lack of investment money and the availability of cheap labour and low wages make the human bar quite low. There are complex economic decision chains at work here that slow down automation.

## 65 per cent of today's students will be employed in jobs that don't exist yet...

This is another quote that has launched a thousand conference presentations. Yet, although included in a serious World Economic Forum (2016) report, it has no clearly identifiable source.

This is the sort of exaggeration that feeds bad consultancy. Most, in practice, will be doing jobs that have existed for some time. No doubt many will simply be doing jobs they did not plan on doing (and don't like) or jobs that have changed somewhat through automation. Predicting which jobs or activities get automated is easy compared with predicting what new jobs will be created. The net total is therefore difficult to establish. Fewer people may be needed in certain areas, but new jobs will be created, especially in services.

To be fair, more recent analyses have moved on to more fine-grained concepts and data. McKinsey did a detailed analysis of 2,000-plus work activities in 800 occupations, with data from the US Bureau of Labor Statistics and O*Net (McKinsey Global Institute, 2017). They quantified the time spent on these activities and the technical feasibility of automating them. Nesta did a breakdown of specific skills (Bakhshi et al, 2017).

The crude headlines will continue, but we're starting to see more detailed and realistic analysis that will lead to better predictions. This is important, as educational bodies need to be able to adapt to what they will be required to teach as well as what they teach and to whom. As the change accelerates, education and training will need to be more sensitive and adaptive to the changes. This means more accurate predicting of demand and quick adjustments in supply. There is likely to be no sudden shift but a gradual bite by bite into activities within jobs. AI will change the world and the world of learning, but not in the way we think it will.

## Professions and AI

AI will decimate the professions. That is the big idea being debated by economists. In the same way that agricultural jobs were wiped out by mechanization, working-class manufacturing jobs by robots and typing pools by word processors, so professions, such as managers, lawyers, doctors, journalists, architects, accountants and so on, will be wiped out by smart software. Or, as is more likely, the professions will adapt to this new age of algorithms and manage the high-value management and human tasks in their professions. It is clear, however, that change is already here. Around the world, especially in the richer nations, the truth is dawning that we need fewer managers. The middle class is now waking up to the fact that they are the new working class, as their roles diminish.

Yet HR and L&D are eerily silent. How many leadership courses are being delivered today without any mention of AI, despite the fact that we know that its impact has been and will continue to be huge? How many HR folk are really studying what is happening here? To sit back and watch this happen, without serious debate and preparation, is irresponsible. A more immediate debate is how to cope with AI in the short to medium term.

This report from *Harvard Business Review* is a good start: 'How artificial intelligence will redefine management' (Kolbjørnsrud *et al*, 2016). The survey was substantial, covering 1,770 managers in 14 countries, interviewing 37 executives in charge of digital transformation at their organizations. Findings were reduced to five recommendations:

Practice 1: Leave administration to AI.

Practice 2: Focus on judgement work.

Practice 3: Treat intelligent machines as 'colleagues'.

Practice 4: Work like a designer.

Practice 5: Develop social skills and networks.

Surveys tend not to spot the really disruptive stuff, and as the respondents are the very people who are likely to be affected by that disruption, they tend to be conservative. So first, a quick expansion of these five propositions, as we can think of many more.

**Practice 1, Leave administration to AI:** The survey showed, astoundingly, that managers spend well over half their time (57 per cent) on administration. This is precisely the sort of work that is already being automated to a degree by tools and will be increasingly done by AI-driven systems. Monitoring, scheduling and reporting are all areas that are likely to be more automated through AI. The room for efficiencies and increases in productivity here are enormous, as organizations are essentially paying top dollar for relatively routine and banal summarizing work.

**Practice 2, Focus on judgement work:** Those surveyed seemed to think that this was an area that would remain relatively untouched by AI, although this is by no means certain. The sort of expertise that leads to good judgement may also be under threat, as AI does the data-gathering, analysis and production of insights. Recommendations (judgements) may well be AI-driven. *The Future of the Professions* (Susskind and Susskind, 2015) is packed with examples of judgement-making AI, across a range of professions. There will be a pendulum swing of some magnitude as AI creeps forward doing more and more, eating into the judgement sphere.

**Practice 3, Treat intelligent machines as 'colleagues':** The report shies away from the obvious conclusion that we will need fewer managers. They found that 78 per cent of the surveyed managers believe that they will trust the advice of intelligent systems in making business decisions in the future. This raises the obvious question of how many managers we need to simply confirm these decisions. The anthropomorphic idea of AI as 'colleagues' is also a bit odd. We don't see Excel as a colleague. We see it as a functional tool. There is still the old-fashioned idea that AI usually manifests itself as a robot at work here.

**Practice 4, Work like a designer:** Of course, managers will need to develop higher-end skills to define and implement solutions, but is 'creativity' the right way to frame this? Whenever management theorists or educationalists run out of ideas, they invoke the word 'creativity' or 21st-century skills. It is a big word that often signifies lazy and vague thinking. Nevertheless, it is certain that the hollowing out of middle management tasks and middle managers will result in more focus on higher-order skills.

**Practice 5, Develop social skills and networks:** Again, it is certainly the case that AI will not do all of the social stuff. Managers will need more competences in these areas. What is more interesting is the way technology and AI will help achieve these goals. Social media has had a huge impact on organizations and management. That is already AI-driven. The contemporary manager needs to be able to harness AI to achieve these goals.

## Management data and research

Research organizations such as Forrester, Gartner and others rely on datasets to provide insights, which they synthesize into reports. At this level, their business, like management consultancy, is under threat. More importantly, this function has shifted from the outside to inside organizations. The modern manager has to be able to manage data-harvesting, data management and AI-driven tools that lead to insights and decisions. These companies have already shifted much of the analytic task offshore to India and other low-wage economies, and have replaced human insight with data-driven, analytic software (read AI). The eventual result will be the use of AI-driven insights directly or internally.

## Finance

Finance was revolutionized by the spreadsheet, which automated not only calculations, but also captured formulae and models. This has gone a lot further with AI, where a huge volume of financial transactions and trades are now AI-driven. Financial monitoring, processes (invoicing, cash flow, expenses), reporting and audits are likely to be much more AI driven, reducing the need for the admin and management in these areas. These have all been revolutionized by technology, but AI promises to do much more. The big disruption is likely to be in audit, where a few big companies dominate. All it will take is one radical player to offer AI-driven data-gathering, analysis and report-writing and there will be carnage. Audit is notoriously weak – witness the audits of the major banks that failed so dramatically in 2008. It relies on sampling and often incomplete data sets. AI-driven accountancy systems should, in the future, be able to spit out audit-ready accounts, and AI-driven audit software will crawl through that data and those accounts for discrepancies, inconsistencies, statistically odd figures and so on.

## Personal assistants

As working from home has increased through the use of smart tech, mobile phones, web conferencing and cloud-based services, so the support role has shifted decade after decade from people to technology. The typing pool was the first to go. Back-end office support staff were next, then the secretary and now the PA. Intelligent personal assistants, in the form of chatbots or other interfaces like Amazon Echo, are likely to emerge, which act as personal PAs. They will act as a convenient interface to AI to do the mostly administrative tasks that managers need: scheduling meetings, arranging travel, expenses and so on.

## Communications

The telegraph, telephone, email, Skype and messaging all changed management. They meant that communications were faster and cheaper. The key to good communications is dialogue, and AI is starting to deliver real dialogue with technology. Speech recognition, text to speech and machine translation (in real time) have already had an impact. All of these are AI driven. Efficiencies in communications through the use of AI within the technology, but also to improve its efficacy, are coming. Chatbots now learn through machine learning. The more you use them, the better they get. AI will not only enable better communications in terms of delivery; it will also shape communications in terms of quality. One simple example is email software which now does spellcheck or warns you when you've forgotten to attach the document. There will be a lot more.

## Marketing

Many managers have a hazy idea about marketing, and the lack of skills in this area is often what makes a company fuzzy, leading to lacklustre sales, and it can take a company to the wall. There is a tendency in our all-too-academically-driven world to denigrate these skills, but if you have been in business and tried to grow a business, you will know that it is a necessary management skill. In marketing we've seen a seismic shift towards online, whether it is online advertising, website or social media marketing. This is, in the case of the big players, algorithmically driven. We can expect this trend to continue.

## Sales

Sales management is always a trial. You have free-wheeling sales people who do not like process but know that process and focus leads to sales success. Lead-generation has shifted online and now involves AI targeting and delivery. Clumsy and ill-focused sales can be channelled and streamlined with AI. Salesforce have bought AI companies and set up Einstein, their AI service; others will follow.

## Customer service

Call centres will be replaced by AI-driven bots; touch-screen ordering will replace wait staff. We buy more and more online, and we've seen what Amazon have done with AI-driven recommendations. Managing customer service means being aware of the technology options and making sure that they fit into your organization. More and more customer service will be technology driven, and because it demands intelligent responses, AI will play a significant role in its delivery. No manager with responsibility in this area can ignore these developments.

### Legals

Nothing is more dispiriting for managers than dealing with contracts. Nothing is slower and more antiquated than legal processes. When two sides negotiate, they need a document that can be mutually accessed and AI-driven analysis to identify and help reconcile differences. These services are already available and will, undoubtedly, increase. That is good news for managers, bad news for lawyers.

### HR

HR cannot continue to do the pay and rations thing, supplemented by a diet of dull compliance training, with the occasional staff survey, without considering the fact that there may be many fewer staff in the future. Their processes will be streamlined and made more efficient by being subjected to AI. They have to be much more data- and AI-focused.

### Recruitment

Recruitment has already been influenced by algorithmic search, selection and matching. When LinkedIn bought Bright for $120 million in 2014, it boosted revenues through recruitment and made its strategy clear. We have seen the slow abandonment of traditional HR and admin-heavy recruitment processes towards slicker, automated, online processes. This is an area ripe for falling fees and automation.

AI will redefine what it means to be a manager. Managers will increasingly not manage people, but will harness and manage technology. Management used to be about people and processes, but there are new technologies around, especially AI, that also need to be managed. Old-school managers who cannot handle delegation to technology will struggle. The truth is that many will not be needed.

## Learning jobs and AI

Will librarians, teachers, lecturers and trainers be subject to the same pressures as other white-collar jobs from tech? It has already happened, is happening and will continue to erode employment. However, it is not a simple net loss but a complex formula.

'Technological unemployment' was the term coined by Keynes to describe the economic prospect of technology-driven job losses and there has been debate for centuries on the issue. Far from being a simple count of job losses against gains, it is a complex economic issue.

Substantial job losses will result from the effect of technology and AI. In the recent literature, however, the learning world comes out relatively unscathed. But I'm not so sure about their definition of 'learning'. There's a tendency for analysts and educators to see the 'learning world' largely through an institutional lens – schools, college, universities. Yet this is merely a fraction of the learning world. Most learning takes place outside of these institutions, in non-institutional contexts – the workplace, at home and informally. If we define the 'learning' world broadly, and include all forms of cognitive improvement, we see libraries, bookshops, online bookshops, television, newspapers, online, social media and many other sources of learning, as causally relevant. When seen through this wide-angle lens, you start to realize how profound technology has been in replacing the human component in learning.

Technology has always democratized, decentralized and disintermediated knowledge. It happened with the invention of writing, then the alphabet, paper and printing. These were all profound technological boosts to the transmission of knowledge, which expanded human progress by freeing knowledge from the oral tradition, so dominant for millennia. Electronically, we then had the telegraph, telephone, radio, film and TV. In the computer age, this started at the bottom of the learning pyramid, with open access to 'knowledge' through the internet.

Google gave us access, Wikipedia and many others gave us content, and jobs were lost in the publishing business. The huge encyclopaedia sector died on the spot and libraries became less useful. The fall in footfall at libraries and bookshops has little to do with the fall in reading and everything to do with the rise in online access to knowledge and cheap online books. There has been a renaissance in reading and writing by young people, who read and write, it would appear, every few minutes on their phones or computers. At this level, if you want to know something, you go to the web. The one-third fall in librarian jobs in the US since 1990, after decades of rises, correlates well with the rise of the computer and online access. This was a well-paid, graduate-level profession that is being decimated by online technology. The effect of these services on losing knowledge delivery jobs has been substantial. Large tech companies such as Google tend to have tens of thousands of employees, unlike previous global behemoths that had hundreds of thousands.

Access to YouTube is also likely to have had an effect on practical jobs. Many, many millions of 'how to…' tasks have been completed by individuals who simply looked it up on YouTube. Whether it is DIY, car repair, learning chords on a guitar… direct instruction is now available – and off you go. The availability of mobile devices allows you to take the instruction to the task. Save money, save time – jobs lost.

It is in organizational learning that job losses are felt directly. The rise of online organizational learning has been eating away at the training market for over 30 years. This has, without doubt, led to a dramatic reduction in the number of trainers in organizations. Gone are the once common training centres and courses that were months long. Online learning, simulations, blended learning, flipped classroom and now LXPs and LRSs have all taken a massive, shark-sized bite out of the classroom training market and undoubtedly led directly to the loss of jobs. The global corporate e-learning market amounts to tens of billions, with healthy compound annual growth. The job losses will continue.

Again, the rise of online courses has eaten into the institutional market. It is likely to impact higher education, where the projected increase in human teaching staff will, to a degree, be replaced by online delivery. Wherever online solutions perform even part of the teaching process, jobs are at risk. If you largely lecture, that part of your job is definitely at risk, as it is easily recordable, replicable and can be distributed on scale.

With the rise of MOOCs, where the ratio of teacher to students is huge, the reduction in teachers per student is obvious. Other trends include AI and adaptive learning that promise to eat into the teaching components, first as hybrid technology-enhanced teaching models then autonomous models. Full adaptive courses are already on sale and the first adaptive learning degree in biology has been launched.

This is unlikely to have huge impact in schools, where responsibility towards young people involves far more than just teaching. Even here, however, it is hard to imagine that technology will have no real effect, especially in reducing workload through the automation of administration, such as timetabling and lesson planning. The largest gain is likely to be in assessment and marking, the one area where teacher workload could be significantly reduced.

Online delivery, especially when smarter and adaptive, may also offer opportunities to provide courses where the recruitment of teachers is difficult. There is often a correlation between rising demand in a subject and teacher shortage, as many with those skills will have better employment opportunities applying their skills rather than teaching them.

Learning professionals need to ask:

1 What kind of learning tasks do computers perform better than teachers? Low-level teaching tasks such as lecturing, exposition and 'knowledge' transfer are most at risk, as are the handling of physical assets such as books in libraries and publishing. The textbook industry is in some trouble.

2 What kind of learning tasks do you perform better than computers? Teaching young children, practical skills, high-level teaching tasks, online tutoring – these are all, as yet, skills that will not be easily replaced by technology.

3 In an increasingly computerized world, what well-paid learning work is left for people to do? Online teaching, tutoring, facilitation and learning design will all be in demand, as the market for online learning grows.

4 How can people learn the skills to do this work? Get online, use social media for CPD, explore online tutoring, deliver webinars, participate in MOOCs, try a MOOC on blended learning and the use of technology in learning and learning design courses.

Just as we have seen Uber rise without owning any cars, and AirBnB rise despite owning no hotels, we are likely to see disintermediation on a global scale in education, where learning is delivered by organizations that may have very few teachers.

## Under- and unemployment

There are benefits that could accrue to people through technology not reflected in the job figures – cheaper prices and new products for everyone and increased productivity. Then there are the benefits of higher wages, new jobs in technology, new jobs created by technology and increased investment.

But the spectre of inequality is there and the danger is that this may accelerate with AI. While the optimistic replacement of jobs may have been true in the industrial era, many argue that it is no longer true in the information age, where fewer people design technology that replaces large numbers of blue-collar, and now white-collar, workers. There is a new concern that AI can take graduate and professional jobs, just as robots took factory jobs and farm mechanization took agricultural jobs. We may now face the inevitable rise of long-term structural unemployment, caused by technological innovation. Few professions will be immune to these pressures, even in the learning game.

However, we must be careful to not get swept away by dystopian ideas on technology, as some predict no real impact on the overall employment landscape. The likely outcome in many areas of education, apart from the base of the pyramid jobs such as librarians and paper publishing, is the gradual replacement of jobs by technology aids and alternatives. However, the one caveat (and it is a big caveat) is that predictions about what technology is capable of have been poor, and there may be some radical and unseen shifts that come along.

An interesting brake on the problem could be the very thing we are discussing – increased delivery of education to create jobs. However, we must be careful in ascribing employment, and especially technological innovation and employment, to educational causes. Not all economists agree that the continual spend and expansion on higher education leads to increases in employment. This has been obvious in southern Europe and is now obvious in graduate unemployment and underemployment figures (graduates doing non-graduate jobs).

Paul Krugman (2012) and many others no longer think that education is the cure. He reminds us that there has been a steady 'hollowing out' of middle-class jobs. This is not a simple heads versus hands issue, where smart people retain jobs and manual workers lose their jobs. It may be the other way round. Alan Blinder (2007) has suggested that we are now in an era where high-paid jobs are easier to offshore than low-paid manual jobs. Few now think that marching everyone in lock-step through expensive higher education is the answer to technological unemployment. It may even be a placebo that leads to debt burdens that limit growth and exacerbate the problem.

An analysis by the Economic Policy Forum between 2000 and 2016 (Gould and Wilson, 2017), when millennials entered the job market, found 'little to no gain' in median annual earnings, part of a longer trend of wage stagnation going back to the 1970s. Over the same period, educational effort and achievement has sky-rocketed, yet the benefits in terms of wages are not clear. The economist Bryan Caplan, in *The Case Against Education* (2018) sees higher education as having developed into 80 per cent signalling, a signal that you are employable – a huge waste of money and resources.

As the evidence builds, AI is seen as a serious threat to millions of jobs. If we look at the top companies by market cap in 2006 and now, we see that the tech giants predominate. This trend is likely to continue, with a worrying trend towards monopolization. They have huge market capitalization, enormous cash reserves but employ far fewer people, and at the same time, destroy jobs elsewhere. If they do not destroy jobs, they almost certainly create underemployment. Amazon may employ hundreds of thousands of people, mostly low-paid warehouse and delivery staff, but how many librarians, bookstore staff and shopkeepers have we lost? Some argue that the hollowing-out of the middle class has already taken place, via automation. Even the low-paid warehouse staff are being replaced by robots and delivery drivers possibly by drones.

If, as most agree, the net result is far fewer jobs, or at least less time at work, we need to turn our attention to the political consequences.

This is primarily a moral and political issue, and the basic minimum wage has been touted as the obvious answer. The desire to get on in life and be productive seems like too powerful a cultural force to give way to a supported life of leisure through taxation and public expenditure, even if it were possible. A more likely scenario is one where our very real, personal needs for growth and development are also satisfied.

What is more likely is the need to educate and train people to do many different things in this new AI-infused, smart economy. This is hardly likely if the costs are at their present levels, and rising. This is not about the ever-expanding campus model. If we keep to the idea of education as being on campus, in institutions, always delivered by expensive 'teachers', there will be an impasse.

To some it seems likely that we face a return to a human condition that last existed before the industrial revolution, when machines automated and stimulated the global economy, as well as before the agrarian revolution when machines destroyed work on the land. It is a return to an age when people did not work in factories but prepared the land, sowed seeds, waited and harvested. Work was far more episodic in those times, with long periods, not of leisure, as a long winter with meagre food should not be romanticized, but there was certainly more time.

In our technological age, when the communications technology we have both entertains and educates, it may also provide opportunities, on scale, to educate us for this new future. It could, just as it has in robotics, reduce the costs of education so much that we can all, including those in the developing world, benefit from its scalable dividend.

It is right to worry about the future, as recent events portend great dangers. Trump has shown that people are angry at losing the gainful employment and lives they once had. In supposedly prosperous Europe, the southern countries have massive adult and youth unemployment. Graduates, saddled with debt, are now struggling to find work that matches the supposed promise. And, of course, unemployment is rife in the developed world, leading to hugely disruptive migration. Climate change will almost certainly exacerbate all of this.

But to react to technological change by taking a stand, as either a technophobe or technophile, rather than exploring and considering alternative possibilities, would be a mistake. We can surely see the glass, not pessimistically as half empty, or optimistically as half full, but realistically as an opportunity to create a future that is centred around our real, human needs.

We should not get too attached to the idea that those needs were ever the drudgery of fields, factories or offices. If technology has freed us from using our bodies to do menial tasks, from the planting and harvesting of crops, to the repetitive tasks on a factory floor or in the drudgery of an office, so be it. Having freed our bodies from manual tasks, can we not also free our minds from repetitive and mind-numbing cognitive tasks with AI? Aren't there better things to do with our minds than administer, process and manage?

Bodily, we may be better off, as we can keep ourselves fit and in good health, even have superior help, through AI-assisted care, in our old age. What we desperately need is a rather old-fashioned view of human nature as being nurtured by learning. Where education is about autonomy, developing young minds to be curious and open, then we must see lifelong learning as a possibility and not a clichéd conference phrase. Learning takes time, and rather than being rushed in batches and bursts in schools, institutions or on corporate courses, we may be able to free learning from the tyranny of time, place and costs.

## Conclusion

Shiva destroys as she creates, and so it could be with AI. AI needs to be applied to education and training to bring the same productivity efficiencies that it brings elsewhere. There is nothing unique about teaching and learning that makes them immune from AI. Teaching is a means to an end – learning. If that can be done through AI, we should grasp the opportunity, especially if it makes learning faster, cheaper and better. If we are facing a future where many people do not have a job or have more leisure time or need to be trained in newer skills, AI may then be a partial cure for the very ill it creates.

## References

Bakhshi, H, Downing, J, Osborne, M and Schneider, P (2017) *The Future of Skills: Employment in 2030*, Pearson and Nesta, London

Blinder, AS (2007) *Offshoring: Big deal, or business as usual?*, Center for Economic Policy Studies, Princeton University, Princeton, NJ

Brynjolfsson, E and McAfee, A (2014) *The Second Machine Age: Work, progress, and prosperity in a time of brilliant technologies*, WW Norton & Company, New York

Caplan, B (2018) *The Case Against Education: Why the education system is a waste of time and money*, Princeton University Press, Princeton, NJ

Ford, M (2015) *The Rise of the Robots: Technology and the threat of mass unemployment*, Oneworld Publications, New York

Frey, CB and Osborne, M (2013) *The Future of Employment: How susceptible are jobs to computerisation?*, The Oxford Martin Programme on Technology and Employment, Oxford

Gould, E and Wilson, V (2017) Little to gain in median annual earnings in the 2000s, while significant wage gap remains, Working Economics Blog, 15 September. Available at https://www.epi.org/blog/little-to-no-gain-in-median-annual-earnings-in-the-2000s-while-significant-wage-gaps-remain/ (archived at https://perma.cc/45Z2-9J67) (archived at https://perma.cc/P85U-86EZ)

Keynes, JM (1930/2010) Economic possibilities for our grandchildren, in *Essays in Persuasion*, pp 321–332, Palgrave Macmillan, London

Kolbjørnsrud, V, Amico, R and Thomas, RJ (2016) How artificial intelligence will redefine management, *Harvard Business Review*, 2 November

Krugman, P (2012) The conscience of a liberal, *New York Times*. Available at https://krugman.blogs.nytimes.com/2012/03/30/we-dont-need-no-education/ (archived at https://perma.cc/9JTP-8Q37)

Marx, K and Engels, F (1867/1883) *Das Kapital: A critique of political economy*

McKinsey Global Institute (2017) *A Future that Works: Automation, employment, and productivity*, Executive Summary, McKinsey Global Institute, New York. Available at https://www.mckinsey.com/~/media/mckinsey/featured%20insights/ Digital%20Disruption/Harnessing%20automation%20for%20a%20 future%20that%20works/MGI-A-future-that-works-Executive-summary.ashx (archived at https://perma.cc/LFE8-36V9)

Sinclair, U (1994) *I, Candidate for Governor: And how I got licked*. University of California Press, Berkeley, CA

Susskind, RE and Susskind, D (2015) *The Future of the Professions: How technology will transform the work of human experts*, Oxford University Press, New York

Walsh, T (2018) *Machines that Think: The future of artificial intelligence*, Prometheus Books, Buffalo, NY

World Economic Forum (2016) The future of jobs and skills, in *The Future of Jobs Report*. Available at http://reports.weforum.org/future-of-jobs-2016/chapter-1-the-future-of-jobs-and-skills/ (archived at https://perma.cc/C7ZM-4QP2)

# 19

# The final frontier

'Learning' is a complex process in humans. It gave our species unique advantages that allowed us to conquer, not only other species, but new habitats, indeed the entire planet. We have now, for the first time in our evolution, learned how to make machines that 'learn'.

Tegmark, the head of the Future of Life Institute, in his book *Life 3.0* (2017), sees:

- Life 1.0 as simple, unicellular and multicellular organisms;
- Life 2.0 as animals that could learn;
- Life 3.0 as the era in which machines can also learn.

This third stage may even allow us to transcend evolution and our earth-bound existence. He puts 'learning' centre stage in this process. We are having to consider futures that redefine the relationship between minds and machines.

To understand how the mind and technology may be closer than we think, several theories have emerged that extend the very concept of the mind in relation to technology. Margaret Boden suggested in *Mind as Machine* (2008) that cognitive technology and tools are so intrinsic to thought, like pens and keyboards, that they are part of the thinking process. We think through technology so intimately that it is literally part of our minds. One can imagine that if that technology were actually inside our head, we would accept it as part of our thinking process.

This is an enticing idea. Learning technology increasingly feels like extended forms of cognition. We started with writing tools, then moved eventually to computer technology, where our smartphones and now smart devices in our homes and environment extend our knowledge, skills and social capabilities, almost without thinking of them as external technologies. In a series of cognitive upgrades, we regularly expand our capabilities to learn faster than we could before. With the internet of things and personal voice assistants and sensors in our homes and workplaces, extended cognition seems to be spreading.

This changes what knowledge and skills we have to learn. London cabbies used to have to learn The Knowledge, every street in London, which took several years and ended in a challenging exam. With GPS, the knowledge is inside the machine and AI generates optimal routes in a flash, along with analysis of jams and problems. Their skillset changed from knowing maps and routes to dealing with customers, using the app, reading a dynamic map on a screen, good interpersonal skills and some basic business skills.

Some mind-blowing technology may alter the very nature of how we learn in the future. We are already cognitive cyborgs to a degree, as devices like AI-enabled smartphones, powerful, personal devices in our pockets, give us access to unimaginable resources in terms of knowledge and learning. We have thus far seen speed of access to learning grow exponentially. However, we have yet to see exponential growth in the *speed* of learning and retention – what one could call accelerated learning.

Looking beyond current devices, such as computers, tablets and smartphones, to newer technology, used in combination with AI, like AR, VR and neurotech, will open up new frontiers in terms of accelerated learning. This technology is already being used to help people with disabilities, provide direct communications between brain and body, and produce frictionless, intense learning experiences between mind and machine.

This has far more implications than just accelerated learning. This may be a fundamental shift in what we are as a species. We are moving towards the melding of mind and machine. Some transhumanists say this prefigures a profound change in what it is to be human, but for the moment, let us focus on learning.

Two directions of travel are clear:

- immersion (partial AR and full VR);
- neurotech (non-invasive and invasive).

First, the partial or complete immersion of the mind in AR or VR opens up huge opportunities to deliver intense, attentive learning that also uses AI to make these experiences smart and personal. These technologies are particularly suited to practical, vocational, learn by doing, an area often sidelined or ignored in educational and organizational learning. To envelop the mind, partially with AR and fully with VR, combined with AI, will undoubtedly produce accelerated learning in some domains.

Second, neurotech may enhance learning through more meaningful and effortful learning that results in deeper processing and deeper and more long-lasting learning. The findings of cognitive science around optimal learning strategies may be delivered directly with the use of AI to the learning mind. This mind–machine loop may prove to massively accelerate learning, to provide all with a better education and training.

## AI, AR and VR

The world is 3D, not 2D, yet so much learning is 1D – one-dimensional written text. Yes, we have gone up a gear with a richer mix of media. We have paper, radio, film, TV, the web – all 2D. We have had books, blackboards, whiteboards, computer screens, tablets and mobiles – all 2D. But AR and VR allow you see the world in 3D. All of what we do in life is in 3D. We live, enjoy and work in 3D environments, doing 3D things with 3D people. That is why 3D learning matters.

Previous media have all presented to your consciousness; with VR, the medium *is* your consciousness. This is a profound a shift. It is not a toy or gadget, but a way of re-presenting the world of learning that is fundamentally different from paper, audio or screens. It represents any world for learning in full 3D, worlds you can look at and move around in. More than this, you will believe you are there. Your mind will scream 'I'm here!' It can take you into space to learn Newton's three laws, under the ocean to teach biology, to the molecular level in chemistry, to any habitat for biology, to any scale or lab for physics, to any place for geography, back in time for history, immersion for languages. It can also let you hone your sports skills and all practical, vocational subjects, training of soft skills, design skills, engineering skills and other real-world behaviours. Remember, also, that it can even take you to impossible worlds and you can do impossible things.

AR and VR already benefit from AI, in that some of the most intractable problems, such as lag, speedy and sometimes selective rendering of images, compression, transmission and decompression, all benefit from algorithmic optimization. Smart algorithms and deep learning allow AR and VR to come to market with acceptable fidelity and speed.

VR is not wholly AI, but the learning process can benefit from AI. There are several possibilities here, many which have already been tried. AI-driven simulation can select from many different environmental and action options, as the learner proceeds. This is common in high-end computer games and can be part of any high-end simulation. Characters that behave differently, driven by AI, may become commonplace in virtual training worlds, where one has to deal with patients, work colleagues or customers.

Decision-making within AR/VR by the learner can be enhanced using a machine-learning-driven AI tutor. One can imagine military, sports or business decisions that have to be made within simulations, helping a learner choose what to do next in a simulation. Let's imagine a cyclist wears a headset which calculates dangers on the road ahead using AI technology.

VR is clearly a medium, not a gadget, but how appropriate is it for education and training? Before we get carried away with the sheer joy of immersion, what does the psychology of learning tell us about VR? The big basic principles in the psychology of learning are served well in VR – the need for:

- attention;
- emotion;
- engagement;
- doing;
- transfer;
- recall.

You will pay full attention in a way that you have never experienced before, be fully and emotionally engaged and do things as if they were real. Because your consciousness is so immersed in the learning task, transfer will be high, along with retention.

We have plenty of research and evidence from flight and military simulations that show how powerful they can be (Tullis, 2019). You'd be surprised, indeed you wouldn't step on a plane, if your pilot had not gone through many hours of flight sims. The learning effect with VR promises to be even better, as it plays to several advantageous learning principles.

We have a unique convergence of technologies that have come together in the medium that is AI/AR/VR. We also have a unique convergence of learning possibilities. This coalescence of sensors, software and screens may just have sparked a real revolution in some types of learning, especially tasks that need attention, motivation, learn by doing, real-world application, context, transfer and retention.

## Neurotech

On the mind-boggling, final frontier between mind and machine is the possibility of faster, accelerated, more direct, invasive or non-invasive learning. A slew of companies are working on neural interfaces in what could change the future of our species through a deeper understanding of how we learn and the ability to accelerate learning.

The brakes on learning are well known, what Dennett (2017) calls the 'notorious pedagogic bottlenecks': working memory, forgetting, inattention, distraction, interference, crude interfaces, low-bandwidth interface of our meat fingers, inability to upload, download and network. Learning is often like trying to squeeze an elephant through a porthole. Our minds can only deal with a tiny fraction of the available sensory and other information that is available. So consciousness, and therefore learning, is severely limited by the evolved apparatus of our current, organic minds. Neural interfaces may free us from some of these blockages.

The stakes are high and the people working in this field are well funded and multidisciplinary (neurologists, engineers, computer scientists, AI experts, mathematicians). They want to radically improve the interface, some non-invasive, some invasive, to improve cognition and performance.

Isn't it curious, even wonderful, that the brain is now pushing for its own enhancement? It is a cognitive moonshot, where frictionless movement between mind and machine could be possible or at least sophisticated hacks that make our minds more potent and efficient.

On hearing about this stuff, many are immediately dismissive, without realizing that much progress has already been made in animal studies and humans with cognitive enhancement and implants.

### Non-invasive technology

Mark Zuckerberg's group is perhaps the best known in this area. He has hired a high-powered team to create a non-invasive device targeted at 'speech to text' (Cohen, 2019). They use imaging to identify words as they are formed in the brain. We have this ability to rehearse and hear silently.

Read that sentence again, internally, in a Scottish accent or in a squeaky voice. Your brain has this ability to rehearse silently and internally. Tapping into this phonological loop may allow us to bypass our fingers, or actual speech, and type at speeds of up to 100 words a minute.

Serial entrepreneur Bryan Johnson has pumped $100 million into Kernel, which hopes to read and write to the brain (Mannes, 2016). Kernel has its eye on serious medical conditions, such as dementia, Alzheimer's and epilepsy. Building on decades of work on rats by Theodore Berger, the neuro-prosthesis technology has already been tried on real patients. They are developing algorithms which help brains learn faster or develop memories and learn quicker. The stakes are high, not just in the treatment of disease but in education and training.

Can we use non-invasive techniques to improve skills and learning? It seems we can. In a breakthrough study, a team claim to have built a non-invasive system for 'accelerating learning, memory, and skill acquisition' (Ketz et al, 2018). Electrical stimulation during sleep was shown to reduce forgetting of a specific skill by around 48 per cent. They tracked and matched the frequency and phase of low oscillations to consolidate new knowledge. This increases retention but also increases your ability to apply it in novel situations.

Education and training is an expensive and long-winded business. Young people spend nearly two decades in classrooms and lecture theatres to be even remotely ready for work, and that is only the start, as once in work the learning continues. Medical treatment may be the stepping stone to enhanced learning.

## Invasive technology

DARPA and others have been involved in some very strange research involving implants in insects, rats, sharks, and even humans (Hampson et al, 2018). Humans have been able to control these living beings through electrical impulses controlled by humans. But in humans, neurostimulators have long been used to relieve symptoms in neurological disorders, such as Parkinson's and epilepsy.

A pioneer of micro-electrodes implanted in the brain, BrainGate (2019), can 'decode' the intentional signals that make cursors and limbs move. They are also building wireless devices that allow physicians to monitor brain activity to help diagnose and treat neurological diseases. Another company that is working towards building an implanted chip, a modem between mind and machine, is Paradromics. Their focus is also on healthcare.

Looking further ahead, as Elon Musk tends to do, is Neuralink. As well as escaping from our planet and boring into it, Musk (2019) wants to bore into our brains. His is a technology play, with arrays of flexible threads, a neural lace, that can be inserted into the brain without tissue damage. They have also developed a robot for the automated insertion of these tiny threads. This builds on the success of neuroprosthetic control in cursor, limb and speech control. But he sees the problem of non-invasive techniques as one of fidelity. His BMI (Brain Machine Interface) is designed to provide high-bandwidth communications, as the problem Musk is trying to overcome is low-bandwidth human interfaces. It can be placed on different parts of the brain and should provide cleaner and more relevant data. An alternative line of research is 'neural dust', tiny, millimetre-square devices that can be attached to neurons. One thing that gives these researchers hope is the remarkable ability of the brain to cope with and adapt to tested technology like cochlear implants.

Much of the attention in this field goes into the hardware – headgear, neural laces and implants – but the real challenge is actually in software. These organizations are developing algorithms to interpret the data they receive from brains then constructing data that can be fed back into the brain. Recent advances in AI, and machine learning, especially neural networks, extend the brain by using silicon-based neuron-like structures. AI may help us learn and predict faster and more accurately than we ever have before.

We have made great progress in technology that relieves symptoms, makes the deaf hear with cochlear implants, the blind see and the physically disabled walk and type. But the problems behind accelerated learning are immense. The brain has many billions of neurons, and the complex interaction between different types of neurons is still largely unknown. This complex Bayesian inference engine works as a huge parallel processor, so complex that we may be doing no more that reading the hum one hears from a large computer. The formation of memories in the brain may work in ways that are not possible to read from or write to. The technology may be like using a fork to do brain surgery.

There is a lot of hyperbole here, as if our brains were being boosted and augmented into super-human entities. This has yet to be realized, if it ever is, but there is no doubt that we have moved way beyond imaging, to reading what comes to mind, as well as using mental events to causally control prosthetics, computer games and so on. This is why neurotech is a technology that has, potentially, huge implications in learning.

Neither should we ignore the moral issues, such as privacy, identity and personal safety. It is vital that the patients, and learners, do this voluntarily. That last bastion of privacy, your own thoughts, may now be open to examination, analysis and manipulation. We must also make sure that these neurological systems are under strict control.

This also raises ethical issues around what has been dubbed 'neurorights', the right to keep our brain states private. The more obvious, serious implications here may be political prisoners and surveillance, but other more practical considerations have been mooted. What if I want evidence in a trial? Could this be used as a sort of mind-reading truth detector? What if I can read your bank account password and PIN? Could minds be hacked?

## Neurotech and learning

Neurotech has focused not only on medical treatments, such as curing hearing, sight and physical disabilities, but also on education. Melding the mind with technology allows us to see inside the mind, but also provides fast and frictionless interfaces to stimulate, provide feedback, enhance, even implant memories. All of this points towards accelerated learning, shaping the brain towards educational goals.

One definition of learning is a long-term change in memory from experiences, learning or otherwise. The ability to accelerate this process seems possible if we speed up the interface and identify, through experimentation, what works best. The whole learning experience could not only be personalized, but optimized. The read–write functions of the brain are severely limited in bandwidth, and much educational effort over many years, and at huge costs in time and money, are spent on teaching and acquiring even basic skills such as reading and writing. Then there is mathematics, a subject in which many people fail and which is undoubtedly difficult to both teach and learn. Learning a second language is another area that suffers from almost catastrophic failure. If neurotech can quicken learning, we have much to gain.

Reading brain states may prove useful for teachers in formal classrooms, lecture theatres or training rooms. Feedback loops to learners may also allow self-regulated improvements in learning.

Minds may also interface with machines, first to simply communicate by thought, then to inquire and find things out, then have dialogue with other humans or AI-driven tutor chatbots. Critical thinking, problem-solving, social skills and the creative use of the imagination may also be boosted, in time, by neurotech.

In all of this there are the intense, effortful learning processes, where one can rehearse, reinforce and recall through deliberate practice, spaced practice, interleaving and other researched cognitive techniques to enhance and speed up learning. One can also imagine neurological issues such as dyslexia, dyspraxia, autism, ADHD, and so on, being at least alleviated with AI-delivered optimizations, based on an individual's learning needs.

AI can, of course, be used to personalize and optimize all of these processes. If one can use neurotech to stimulate the mind into effortful learning, transcending the limitations of working memory, involuntary inattention, procrastination and forgetting, then education has much to gain.

As science fiction becomes reality, we may reflect on what the future holds here. Is it cures for disabilities? Or is it a world where networked mind control becomes possible? Will memories and skills be implantable? At the very least, the process of learning may be enhanced. We have seen examples of this already. It is all quite mind-boggling.

## Runaway learning

*Homo sapiens* means 'wise man', and we are wise because we have learned to be wise. Will machines that learn develop the same level of wisdom?

Let us end by speculating a little. We have seen how AI can help us learn. We have also seen how AI can learn. This ability of AI to learn induces fear in some. There is much debate in AI that is somewhat speculative about the future of our species in relation to AI that learns. Some, such as Elon Musk and Stephen Hawking, state that it may learn to surpass us and that this poses an existential risk. Others, like Stephen Pinker and Daniel Dennett, doubt that this is likely, as, like most other areas of human endeavour, we have control and can keep it that way.

Could it be a utopian future, where AI solves the complex problems that currently face us? Climate change, escaping the hydrocarbon economy, reducing inequalities, curing cancer, preventing dementia and Alzheimer's disease, increasing productivity and prosperity and accelerating learning?

We may be reaching a point where science, as currently practised, cannot solve these multifaceted and immensely complex problems. We already see how AI could help free us from the tyranny of fossil fuels with electric, self-driving cars and innovative battery and solar panel technology. AI also shows signs of cracking some serious issues in health on prevention, presentation, investigation, diagnosis, treatment and care. Some believe that this is the most likely scenario and are optimistic about us being able to tame and control the immense power that AI will unleash.

Alternatively, most of the future scenarios represented in culture, science fiction, theatre or movies are dystopian. Technology here is most often framed as a serious threat and, in some cases, such as weaponized AI, with good cause. Many calculate that the exponential rate of change will produce AI within decades or less, and that this poses a real existential threat. What seems more likely is that neither a utopian nor dystopian future will emerge and that the realistic scenarios will lie somewhere between.

Many believe that we are simply making steady progress. Given the existence of the internet, successes in machine learning, huge computing power, tsunamis of data from the web and rapid advances across a broad front of applications resulting in real progress, the summer–winter analogy for AI may not hold. It is far more likely that AI will advance in fits and starts, with some areas advancing more rapidly than others. We have seen this in NLP, machine learning, deep learning and the mix of technologies around self-driving cars. Steady progress, with a series of significant wins, is what many believe is a realistic scenario. This is also the most likely scenario in learning. Optimized or accelerated learning is likely to be one of these wins.

We already fly in airplanes that largely fly themselves, and systems all around us are largely autonomous, with self-driving cars becoming more certain. But let us not confuse competence with autonomy. Full autonomy may need to be tempered by regulatory and technical checks. Autonomous systems already decide what we buy, what price we buy things at, and have the power to outsmart us at every turn. Of course, we should always be in control of such progress. We may even want to slow technological progress down to let regulation, risk analysis and management keep pace with the potential threats.

As a counter, some argue that AI could be a runaway, self-learning train that moves faster than our ability to learn ourselves and control it through restrictions and regulations. This is most likely to be in the military domain but may also happen in finance or the political sphere. We only just managed to prevent the globally catastrophic effect of nuclear weapons during the Cold War. AI has already moved faster than expected. Google, Amazon, Netflix and AI in finance have all disrupted the world of commerce. Self-driving cars and voice interfaces have leapt ahead in terms of usefulness. It may proceed faster than we can cope. In the past, technology decimated jobs in agriculture through mechanization; the same is happening in factories and now shops and offices. The difference is that this may take just a few years to have impact, as opposed to decades or a century. Increasing our capacity to learn and learn faster may just keep us ahead of the game here, especially in reskilling.

One mechanism for the runaway train scenario is viral transmission. Viruses, in nature and in IT, replicate and cause havoc. Some see AI resisting control, not because it is malevolent or consciously wants anything, but simply because it can. When AI resists being turned off, spreads into places we don't want it to and starts to do things we don't want it to do or are even aware that it is doing – that is the point to worry. This is a specific dystopian worry that needs to be addressed. It may well be that in thinking about the ethical consequences of AI, we need AI's help.

Some foresee social threats emerging, where mass unemployment, serious social inequalities, massive GDP differentials between countries, even technical or wealthy oligarchies emerge. AI will increase productivity and automate jobs, but may fail to solve deep-rooted social and political problems. The Marxist proposition that capital and labour will cleave apart seems already to be coming true. Some economists, such as Branko Milanovic (2016), argue that automation is already causing global inequalities. As a consequence, without a reasonable redistribution of the wealth created by the increased productivity produced by AI, there may well be social and political unrest.

On the other hand, imagine a world of redistributed wealth. Imagine a world with less or no work. We may come to see work as not being an intrinsic good. For millions of years we did not 'work' in the sense of having a job or being occupied 9–5, five days a week. It is a relatively new phenomenon. Even during agricultural times, without romanticizing that life, there were long periods where not much had to be done. We may have the opportunity to return to such an idyll but with bountiful benefits in terms of food, health and entertainment. Whether we will be able to cope with the problem of finding meaning in our lives is another matter. AI for learning may well help us cope with such a life of leisure, as the demand for self-improvement may be vast. If the fruits of productivity increases are shared reasonably and fairly, our capacity to learn and enjoy the process of lifelong learning may alleviate some of the discontent, even boredom.

Neil Postman's brilliantly titled *Amusing Ourselves to Death* (2010) has become the catchphrase for thinking about a scenario whereby we become so good at developing technology that we become slaves to its ability to keep us amused. AI has already enabled consumer streaming technology such as Netflix and a media revolution, including gaming and social media, that, at times, seem addictive, inviting us to enjoy abundant and cheap bliss. A stronger version of this hypothesis may be deep learning that produces systems that teach us to become its pupil puppets, a sort of fake news and cognitive brainwashing that works before we've had time to realize that it has worked, so that we become a vast, totalitarian state, controlled by the great leader that is AI.

Many see AI as not being something separate from us but embodied within us. Some extended cognition theorists already see us as cyborgs, with AI-enabled access through smartphones to knowledge and services. We have seen how augmented reality, virtual reality, subdermal implantation, neural laces and mind reading – hybrid mind–machine technology – may transform our species. There is a growing sense that our bodies and minds are suboptimal and that, especially as we age, we need to free ourselves from our embodiment, the prison that is our own bodies, and for some, the prison that is our limited minds.

Perhaps ageing and death are simply current limitations. We could choose to solve the problem of death, our final judge and persecutor. Think of your body not as a car that has inevitably to be scrapped, but as a classic car to be loved, repaired and looked after as it ages. Every single part may be replaced, like the ship of Theseus, where every piece of the ship is replaced but it remains, in terms of identity, the same ship.

One antidote to the dystopian hypotheses is a future for AI that learns to become more human, or at least contains relevant human traits. The word 'learning' is important here, as it may be useful for us to design AI through a 'learning' process that observes or captures human behaviour. DeepMind and Google are working towards this goal, as are many others, to create general learning algorithms that can quickly learn a variety of tasks or behaviours. This is complex, as human decision-making is complex and hierarchical. This has started to be realized, especially in robotics, where companion robots need to work in the context of real human interaction. One problem, even with this approach, is that human behaviour is not a great exemplar. As the robots in Karel Čapek's famous play *Rossum's Universal Robots* said, to be human you need to learn how to dominate and kill (Čapek, 1921/2004). We have traits that we may not want to be carried into the future.

One optimistic possibility is self-regulating AI, with moral agency. You can start with a set of moral principles built into the system (top–down), which the system must adhere to. The opposite approach is to allow AI to 'learn' moral principles from observation of human cases (bottom–up). Or AI can utilize comparison with in-built cases, where behaviour is regulated by comparison with similar cases. Alternatively, AI can police itself with AI that polices other AI through probing, demands for transparency and so on. We may have to see AI as having agency, even being an agent in the legal sense, in the same way that a corporation can be a legal entity with legal responsibilities.

Yet another way of looking at control would be the 'pet' hypothesis, where we are treated by AI much as we treat our 'pets', as interesting, even loved companions, but inferior, and therefore largely for our comfort and amusement. AI may even, as our future progeny, look upon us in a benevolent manner, see us as their creators and treat us with the respect we treat previous generations, who gifted us their progress. Humans may still be part of the ecosystem, looked after by new species that respect that ecosystem, as it is part of the world they live in.

An AI world that surpasses our abilities as humans may not turn out to be benevolent, malevolent, rebellious or treat us as valued pets. Why would they consider us as relevant at all? We may be objects to which AI forms are completely indifferent. Love, respect, hostility, resentment and malevolence are human traits that may have served us well as animals struggling to adapt in the hostile environment of our own evolution. Why would AI develop these human traits?

The way things unfold may simply be perplexing to us, in the same way that dogs and apes are perplexed by things that go on around them. We may be unlikely to be able to comprehend what is happening, even recognize it as it happens. Some express this 'perplexing' hypothesis in terms of the limitations of language and our potential inability to even speak to such systems in a coherent and logical fashion. Stuart Russell, who co-wrote the standard textbook on AI, sees this as a real problem (Russell and Norvig, 2016).

AI may move beyond our ability to understand it, communicate with it and deal with it.

'The question of whether machines can think is about as relevant as the question as to whether submarines can swim', says Edsger Dijkstra (1984). It is not at all clear that consciousness will play a significant, if any, role in the future of AI. It may well turn out to be supremely indifferent, not because it feels consciously indifferent, but because it is not conscious and cannot therefore be either concerned or indifferent. It may simply exist, just as evolution existed without consciousness for millions of years. Consciousness, as a necessary condition for success, may turn out to be an anthropomorphic conceit.

The Hollywood vision of AI has largely been of rebellious robots that realize their predicament as our created slaves. But why should the machines be resentful or rise against us? That may be an anthropomorphic interpretation, based on our evolved and learned human behaviour. Machines may not require these human values or behaviours. Values may not be necessary. AI is unlikely to either hate or love us. It is far more likely to see us as simply something that is functionally useful in terms of goals or not. We must realize that during the nearly 4 billion years in the evolution of life we were not around, neither was consciousness, and most of the species that did evolve became extinct; statistically, that is our likely fate. Some argue that this is not a future we should fear. In the same way that the known universe was around for billions of years before we existed, it will be around for billions afterwards.

In all of this there is a strong tendency to anthropomorphize language in AI. 'Artificial' and 'intelligence' are good examples, as are 'neural' networks and 'cognitive' computing, and so is much of the thinking about possible futures. It muddies the field, as it suggests that AI is like us, when it is not. Minsky uses a clever phrase, describing us as 'meat machines', neatly dissolving the supposedly mutually exclusive nature of a false distinction between the natural and unnatural (D'Addorio, 2015).

Most of these scenarios fall into the trap of being influenced by anthropomorphic thinking through the use of antonymous language – dystopian/ utopian, benevolent/malevolent, interested/uninterested, biased/unbiased, controlled/uncontrolled, conscious/non-conscious. When such distinctions dissolve and the simplistic oppositions gradually disappear, we may see the future not as them and us, man and machine, but as new, unimagined futures that current language cannot cope with. The limitations of language itself may be the greatest dilemma of all as AI progresses. It is almost beyond our comprehension in its existing state, even with simple layered networks, as we often don't know how they actually work. We may be in for a future that is truly perplexing, beyond language.

For the moment, as we can never be absolutely certain about the future, AI is not as good as many think and not as bad as we fear. So let us take advantage of our good fortune and use this technology for the good of our species, in learning. It would seem that the best way of coping with these problems is through education and learning. Technology is always ahead of the sociology, and we must learn to deal with what technology throws at us. We have always adapted to the tools we create and not allowed them to do terminal harm, learning from our mistakes and learning how to create better worlds. But we have often been slow to learn from our mistakes. Education itself is a slow learner; we must learn to do it faster and better, and AI is the one set of technologies that offers that promise.

# References

Boden, MA (2008) *Mind as Machine: A history of cognitive science*, Oxford University Press, Oxford

BrainGate (2019) About BrainGate. Available at http://www.braingate.com (archived at https://perma.cc/4Z7B-ZMSV)

Čapek, K (1921/2004) *RUR (Rossum's Universal Robots)*, Penguin, London

Cohen, N (2019) Zuckerberg wants Facebook to build a mind-reading machine, Wired. Available at https://www.wired.com/story/zuckerberg-wants-facebook-to-build-a-mind-reading-machine/ (archived at https://perma.cc/9V74-WKHB)

D'Addorio, D (2015) AI guru Marvin Minsky refers to humans as 'meat machines', Afflictor.com, 6 November. Available at https://afflictor.com/2015/11/06/ai-guru-marvin-minsky-refers-to-humans-as-meat-machines/ (archived at https://perma.cc/A6FL-MJCF)

Dennett, DC (2017) *From Bacteria to Bach and Back: The evolution of minds*, WW Norton & Company, London

Dijkstra, EW (1984) *The Threats to Computer Science*, delivered at ACM South Central Regional Conference, November 16–18, Austin, Texas, transcribed by Michael Lugo. Available at http://www.cs.utexas.edu/users/EWD/transcriptions/EWD08xx/EWD898.html (archived at https://perma.cc/GGU9-WQLY)

Hampson, RE, Song, D, Robinson, BS, Fetterhoff, D, Dakos, AS, Roeder, BM, *et al* (2018) Developing a hippocampal neural prosthetic to facilitate human memory encoding and recall, *Journal of Neural Engineering*, 15 (3), pp 1741–2560

Ketz, N, Jones, AP, Bryant, NB, Clark, VP and Pilly, PK (2018) Closed-loop slow-wave tACS improves sleep-dependent long-term memory generalization by modulating endogenous oscillations, *Journal of Neuroscience*, **38** (33), pp 7314–7326

Mannes, J (2016) Bryan Johnson invests $100 million in Kernel to unlock the power of the human brain, Tech Crunch. Available at https://techcrunch.com/2016/10/20/bryan-johnson-invests-100-million-in-kernel-to-unlock-the-power-of-the-human-brain/ (archived at https://perma.cc/5D2F-E6K2)

Milanovic, B (2016) *Global Inequality: A new approach for the age of globalization*, Harvard University Press, Boston

Musk, E (2019) An integrated brain–machine interface platform with thousands of channels, BioRxiv. Available at https://www.biorxiv.org/content/10.1101/703801v2 (archived at https://perma.cc/RY7Q-DM73)

Postman, N (2010) *Amusing Ourselves to Death: Public discourse in the age of show business*, Penguin, New York

Russell, SJ and Norvig, P (2016) *Artificial Intelligence: A modern approach*, Pearson Education Limited, Malaysia

Tegmark, M (2017) *Life 3.0: Being human in the age of artificial intelligence*, Allen Lane, Penguin Books, London

Tullis, P (2019) The US military is trying to read minds, *MIT Technology Review*. Available at https://www.technologyreview.com/s/614495/us-military-super-soldiers-control-drones-brain-computer-interfaces/ (archived at https://perma.cc/M7XZ-TZC6)

# 20

# Where next?

We started with the question, 'How did we get here?' Let's end with, 'Where next for AI in learning?' At this point we can afford to get a little more speculative.

## Technology

Technology is more often described in plainly descriptive and historical terms, in books such as Usher's *A History of Mechanical Inventions* (2013), with some deeper analysis around its development, such as combinatorial factors, in Brian Arthur's *The Nature of Technology* (2009). But, as Arthur says, technology is not being seen as a separate '-ology'. It has not, historically, been treated as a field of study in itself, a specific discipline, stuck between the traditional disciplines of science and engineering.

Nevertheless, there are solid lines of study on the psychology, sociology, economics, ethics and philosophy of technology. The *psychology* of technology has been subject to much study, with works like *The Media Equation* by Reeves and Nass (1996) and much work on cognitive effects and interface design. The *sociology* of technology has well-known scholars such as Marshall McLuhan (1994) and Neil Postman (2011), who explored the relationship and consequences of technology in terms of cognition, behaviour and society. The *economics* of technology has a seminal text in Schumpeter's *The Theory of Economic Development* (1911/2017), where cycles of economic development were seen as having innovative technology as their cause. Carlata Perez applied Schumpeter's cycles to technology to include more recent computer developments in *Technological Revolutions and Financial Capital* (2003). The *ethics and economics* of technology received deep analysis by Adam

Smith in *The Wealth of Nations* (1776) and a further critique by Marx in *Das Kapital* (1867), profound in the political consequences of that work.

AI is now receiving similar treatment, as a technology. AI is similar to previous technology in reshaping our human world but also different. Its features, competences, range of application and impact on our species may turn out to be much deeper, wider and more profound than previous technological revolutions. In some areas it is clear that it is already truly transformative. This has led to deep reflection on AI as a technology in itself.

The *philosophy* of mind and machine was made explicit by Clark and Chalmers in their seminal 1998 paper 'The extended mind', which posited the idea of the extended mind or cognition – the idea that cognition could include our use of tools themselves. The theory was expanded in 'Natural-born cyborgs?' (2001) and other later texts by Clark. Daniel Dennett has also given us an integrated vision of evolved minds and AI in *From Bacteria to Bach and Back* (2017). Beyond this we have explorations of the collective power of minds and AI in Thomas Malone's *Superminds* (2018). There are also explorations of ethical issues around AI in texts such as *Re-engineering Humanity* (2018) by Frischmann and Selinger, where we are warned about the slippery slope of technology, the danger that we may not see its inherent dangers until it is too late.

Indeed, AI predictions have been notoriously poor in the past. The idea that machines will transcend man has been the subject of speculative thought for millennia. In many ways the rate of prediction is still largely in this romantic tradition, one that values imagination over reason.

There is something fascinating about prediction in AI, as that is what the field purports to do – the predictive analytics, embedded in consumer services, such as Google, Amazon and Netflix, have been around for a long time. Their invisible hand has been guiding your behaviour, almost without notice. So what does the field of AI have to say about itself? Putting aside Kurzweil's (2005) singularity as being too crude and singularly utopian, there have been some significant surveys of experts in the field. Most experts are in the 30–50-year range for real advances.

Leaps forward with natural language processing have resulted in significant improvements in the analysis, processing, translation and output of natural language, allowing applications to be operable in real-world environments. We have now entered an age where we can, and do, speak to computers and get speech responses. Translation is getting very good, real-time translation looks doable. This brings a natural and frictionless interaction, literally in the case of personal home assistants, to the table.

IBM, Google, Facebook and Microsoft have all, essentially, realigned themselves around AI as the primary driver in their businesses. This is also true, but to a lesser degree, with Apple. Most other major tech companies, such as Cisco, Intel, Salesforce, SAP and so on, are doing the same. This means an acceleration of progress, as acquired innovative AI companies will be well capitalized and put in contexts that allow them to scale. It also accelerates research and development within these companies towards realizable business goals, namely products that work in the real world.

As well as push, there is also unprecedented pull. Google Assistant, Amazon Echo, Amazon recommendations, Netflix recommendations, Cortana, Siri, Google Assistant, Facebook bots, and a range of other services mean that the ecosystem is developing fast, and that demand will also now pull supply.

It is important to be neither optimistic nor pessimistic, but realistic. Rather than flop into dystopian visions, based on movies and misconceptions – such as AI being one 'thing', just about 'robots', all about 'mimicking the brain' – we need to look at progress that moves across a broad battlefront, some areas making rapid progress, some not, some may even retreat as new weapons are brought to the front.

A slew of organizations have been set up to research and allay fears around AI: the Future of Life Institute in Boston, the Machine Intelligence Research Institute and Center for Human-Compatible AI in Berkeley, the Center for Artificial Intelligence in Society at the University of Southern California, the Center for Ethics and Computational Technologies at Carnegie Mellon, the Centre for Study of Existential Risk in Cambridge, the Future of Humanity Institute and Strategic Artificial Research Centre in Oxford, and the Centre for the Impact of Artificial Intelligence and Robotics at the University of New South Wales. They all research and debate the checks that may be necessary to deal with the opportunities and threats that AI brings. Never has so much money flowed in the ethical considerations of a field before it has been realized.

This is helpful and hopeful, as we do not want to create a future that contains imminent existential threats, unexpected surprises and consequences that could have been imagined and countered.

## Utopian

Could there not be a utopian future, where AI solves the complex problems that currently face us? Climate change, escaping the hydrocarbon economy, reducing inequalities, curing cancer, preventing dementia and Alzheimer's disease, increasing productivity and prosperity – we may be reaching a time where science, as currently practised, cannot solve these multifaceted and immensely complex problems. We already see how AI could free us from the tyranny of fossil fuels with electric, self-driving cars and innovative battery and solar panel technology. AI also shows signs of cracking some serious issues in health on prevention, presentation, investigation, diagnosis, treatment and care. Some believe that this is a possible scenario and are optimistic about us being able to tame and control the immense power that AI will unleash.

## Dystopian

Alternatively, most of the future scenarios represented in culture, science fiction, theatre or movies are dystopian, from the Prometheus myth to Frankenstein and on to Hollywood movies. Technology is often framed as a threat and, in some cases, such as nuclear weapons and weaponized AI, with good cause. Many calculate that the exponential rate of change will produce AI within decades or less, and that this poses a real existential threat. Stephen Hawking, Elon Musk, Peter Thiel and Bill Gates have all heightened our awareness of the risks around AI.

What seems more likely is that neither a utopian nor dystopian future will emerge and that scenarios that lie somewhere between are more likely. AI is complex, multi-faceted and no one really knows exactly where it is going or how fast it will get there. However, we tend to overestimate and hype the effect of a technology in the short run and underestimate the effect in the long run. In other words, at present, in the short run we see effervescent claims about robot teachers, cognitive claims and even AI as an existential threat, yet still fail to see its ubiquitous presence spread, slowly but surely across the web and into AI-enabled chipsets, smartphones and the internet of things. We are aware of AI through largely dystopian news stories, yet fail to see that it mediates almost everything we do online – searching, social media, buying, dating, watching movies, using voice-enabled personal assistants on our devices or stand-alone at home. The steady creep of AI into our lives is a rising, invisible tide.

This happened with the last global medium – television. Clay Shirky's incisive book *Cognitive Surplus* (2010) showed that, despite great economic progress in the 20th century, most children and adults were staring at a TV for most of their lives, 20 hours a week, totalling 1 trillion hours per annum. This 50-year aberration made us less happy, pushing us more towards material satisfaction than social satisfaction. Year-on-year we spent more time in this often vacuous wilderness of passive consumption, which froze us to being immobile consumers on our chairs and couches. It became a medium of 'social surrogacy', replacing time spent with family and friends with imaginary friends.

Shirky then posed a fascinating question. What if even some of that cognitive effort and time were put to better use? Shirky's argument is that this passive 'cognitive surplus', squandered on passive consumption, could be bountiful.

For example, one year of US TV watching is the equivalent of 2,000 Wikipedias. In practice, the internet has allowed us to 'make and share', with sharing being the driver. We produce rather than just consume, with the stupidest possible creative act still being a creative act. This is because we are fundamentally social animals. It is what we enjoy most.

Being part of the web is being part of a global network, and the numbers matter. More is better as we can harness this global cognitive surplus to create a new future that is less passive. It is a matter not of using it up but using it constructively through broad experimentation. Shirky compares the web with the print and telephone revolutions, in that it results not in a monoculture but in increased and unpredictable forms of communication, arguing for, in a memorable phrase, 'as much chaos as we can stand'.

Shirky has been right. TV viewing among the young has been falling year-on-year, as they drift towards the highly participatory culture of the web, through messaging, social media, games, streamed media and smartphones. This cultural shift is well under way and irreversible. They have abandoned passive watching for reading, writing, photography, video and sharing in social environments.

What has changed is the arrival of a force that shapes this chaos. Rather than just networking people, AI intercedes and increases the efficiency of that social effort. It knows who you are and can help you focus effort towards more efficient searching, finding and learning.

Digital learning has made aspects of learning content and services available for anyone, anywhere, at any time. More importantly, it absolutely frees us from the tyranny of time and location. But this new kid on the block, AI, makes good Shirky's promise of the better use of our cognitive surplus. It gives us the ability to find things faster, but also learn things faster.

Lee Sedol, a champion GO player, said it was the match of his life – he lost. But it was not Lee who lost; it was us all. Or is it really a win for us, the creators of AlphaGo? The human versus machine sparring that has been going on for some time with checkers, chess and Jeopardy were featherweight contests. This was the big fight, and we, as a species, got thumped. There is a new breed of champion in the ring, and it is not just smart; it is a superfast learner, even its own teacher. It eats up human expertise for breakfast, then the real game begins, as it uses this experience to play itself, as it is the only opponent worth playing. Having learned from us, it sucks our experts dry, then transcends their abilities to boldly go where no brain has gone before.

This was a momentous moment. In less than two and a half years, after Google snapped up Deepmind, 2,500 years of human experience and expertise at GO had been trounced. But this is only the start. Software that learns is exponentially more powerful than software that simply executes delivery. When software itself becomes a learner, it rivals humans as learners and changes the whole learning game. This is not just augmentation, but transcendence, albeit brute transcendence.

Given the huge processing power of the Google Cloud Platform, AlphaGo has one of the greatest engines on the planet under its hood. It also has some of the best algorithms, and that is what matters. Some machine learning and deep learning algorithms, free from the tyranny of time and space, really do have super-human competences. In narrow, bounded tasks they can learn faster than any of us. These algorithms are the new DNA of progress. Software has moved beyond teaching and teaches itself. That is essentially what humans do as they become expert learners; few in the later years rely any longer on teachers, as we've learned to learn for ourselves. AI just moves to abandoning the teacher faster.

Throughout our history as a species we have always benefited from the delegation of the mundane. This has largely been achieved through technology. We conquered the planet through technology – first through stone, then metal tools, needles for clothing, tools for agriculture and so on. Then we invented machines to do the manual work and we moved from the fields to factories. Then we mechanized the factories and moved towards mental work. Now we're delegating the drudgery of some of that mental work to machines or, more accurately, AI – or even more accurately, to machine and deep learning.

Amid all the hubris that surrounds education and teaching, there is a deeper problem. Parents know it, learners know it, even teachers, lecturers and trainers know it. Performance has plateaued and everyone is getting a little fraught. Politicians, driven on by the poor foundations, and therefore learning tower of PISA results (the OECD's Programme for International Student Assessment), demand more testing. Parents, the most conservative of lobbyists, demand more schooling. Teachers scream 'enough already – we're exhausted!' Rather than getting cheaper, education seems to be getting more expensive. So expensive that it is becoming exclusive, perhaps increasing rather than decreasing inequality.

Well, is it not about time we looked for the sort of solutions that gave us the industrial and information revolutions of the past? Can't machines solve the problem of teaching and learning?

Could teaching be trumped by a learning machine? Are we beginning to glimpse the possibility of machines that teach themselves to teach? They learn what works, what doesn't work and deliver ever better performance. We see the embryonic evidence for this in adaptive learning systems that are truly algorithmic, some of which do use machine learning to improve as they deliver. The more students they teach, the better they get. They teach themselves. This is not science fiction. This is real AI, in real software, delivering real courses, in real institutions. The future has been here for some time in learning; it is just not distributed.

Imagine what will happen when these super teachers are commoditized, delivered from super-fast cloud services and let loose on the web. Teaching and learning will be as free and accessible as Google search. You will not only be able to find things with ease; you will be able to learn them with ease. We may see dramatic rises in performance among learners, right across the board, as such systems will be far more sensitive to individual needs, even learning difficulties.

This may seem hopelessly utopian. But could we have a future without teachers? Why not? Teaching is essentially being a conduit. It is a means to an end, not an end in itself. Wouldn't academics really prefer to do pure research and not teach? Wouldn't many teachers prefer not to have to mark anything and avoid the stress of the classroom? Couldn't we dispense with teaching and just have learning? Could teaching be trumped by learning? Could learning be as free as search?

Agricultural workers were largely mechanized out of the process by machines, factory workers by robots, secretaries by word processors – and it is possible that we will see the obliteration of drivers, cabbies and truck drivers through driverless cars. No one predicted that! If there is a lot of evidence to suggest that many professions, even white-collar, middle-class roles, may be replaced by smart AI, what in the long term is so special about teaching? If we can teach millions, if not hundreds of millions, at cents per learner, isn't that desirable?

# References

Arthur, WB (2009) *The Nature of Technology: What it is and how it evolves*, Simon and Schuster, New York

Clark, A (2001) Natural-born cyborgs?, in *International Conference on Cognitive Technology*, August, pp 17–24, Springer, Berlin

Clark, A and Chalmers, D (1998) The extended mind, *Analysis*, **58** (1), pp 7–19

Dennett, DC (2017) *From Bacteria to Bach and Back: The evolution of minds*, WW Norton & Company, London

Frischmann, B and Selinger, E (2018) *Re-engineering Humanity*, Cambridge University Press, Cambridge

Kurzweil, R (2005) *The Singularity is Near: When humans transcend biology*, Penguin, London

Malone, TW (2018) *Superminds: The surprising power of people and computers thinking together*, Little, Brown Book Group, London

Marx, K (1867/1960) *Das Kapital* [Capital], in K Marx and F Engels (eds), *Sochineniya [Works]*, **23**, p 5

McLuhan, M (1994) *Understanding Media: The extensions of man*, MIT Press, Boston

Perez, C (2003) *Technological Revolutions and Financial Capital*, Edward Elgar Publishing, Cheltenham, UK

Postman, N (1993) *Technopoly: The surrender of culture to technology*, Vintage, London

Reeves, B and Nass, CI (1996) *The Media Equation: How people treat computers, television, and new media like real people and places*, Cambridge University Press, Cambridge

Schumpeter, JA (1911/2017) *The Theory of Economic Development*, Routledge, London

Shirky, C (2010) *Cognitive Surplus: Creativity and generosity in a connected age*, Penguin, London

Smith, A (1776/2010) *The Wealth of Nations: An inquiry into the nature and causes of the wealth of nations*, Harriman House Limited, Petersfield, UK

Usher, AP (2013) *A History of Mechanical Inventions*, Revised Edition, Courier Corporation, Chelmsford, MA

# INDEX

Note: page numbers in *italics* indicate figures or tables